ALSO BY DAVID RIEFF

Going to Miami
Los Angeles: Capital of the Third World
The Exile: Cuba in the Heart of Miami

Slaughterhouse

BOSNIA AND THE FAILURE OF THE WEST

David Rieff

SIMON & SCHUSTER

New York   London   Toronto   Sydney   Tokyo   Singapore

SIMON & SCHUSTER
Rockefeller Center
1230 Avenue of the Americas
New York, NY 10020

Designed by Irving Perkins Associates

Manufactured in the United States of America

10   9   8   7   6   5   4   3   2   1

Library of Congress Cataloging-in-Publication Data
Rieff, David.
    Slaughterhouse : Bosnia and the failure of the West / David Rieff.
    p.   cm.
    Includes index.
    1. Yugoslav War, 1991– —Bosnia and Hercegovina. 2. Yugoslav War,
1991– —Atrocities. 3. Bosnia and Hercegovina—History—1992– 4. United
Nations—Bosnia and Hercegovina. 5. Yugoslav War, 1991– —Personal nar-
ratives, American. 6. Rieff, David. I. Title.
DR1313.3.R54   1995
949.7'42024—dc20   94-40148
                                                             CIP

ISBN 0-671-88118-3

"Blood and Lead" from *Out of Danger* by James Fenton
Copyright © 1994 by James Fenton
Reprinted by permission of Farrar, Straus & Giroux, Inc.

To the memory of Dr. Hakija Turaljic, Vice-President of the Republic of Bosnia and Herzegovina, who was killed by Bosnian Serb fighters on the airport road in Sarajevo while riding in a French armored personnel carrier and ostensibly under the protection of United Nations soldiers.

Listen to what they did.
Don't listen to what they said.
What was written in blood
Has been set up in lead.

Lead tears the heart.
Lead tears the brain.
What was written in blood
Has been set up again.

The heart is a drum.
The drum has a snare.
The snare is in the blood.
The blood is in the air.

Listen to what they did.
Listen to what's to come.
Listen to the blood.
Listen to the drum.

—JAMES FENTON

I

This is the story of a defeat. When I first went to Bosnia in September 1992, the victory of ethnic nationalism and of fascism was already probable but not yet assured. Reports of the Serb genocide of the Bosnian Muslims had already leaked out thanks to the heroic efforts of a few aid workers and journalists, but most people in the West seemed unable to confront the bad news. I arrived in the Balkans the month after Roy Gutman of *Newsday* had revealed the existence of an archipelago of secret concentration camps that the Bosnian Serbs had set up in northern Bosnia, and after Ed Vulliamy of the *Guardian* and a British film crew from ITN had been the first foreigners to get inside them. By the time I got to northern Bosnia, some camps had been moved. Others, including the most infamous— Omarska, Manaca, Trnopolje—were being closed. But in other ways matters in the region seemed to be growing worse. What the world was learning to think of as the ethnic cleansing of the non-Serb population was occurring in the towns and cities as well as the villages and was becoming ever more widespread and brazen.

I had come to write one report for an American magazine on ethnic cleansing, without even really understanding what the term meant. I ended up returning again and again. It is said that the press corps became too involved with what was going on in Bosnia, that it should have remained more dispassionate. There is some truth in this. It is hard to be dispassionate about ethnic cleansing and mass murder. After a few visits to Bosnia, I wanted to be nowhere else. Before long, I had put everything else on hold, resolved to write as frankly incendiary a narrative as I could of my journeys to the slaughterhouse that the Republic of Bosnia-Herzegovina became in the spring of 1992. If the bad news about Bosnia could just be brought home to people, I remember thinking, the slaughter would not be allowed to continue.

In retrospect, I should have known better than to believe in the power of unarmed truths. The skies did not darken over Auschwitz and they would not darken over the hills of Bosnia. That is one of the things I have learned in the last two years. But when I first started going to Bosnia, my hope was to add my voice to those far braver than I who were risking their lives to bear witness to what was taking place there. Until well into the winter of 1994, as long as there still seemed to be a chance that the Bosnian cause might not be extinguished, it also seemed important to illustrate why I and many other foreign writers, photographers, and television journalists kept choosing, often over the objections of friends and superiors, to spend time on the Bosnian side. We did not just think that what was going on was a tragedy—all wars are tragic—but that the values that the Republic of Bosnia-Herzegovina exemplified were worth preserving. Those ideals, of a society committed to multiculturalism (in the real and earned rather than the American and prescriptive sense of that much overused term) and tolerance, and of an understanding of national identity as deriving from shared citizenship rather than ethnic identity, were precisely the ones which we in the West so assiduously proclaim. And I had not been long in Bosnia before I came to believe, as I continue to believe today, that we in the rich world had not only a moral obligation to defend Bosnian independence but a compelling interest in doing so as well. That campaign has been lost. What remains is the obligation to bear witness, the obligation to the dead as well as to the living.

Bosnia was and always will be a just cause. It should have been the West's cause. To have intervened on the side of Bosnia would have been self-defense, not charity. America, for all its fissures, is still the most successful multicultural society in history. And the Western European countries are becoming multiracial and multiethnic. If they are *lucky,* they will become multicultural as well. It will not be enough, in this time of blood and fire of which the Bosnian slaughter is only the outrider, to proclaim those values as our own. Freedom cannot be asserted; it must be defended. It cannot hope to live on only in a few gilded corners of the world, any more than species can remain viable if the only places that their safety can be assured are zoos. As the Sarajevo filmmaker Ademir Kenovic, who, though he could easily have left, chose to remain in order to document the siege, once said, "Just because the fire is in the basement, that doesn't mean that the people in the penthouse won't eventually feel the flames."

In believing the Bosnians to have been not only the victims of the fighting, but the people who had right on their side, I do not mean to suggest that one should ignore their own crimes and stupidities, exonerate them of responsibility for the outbreak of the fighting or its duration, or pretend that what has happened in Bosnia is simple. War is a corrupt, debasing experience; it often brings out the worst in people, whatever side they are on, and it rarely leaves their weaknesses unexposed. Always, it is about money and power as much if not more than it is about ideals. It is about vengeance, crime, and the covering up of crimes. It teaches you that your darkest suspicions even about people you admire are likely to be warranted at least part of the time. To give only the most obvious of examples, the heroic defenders of Sarajevo were defending the black market as much as they were defending the city. And yet that does not make what they did less heroic. Like the rest of us, the Bosnians are human beings, not angels.

On the political level, the story was just as complicated. As those of us who knew something of the Bosnian government's behavior before the fighting started realized full well, the commitment of leaders like the President, Alia Izetbegovic, and the Prime Minister, Haris Silajdzic, to the values of multiculturalism and their belief in civil society had been far less firm in peacetime than it was to become after the extinction of their country started to stare them in the face. Before April 1992, Alia Izetbegovic had been the leader of a Muslim national party, and talked more about the rights and requirements of Muslims in Bosnia than about the Bosnian people as a whole. Two years later, he was a *Bosnian* leader, and the ideas he was probably only paying lip service to at the beginning were the ones on which the policies he pursued were based. It is true that this commitment probably began as much as a result of compulsion as of conviction, and that it began to wane in late 1994, as it became clear that the great powers had no intention of doing anything more to help Bosnia survive. From the beginning of the fighting, the Izetbegovic government's strategy was to try to get the West to intervene militarily. It is also true that within Izetbegovic's SDA (Stranka Demokratske Akcije, the Party of Democratic Action), particularly in central Bosnia, the Islamic fundamentalists became more and more important as the conflict dragged on, particularly as the Bosnian army came to depend more and more on Iran, Pakistan, Saudi Arabia, and Turkey for military supplies. But to anyone who spent time in Bosnia, what was remarkable was how deep and abiding the commitment of most people on the government side to multiculturalism turned out to be.

And if, by the fall of 1994, people in Bosnia did begin to identify themselves as Muslims and turn their backs on the multiculturalism they had fought so desperately for almost three years to preserve, this was hardly surprising. They were being murdered as Muslims, made homeless as Muslims. "First, I was a Yugoslav," a friend in Sarajevo said to me once. "Then, I was a Bosnian. Now I'm becoming a Muslim. It's not my choice. I don't even believe in God. But after two hundred thousand dead, what do you want me to do? Everybody has to have a country to which he can belong."

In any case, the mistakes Izetbegovic and Silajdzic had made before the war were not what had caused the war. From the moment Yugoslavia began to break up, it was clear that both Croat and Serb nationalists were less interested in territory than in carving out states with a specific ethnic makeup. Only the Bosnians, for all their mixed signals, stood for a citizen state. From the Serb nationalist vantage point, it was quite simple. If Yugoslavia could not exist, Bosnia should not exist, since with a Serb population of thirty-two percent, it was a refutation of the dream of all Serbs living in their own state. "Had Izetbegovic been an angel," a Belgrade lawyer once said to me, "and he was not, he still would have had his war." And whatever Izetbegovic's original motives, and his failure, before the fighting started, to do more to reassure Bosnian Serbs and Croats, the Bosnia he labored to defend soon became, for all its faults, a living reproach to fanaticism and bigotry. That, and not some preposterous notion that it was or could ever have hoped to become an ideal state inhabited by a uniquely virtuous, uniquely tolerant people, is why Bosnia mattered. It should have been saved. It could have been saved.

Such an intervention would have been neither cheap nor easy. To imagine that it would have been is as great a piece of wishful thinking as to idealize the Bosnians. If it had come, it would have had to come from the North Atlantic Treaty Organization, which alone had sufficient military might and political authority to make the Serbs stop their war. And the war that NATO would have had to unleash would have been costly in lives, money, and lost illusions. It was foolish of so many of those who called for various forms of intervention to have pretended otherwise. They wanted an outcome that required a war to obtain, but they did not want to face the fact that even a just war causes the most terrible suffering. War can bring about many different things, but the one constant in war is the slaughter of innocents. All the loose talk that circulated during the fighting in Bosnia about how the West only needed to lift the one-sided United Nations arms embargo against the Bosnian government and undertake a few "surgical air strikes"—talk that, curiously enough, emanated from the remains of the European and North American left that had rightly derided the concept in all previous interventions from Vietnam to Kuwait—should be seen for the hopeless exercise it was. Those who advocated it can fairly be accused of wanting to deal with a great historical tragedy on the cheap.

The repeated calls for the lifting of the arms embargo against Bosnia, symbolically important though such an action might have been, were perhaps the greatest irrelevancy of all. Those who not only supported it but imagined it would make a difference spoke as if the arms would somehow have reached the landlocked territory still controlled by the Bosnian government by osmosis, or as if the Serb and Croat enemies of Bosnia were going to just stand around as the balance of force on the battlefield was radically altered. Perhaps they thought that because the Bosnian Serb Army had committed great crimes, it was also stupid or incompetent. In fact it was neither, and NATO soldiers would have had to kill and die to get the weapons in. It should be said that, to their credit, at least most of those who opposed intervention seemed to understand its gravity in a way that many of those who backed it did not.

Anyway, that debate is long over now. The West—that dubious euphemism that really means little more than the great powers of Europe and North America—chose to do *anything but* intervene. Instead, they mounted one of the largest and most heroic humanitarian relief efforts in modern history, under the aegis of the United Nations High Commissioner for Refugees, all the while pursuing decidedly unheroic diplomatic negotiations. The purpose of these, as soon became clear, was not to save Bosnia but, as the politicians liked to say, "to contain the crisis." What all the so called peace plans had in common was that the only solution to the conflict was some form of division along ethnic lines.

At first, the affront to Bosnian sovereignty was not complete. The international negotiators—Cyrus Vance, representing the UN, and David Owen, representing the European Community—devised as fair a map of Bosnia as they thought they could persuade the Serbs, who had already conquered seventy percent of Bosnian territory, to accept. Bosnia-Herzegovina was to be divided into ten semiautonomous cantons. Three were to be controlled by the Serbs, three by the Croats, and three by the Muslims. The tenth, which encompassed Greater Sarajevo, was to be governed by representatives of all three national groups in Bosnia. The idea was at least nominally to preserve Bosnian sovereignty in all the territory of the Republic, however little control the central government in Sarajevo would actually have been able to exercise.

When the Vance-Owen peace plan was rejected, in large part due to the unwillingness of the Clinton administration to endorse it, the stage was set for partition pure and simple. The only question remaining—and because it could not be resolved the war dragged on—was what territory the Serbs would keep and what they would hand back to the Bosnian government.

To a very large extent, the diplomats acted as they did because from the start they knew, even if we in the press did not, that there would be no intervention. When governments have made up their collective minds, the influence of the media, the so-called "CNN effect," is greatly overrated. And the European governments had made up their minds that they were not going to do anything more for Bosnia than provide humanitarian relief. Indeed, the courage of the aid workers, United Nations and nongovernmental alike, and the dedication of many of the diplomats, who, when all was said and done could not compel intervention any more than the journalists or aid workers could, may have even made it easier for the Serbs to continue their campaign in Bosnia. For, paradoxically, the fact that something was being done seemed to serve as a pretext behind which the great powers—aka the international community—could hide. Each time the call for intervention mounted in France, or Britain, or the United States, the government ministers of the countries in question, and, with more authority, representatives of the United Nations, who were perceived as having an objectivity about Bosnia many of us who covered the war soon became convinced they did not in fact possess, would quickly insist that the reason no intervention was possible was that it—we soon assimilated the phrase as one might a mantra—"would compromise the humanitarian effort."

In any case, from the beginning of the fighting in the former Yugoslavia, neither the British, the French, nor the Americans had shown any willingness to intervene militarily. United States officials, in particular, consistently reaffirmed their support for the survival of the Yugoslav Federation. On June 21, 1991, the then Secretary of State, James Baker, visited Belgrade and warned the leaders of Croatia and Slovenia that the United States would not recognize their states' independence. European Community officials delivered a similar warning two days later. But, as a CIA report issued earlier in the year had concluded, the breakup of Yugoslavia was already taking place. Four days after the Baker speech, Croatia and Slovenia declared themselves "sovereign and independent states." Two days later, on June 27, a force of JNA troops (the initials stand for the Yugoslav National Army) were on the move from bases in Croatia toward Slovenia. Though there had been clashes throughout the preceding year, this event marked the beginning of the real fighting in Yugoslavia.

The conflict in Slovenia lasted only a few days. To the surprise of the JNA commanders, the Slovene territorial defense forces fought well. The Yugoslav Defense Minister, General Veljko Kadijevic, decided to withdraw the JNA forces rather than pursue the fight. In effect, this was a de facto recognition of Slovenian independence on the part of the authorities in Belgrade. What they were not willing to accept, however, was the independence of Croatia, and the reason for this was ethnic Serb nationalism. There were almost no Serbs in Slovenia. In contrast, Croatia had a substantial Serb minority. And it was in the name of defending these Serbs, rather than in the name of preserving Yugoslavia, that the JNA began offensive operations in Croatia in the middle of July 1991. Their campaign left them with almost a third of Croatia under their control, much of it along the Bosnian border. It was then claimed that this area was no longer part of Croatia but was, rather, the "Serbian Republic of the Krajina." To many, it seemed as if the outlines of Greater Serbia were coming into view as Yugoslavia disintegrated.

The fighting in Croatia lasted until the beginning of 1992. Croatia's little Venice, Dubrovnik, was shelled repeatedly, and the eastern Croatian city of Vukovar was literally leveled to the ground. Under strong pressure from Germany, the European Community decided to recognize Croatia and Slovenia. Cyrus Vance, who had been negotiating a cease-fire between Serbs and Croats for much of the second half of 1991, warned the German Foreign Minister, Hans-Dietrich Genscher, and the then head of the EC, the Dutch politician Hans Van Der Broek, that such recognition made war in Bosnia inevitable. They responded contemptuously and persevered. As Chancellor Helmut Kohl put it on January 15, 1992, "Everyone will soon recognize that this policy [of recognition] was right. Without our decision, this civil war would not end."

In early 1992, Vance did manage to get the Serbs and Croats to agree to a cease-fire in Croatia, albeit one that, despite the deployment of some fourteen thousand United Nations peacekeeping troops, stopped the fighting but did nothing to reverse Serb military gains on the ground. If anything, UN forces in Croatia found themselves in the position of administering an increasingly permanent demarcation line between Serb- and Croat-controlled territory. In theory, the Vance plan had been designed to lead to a political settlement. Serb forces were supposed to disarm, and UN forces take their place. But there was a loophole. The Vance plan naively allowed police units to continue functioning. And what the Serbs did was simply to have their soldiers exchange green fatigues for blue police uniforms. Little else changed in the Serb-held areas of the Croatian Krajina and of eastern Slavonia. And, as Vance had predicted, fighting did come to Bosnia that spring.

Already, in August 1991, Alia Izetbegovic had warned that Slobodan Milosevic, the President of Serbia, "wants the whole of Bosnia. He wants it all." With the Yugoslav Federation more and more Greater Serbia under another name, Izetbegovic, along with the Macedonian President, Kiro Gligorov, had tried desperately to come up with a constitutional solution to the crisis. In December 1991, seeing that Yugoslavia could not be resurrected, Izetbegovic had asked for EC recognition and for UN peacekeeping troops. The latter request was refused, even though at the time the headquarters of the UN force overseeing the cease-fire in Croatia was in Sarajevo. But the EC did respond to Izetbegovic's call for recognition by insisting that the Bosnian authorities hold a referendum on Bosnian independence. It took place on February 29, 1992. Bosnian Muslims and Bosnian Croats, some sixty-three percent of the population of the Republic, voted yes overwhelmingly. But the Bosnian Serb leadership called on their people to boycott the referendum and, in outlying villages, backed up their demand by preventing polling stations from being established. Except in the cities, the Serb boycott was almost entirely successful. The outbreak of fighting was only a matter of time.

In early March, Serb irregulars began setting up roadblocks. This was the way the Croatian fighting had started. By the end of the month, Serb irregulars, openly supported by JNA troops, were seizing territory all over Bosnia. On April 6, 1992, the siege of Sarajevo began. Later in the month, Banja Luka, the second city of Bosnia, fell to Serb forces. The Bosnian slaughter had begun.

I say slaughter because to refer to what has happened there as a war is to distort, and, more gravely, to dignify the real nature of what has occurred. Before the fighting started, Alia Izetbegovic had insisted that there could be no war because one side—his own—would not fight. To have imagined that carnage could have been averted for this reason was only one of the many culpably naive assumptions the Bosnian presidency made. But even to talk of a "Bosnian war" is to talk in similarly naive terms. In reality, war, for all its bestiality, has its dignity and its laws, and soldiers, at least when they are faithful to their codes, rightly claim theirs to be an honorable as well as a terrible calling. To think otherwise is to imagine that nothing is worth dying for, and if Bosnia proves anything it is that such a statement is a shameful lie. But about what the Serbs have done in Bosnia no such claims can or should be made. There was agony aplenty, but nothing agonistic about what took place in Bosnia. The Serbs came, they slaughtered, they conquered, while the world looked on. As Haris Silajdzic, who was first the Foreign Minister and then the Prime Minister of Bosnia, said over and over again, "What is going on is genocide. In the West, many people choose to call it war. But it's not war; it's slaughter."

As I write, the genocide is all but complete. This result has dashed any hope that a book, or a piece of videotape, or a public speech on behalf of Bosnia will do any good in the practical sense. It is too late for all that now. What the brute realities of murder and displacement, destruction and forced population transfer, have accomplished—the new facts on the ground, as the modern political cliché has it—neither words nor good intentions will undo. The destruction of Bosnia-Herzegovina has put paid to that. This does not mean—it is important that defeat not make one sentimental even in the imagination of disaster—that what has happened in Bosnia could not have been worse. One thing that a journey to a war teaches one is that things can always get worse. In the early winter of 1993, at a private dinner in Zagreb, the American Ambassador to Croatia, Peter Galbraith, observed disconsolately that he would not be surprised if the fighting went on indefinitely. "Beirut lasted seventeen years," he said. And shortly before the shell landed in the Sarajevo marketplace in early February 1994, an event that, to the stupefaction of both many Sarajevans and foreigners resident in the city, did finally provoke the great powers to broker the first muscular cease-fire of the conflict—one that they were willing to enforce and that the Serb besiegers recognized could not be ignored—it seemed to me that the bombardment of the Bosnian capital might go on forever. What else was new? The day before, a shell had landed in the isolated Sarajevo neighborhood of Dobrinja, killing ten people, and nothing had changed. Ten days before that, a shell had landed in a housing estate in New Sarajevo and killed six schoolchildren out sledding, and nothing had changed. What was so magical about sixty-eight lives, when compared with the two hundred thousand dead that had predeceased them?

Something, it seemed, though perhaps those of us who were closest to the situation were least equipped to understand just what. Returning to New York in the aftermath of the market massacre, with the airwaves full of the sights and sounds of that explosion, I got a call from an ex-lover—a decent, apolitical woman with no very great interest in Bosnia. "I feel so terrible," she said, and it was clear she meant it. And yet, perhaps churlishly, I wondered why. Why did these dead finally rouse ordinary people to tears and the powerful to a short burst of resolution? But the fact was that they did. The shift in public perception goaded NATO to insist that the Serbs at least stop their shelling of Sarajevo once and for all, even if, as events would show, this firmness did not extend to Gorazde or the other enclaves in the Drina Valley of eastern Bosnia. For all the triumphalist talk, much of it coming out of Washington, where the Clinton administration was quick to claim credit for the cease-fire, the tragedy hadn't stopped, it had only changed its venue.

Still, anyone who cared about the Bosnian people had to be glad for the tenuous peace that was secured for Sarajevo, however unlikely it was that it would endure. But let there be no illusions. Even leaving the fate of Gorazde and Zepa to one side, the lifting of the sieges of Sarajevo and Mostar and a dozen other less well known towns, the confederal arrangements worked out between the Bosnian government and the Bosnian Croat authorities, and, most essentially, the lessening of the rate of killing—the fact that so far tens of thousands of names have not been added to the quarter million who died between the spring of 1992 and the spring of 1994—do not make what has happened to Bosnia less of a defeat. For all of us, not just the Bosnians themselves. To stop the killing is the humanitarian fig leaf under which the partition of Bosnia can go forward. That is, if the Bosnians are lucky.

If, in the humanitarian sense, the worst has not happened—one has only to think of the genocide of the Tutsi of Rwanda in 1994 to understand that—in both the political and the moral sense it has. A group of extreme Bosnian Serb nationalists, well supplied by their allies and mentors in Serbia proper, succeeded through a combination of skillful propaganda and terror in rallying the majority of Bosnian Serbs to the cause of Greater Serbia. They destroyed Bosnia, just as they had said they would. The mystery is how, with the Serbs controlling seventy-two percent of Bosnia and *at best* the plan being for the Bosnian government to regain control of fifty-three percent of the country, anyone can pretend otherwise, or affect surprise that this has led, on the Bosnian government side, to the altogether predictable rise of, if not Islamic fundamentalism in the Maghrebi or Iranian sense, then at least Muslim nationalism. Whatever the long-term prospects may be for the partition that the great powers, particularly France and Britain, had thought desirable almost from the outset of the Yugoslav crisis and finally, in the wake of the market massacre and through the vehicle of a binding cease-fire, succeeded with Russian and American help in imposing early in 1994, Bosnia will not be put back together again as it was before the fighting started.

There will be a Bosnia, of course, as in one guise or another there has been for more than a thousand years, but it will not be the small multiconfessional country made up of ethnic Serbs, Croats, and Muslims that it was before the slaughtering began. The systematic attempt on the part of the Serbs to exterminate the Bosnian Muslims has accomplished that. So has the Serbs' campaign to extirpate their Muslim neighbors from their land and destroy the traces, particularly religious and architectural, of their history there—an event that constitutes the third great genocide of a small European minority to take place in the twentieth century, as even the Bosnian Muslims' critics in United Nations and Western governmental circles agree. Instead of the multiculturalism that, for all its flaws, hypocrisies, and barely submerged antipathies, really did exist in urban Bosnia in cities like Tuzla, Banja Luka, Mostar, and above all the capital, Sarajevo, before the fighting started in April 1992, the destruction not only of two hundred thousand people but of a history of pluralism and tolerance, of that extraordinary amalgam that was Bosnia, all but guarantees that what the future holds in store is piety, iron, and, sooner or later, the revenge of the Bosnian Muslims.

And there is nothing hyperbolic about such a prediction. Anyone who has spent time in Bosnia has heard the grim promises of revenge. Bosnian officers in frontline positions, politicians in their half-lit offices, and Bosnian exiles in cafes in Düsseldorf and Frankfurt, speak in one voice on the matter. "Europe will pay for what was done to us," a Bosnian official told me shortly after it had become clear that the cease-fire in Sarajevo proclaimed in February 1994 really was going to hold. At that time peace seemed, if anything, a stronger goad to bitterness than war had been. Freed of brute exigencies such as trying to get water while ducking snipers' bullets, there was finally time for people to think. And increasingly, ordinary Sarajevans as well as members of the political *nomenklatura* were at last fully taking in the indifference of Europe and of the United States to what had happened to Bosnia. "Clinton will not help us," the official said. "He cares about his health plan, not our survival."

The Bosnians had already grasped, after two years of exposure to UN "peacekeeping," the impotence and sterility of a system of world order that supposedly was enshrined in the charter of the

United Nations. They had learned that there was no world order, old or new. And they had learned that even the principles developed half a century earlier when the UN was founded, in an attempt to bind the world legally to preventing future aggressions just like the one the Belgrade Serbs had unleashed on the country and future genocides like the one the Bosnian Muslims were undergoing, were really just a joke. Bosnia's defenders abroad, like New York's senior Senator, Daniel Patrick Moynihan, might talk about the "shredding" of the international system and call for new measures and, if necessary, military action against the Serbs. From the ground in Bosnia, it did not appear that there was any system to shred. The Bosnians had asked for help. To which the UN had said, "We have no mandate to help"; the Europeans had said, "To help will only level the killing field, and we don't want that"; and the Americans had said, "We'd like to help, but we can't." And so the Bosnians went on dying, refused defense and deprived of the chance to defend themselves.

And this disaster the diplomats called a victory. The UN boasted that it was carrying out its "mandate" under difficult circumstances. The Europeans congratulated themselves on the fact that tragic though the Bosnian situation might be, their diplomacy had successfully "contained" the Bosnian crisis. And President Clinton, having promised during the election campaign that if he was elected, ethnic cleansing would stop and then spent his first eighteen months in office standing by as it continued, angrily rebuked Christiane Amanpour, CNN's correspondent in Sarajevo, for questioning his characterization of American policy as both consistent and successful. "Madam," he said mendaciously, "there have been no flip-flops." No wonder that the seeds of Europe's own "Palestinian problem" were becoming visible long before the firing in Bosnia had stopped. However much Europe and the United States might already be trying to forget Bosnia, and what had happened there—two months into the Sarajevo cease-fire, journalistic and political attention had already shifted to Korea and South Africa, and Sarajevo might have become, as the phrase goes, old news—Bosnia had neither forgotten about Europe nor forgiven it.

* * *

This seemed and still seems to me right, however self-destructive the sentiment may be objectively, to whatever degree it leads to the waste of Bosnian lives in the same way that the intransigent memories of Palestine have led to such a waste of Palestinian lives, and however much it makes me fear for the future of the Old Continent. Europe and the United States could have stopped the genocide, and declined to do so. The UN could have interpreted its mandate to require it to do something to stop ethnic cleansing. Instead of insisting that he was simply an international civil servant, for all intents and purposes a glorified stenographer, there only to do the bidding of the member states, Secretary General Boutros Boutros-Ghali could have made it his priority to defend Bosnia. He, too, had an interest in doing so, since the United Nations is a multiethnic, multicultural entity or it is nothing at all. The permanent members of the Security Council may have shaped the UN's role in Bosnia, but, as much as anything, that is because Boutros-Ghali let them. He did not even defend Bosnia, or the concept of a multiethnic state, verbally. To the contrary, one of the main activities of Boutros-Ghali and his representatives was to do everything in their power to forestall any outside military help the Bosnians might have secured.

These are the facts that make the bitterness of the Bosnians themselves and those of us who cared about Bosnia so deep-seated and unassuageable. This is where the story of Bosnian defeat segues into the story of Western European and North American disgrace. What has taken place in Bosnia has revealed the bankruptcy of every European security institution, from the North Atlantic Treaty Organization to the Council on Security and Cooperation in Europe, exposed the fact that nowhere in these great structures was there either intellectual preparedness or moral fortitude for dealing with the crises of the post–Cold War world or for coming to terms with the likelihood that in the future a great many wars will take place not between states but within states. To content oneself with anatomizing the defeat alone would be to mislead. After all, the defeat of right by might is a commonplace of human history, a fact as ubiquitous, if as unpalatable, as individual mortality. But the unnecessary defeat, the defeat that could have been averted, the genocide that need not have taken place, or, once it had begun, could have been cut short, are things to which it is obscene to be reconciled.

This is what happened. Two hundred thousand Bosnian Muslims died, in full view of the world's television cameras, and more than two million other people were forcibly displaced. A state formally recognized by the European Community and the United States on April 7, 1992, and by the United Nations on May 22, 1992, was allowed to be destroyed. While it was being destroyed, United Nations military forces and officials looked on, offering "humanitarian" assistance and protesting—here, it must be said, to a large degree rightly, since if the UN could have acted differently, the great powers could have given the UN a different mandate had they chosen to do so; the UN implemented the disgrace but it did not create it—that there was no will in the international community to do anything more. Two successive American Presidents, one Republican, the second Democratic, declared over and over that they represented the last remaining superpower and yet simultaneously insisted that they were helpless to launch an intervention or even get the arms embargo lifted. And this was not, as so many pretended, the result of some grim, ineluctable law of history, but rather a testimony to specific choices made by those who governed the rich world and by the civil servants who administered the international system that they had created. In a letter to a friend in which he reported on the public hanging of three thieves he had witnessed during a stay in Rome, Lord Byron, realizing perhaps that his account might give the impression that he had enjoyed what he had seen, added, "I would have saved them if I could." The spokesmen for the great powers took the opposite tack. For more than two years, they protested how much what they were seeing appalled them, but insisted that they were powerless. And individually, in private, doubtless they were. But the nations and institutions they represented were unmoved by the execution of Bosnia. For these, it was a matter of saying, "I would have saved them but I chose not to." Meanwhile the UN looked on "like eunuchs at the orgy," as people said in Sarajevo.

Such is life in the post–Cold War world. (We do not seem to have names for our times, only, in terms like "post–Cold War" and "postmodern," markers of our distance from previous categories.) For more than two years, I went back and forth between New York and Croatia and Bosnia. When I would return, and attempt to reconnect to my life back home, friends would inform me earnestly that there

were no other alternatives. "We" had other agendas, other impedi-
ments to action, other considerations to take into account. "It's the
economy, stupid," candidate Clinton's handlers had repeated. To
which, where Bosnia was concerned, leftists unwilling to contemplate any use of American power to save Bosnia might add, "It's
American imperialism, stupid." Ordinary, decent Americans might
add, "It's our kids, and Bosnia is Europe's problem." And people
versed in all the other tragedies taking place around the globe might
insist, "What about Angola, Sudan, East Timor, Tibet, Haiti,
Rwanda?" I recall one acquaintance mustering a phrase of Hegel's—
not, to my relief, the one made celebrated by Francis Fukuyama
about "the end of history," but the soberer evocation of the "slaugh-
terbench of history"—to buttress his argument that what was taking
place in Bosnia was just the best-publicized instance of the horrors
that were taking place all the time, all over the world.

Before I went to Bosnia, I might have been tempted to agree with
Boutros Boutros-Ghali, who had remarked during his one and only
visit to Sarajevo, on December 31, 1992, that what was going on
there was "a rich man's war." Good Third Worlder that he was, the
Secretary General meant that Bosnia was a white man's war. He had
admonished the astonished Sarajevans, "I understand your frustration, but you have a situation that is better than ten other places in
the world . . . I can give you a list." Then he had left the city. Once I
had started spending time in Bosnia, it was not even a question of
agreeing or disagreeing so much as feeling that all this comparative
martyrology, all these dueling body counts, were as irrelevant as the
vying for ultimate victim status that had become all the rage on better American college campuses in the early nineties. Having been in
Bosnia, I could find no meaning in the exercise of trumping one people's suffering with another's. In either an academic or a political setting, the exercise seemed pointless. "Rate the best Jacobean poets in
order of importance"; "Rate the worst human tragedies in the world."

For my part, I could no longer take seriously the debate as to
whether the siege of Sarajevo was worse than the siege of the An-
golan city of Cuito, or whether the sufferings of the Bosnian Muslims were worse than those of the Christians and animists of the
southern Sudan. I knew what I had seen, what was happening in
Bosnia, and I knew that to dismiss these events in the name of some

other, even more horrific events was, in moral terms, to make the great the enemy of the good. I also knew that what was happening in Bosnia need not have happened, that the West could have prevented the slaughter. To talk of all the other slaughters it should have been paying attention to but wasn't seemed like little more than a sophisticated justification for feeling good about doing nothing. "I'll see your Bosnia, and raise you one East Timor."

To return to the life you led before you have been to a scene of slaughter and bloodshed, at least if you are a citizen of the rich world, is to choke on the cant and the complacency of everything that used to be familiar and pleasurable to you. You start to feel like an alien in the life you yourself have fashioned. In a sense, all writers, to greater or lesser degrees, must condition themselves to be professional outsiders. But for all my familiarity with that way of seeing things, traveling back and forth from a place like Sarajevo or Banja Luka to a place like Manhattan removed me from my friends and my past to a degree I had never dreamed possible. I felt not only as if I had returned from the land of the dead, but as if I too had become somehow posthumous.

And I believe that I am not alone in this. Even seasoned war correspondents have found it hard to recover from what they lived through in Bosnia. If now I write both in support of the Bosnian cause—this despite the fact that temperamentally I have always suspected causes and, in any case, I believe that cause has been lost—and in protest against the callous indifference, the shallow pessimism, and the hypocrisy that have surrounded the murder of Bosnia, I suspect that I am more surprised by my own stance than anyone. In a previous life, the life before Bosnia, I used to flatter myself that indignation was an emotion to which I was virtually immune. Just as I did not expect to end up in Bosnia in the first place, so I did not expect to feel that I would never recover from it.

This has nothing to do with feeling comfortable there, let alone imagining, as people often do when they fall in love with countries or causes, that I somehow "belonged." In all the time I spent in Bosnia, I cannot remember a single moment when I was not at least a little frightened, and I remember many moments when I was terrified. I was then, and I remain, intensely critical of the Bosnian government, in both its policies and its naïveté, and often bored and exasperated by the way the Bosnians talked with such a combination of self-absorption and lack of realism about themselves and the rest of the world. Nevertheless, it has seemed easier to be in Bosnia, however hopeless or exasperating things could seem there, than to listen to the way Bosnia was usually talked of, or, worse still, not talked of, ignored, in the West.

That one heard so little about Bosnia in countries like Germany and Italy that were so near was something I soon got used to. But the emblematic moment for me was when, a year into the slaughter, long after the beginning of the siege of Sarajevo, long after the Bosnian Serb forces had expelled from the valleys of eastern Bosnia most of their former majority of Muslim inhabitants, and long after the overwhelming majority of the mosques of northern Bosnia had been blown up, thus eliminating the traces of a European Islam that had existed in the region for five centuries, President Clinton presided over the opening of the Holocaust Museum in Washington, D.C. It was a blustery day, replete with clenched jaws, somber clothes, and flights of rhetorical purposefulness. The President of Croatia, Franjo Tudjman, who at one time expressed skepticism about the very existence of the Holocaust, was in the audience. So were many of its survivors, including Elie Wiesel, who, to his credit, reproached Clinton for America's Bosnia policy. For his part, the President wanted to confine the conversation to generalities. He did have one suggestion, though. So that the genocide that befell European Jewry during the Nazi period never take place again, Bill Clinton insisted, extraordinary vigilance was necessary. "We must deploy memory," he said.

That President Clinton could speak of memory as if it were something like a moral antiballistic missile system was the least of it. The real moral solecism was to speak optimistically about the future when, as he knew perfectly well, and Wiesel would soon remind him from the podium, another genocide was taking place in Europe. The Bosnian genocide was not identical to what had happened to the Jews, any more than the extermination of the European Jewry had been identical to the genocide of the Armenians in 1915. Genocide had been the goad behind the adoption of such principles of post–World War II international order as the Four Geneva Conventions, the Genocide Convention of 1949, and, above all, the United Nations Charter. And these laws were being systematically violated in Bosnia.

The siege of Sarajevo was itself a war crime. On the battlefield, usually it was rarer to find instances where war crimes *had not* been committed than where they had. And of course, ethnic cleansing was not just a war crime, it was genocide, pure and simple. To utter words like "Never again," as Clinton did at the opening of the Holocaust Museum, was to take vacuity over the border into obscenity as long as the genocide in Bosnia was going on and Clinton was doing nothing to stop it. His words were literally meaningless. For if there was to be no intervention to stop a genocide that was taking place, then the phrase "Never again" meant nothing more than: Never again would Germans kill Jews in Europe in the 1940s. Clinton might as well have said, "Never again the potato famine," or, "Never again the slaughter of the Albigensians." At the rate things were going, in the year 2050 could one expect that a future American President might open a museum to ethnic cleansing?

During the 1992 election campaign, candidate Clinton had promised to use American power to bring this Bosnian genocide to a halt (much later, a Clinton operative would exclaim to me in exasperation, "Why do people nowadays take campaign promises so seriously?"), or, at least, give the Bosnian government the means to fight back. Two years later, Charles Redman, the US State Department official charged by President Clinton to come up with a peace plan for Bosnia, would justify American acceptance of the principle of partition by saying "we had to jump over the moral bridge" to obtain peace. At least the Americans remained committed rhetorically to the idea that the Bosnian government should be allowed to defend itself against Serb aggression, and, by late 1994, had decided they would no longer enforce the arms embargo. The Europeans denied that any aggression had even taken place, and spoke instead of a civil war in Bosnia. They steadfastly opposed lifting an arms embargo that the United Nations had passed more than a year earlier as part of a package of sanctions designed to penalize the Serbs for the war that they were waging against a secessionist Croatia. And they maintained this policy despite the fact that the war in Croatia had ended and it now served only to further the Serb cause in Bosnia. The Serbs and their Bosnian surrogates had more than enough arms.

They had inherited the stores of the Yugoslav National Army, and could get what little they did not have from the Russians and the Greeks. The Croats' position was more complicated. They had initially allied themselves with the Bosnian government when the fighting started in April 1992. A year later, however, as it became clear that even under the Vance-Owen plan Bosnia was to be divided largely along lines of ethnic predominance, the Croats had begun their own campaign of ethnic cleansing against the Muslims. This had backfired when Croat troops were unable to seize the Muslim section of the city of Mostar and when government forces counterattacked successfully in central Bosnia. Finally, in 1994, thwarted on the battlefield and under heavy US and German pressure, the Croats had again made common cause with the Sarajevo government and had even fought with them in a government offensive that drove Serb forces out of the town of Kupres in late October of 1994. Not only had the Croats been able to buy a great many arms on the open market, but the revival of the alliance with the Bosnian government guaranteed them a share in whatever weapons the Bosnian army might be able to smuggle in. Bosnia, after all, is landlocked and everything had to pass through Croatian territory.

The real purpose of maintaining the embargo, of course, had long been to ensure that as few weapons as possible get through to the government side. Although the embargo had been passed by the United Nations Security Council on September 25, 1991, before Bosnia had declared its independence, the fact that only the Bosnian government was really affected troubled almost no one. To the British Foreign Secretary, Douglas Hurd, the military imbalance that the embargo perpetuated actually made it all the more important that the embargo remain in force. "We don't want to level the killing field," he said more than once. It seemed as if what Hurd was really afraid of was that if the Bosnian government forces were better armed they would give the Serbs a fight. Who knew what would happen then? Better, however unhappy such a choice might be, to wish for a Serb victory. At least the fighting would be over.

There were officials within the British government who were more than willing to concede as much. "We should never have accepted the dismemberment of Yugoslavia," wrote a Mr. R. D. Wilkinson of the Foreign Office Policy Planning Staff to the English conservative writer Nora Beloff, "without first having settled the problems of minorities and frontiers, and probably not before having put in hand a humane program of population exchange. The recognition of Bosnia, and indeed the incitement of them to proclaim their independence, was the ultimate act of thoughtlessness." In the American case, what seemed to be involved was an absolutely visceral reluctance to expend the political capital necessary to rescue Bosnia. "We can't let Bosnia endanger the best liberal hope for a generation," a former Colorado Senator and counselor to Clinton, Tim Wirth, was reported to have remarked. And disgruntled Clinton aides told the story that one critical moment when the administration was thinking of sending the Secretary of Defense to Sarajevo, Hillary Rodham Clinton argued passionately against the move on the grounds that this would take health care off the front page for the duration of his visit to Bosnia. Hearing these stories, all I could think of was the dead and how they need not have died. That simple thought still haunts me, whatever its effect might have been on the political fortunes of the best liberal hope for a generation.

The effects of both Anglo-French hostility to Bosnia and American prevarication combined to ensure that throughout the two years of slaughter, it fell to the Bosnian government side to do the lion's share of the dying. Before the fighting began, the Serbs had almost all the guns (unlike Slovenia, Bosnia never established a territorial defense force and only created one after the shooting started), and after combat had begun in earnest, they were able to establish mainly untrammeled supply lines from Serbia proper, across Bosnia, and into Croatia. Ethnic cleansing was in part about making these routes secure from guerrilla attack. The Serbs also seized most of the high ground—the first axiom of military strategy. Whether we were contemplating the heights surrounding Sarajevo, or Mount Vlasic, in central Bosnia, with its commanding view of Muslim and Croat towns spread out below, those of us who spent the war mostly traveling with Bosnian government forces spent our time cowering under bombardment and with cricks in our necks from staring up at the gun positions on the other side. For all the publicity about bearded "Chetnik" irregulars, kitted out in Serbian white-eagle emblems, death's-head pins, and bandoliers of heavy machine-gun ammunition worn to make them look like the original Chetniks—the

monarchist irregulars under the command of General Draja Mihailovic who had fought against Tito's partisans during the Second
World War—most of the Serb fighters in Bosnia looked and acted
like (and more often than not were) members of the regular JNA, the
Yugoslav National Army. Before the Bosnian fighting had started,
their commander, Ratko Mladic, had even commanded a corps during the Croatian war. It was only after the Serbs had conquered a
third of Croatia that he had moved on to Pale, the Sarajevo suburb
that served as the capital of the self-proclaimed Srpska Republika,
the Serb Republic of Bosnia-Herzegovina. Mladic had acquired the
rump of the JNA in Bosnia, its stores and cantonments as well as
most of its regular officers and men, and it showed. "The Serbs are
real soldiers," a Canadian officer serving with UN forces in Sarajevo
told me in the early winter of 1993. "Whatever you think of what
they've done, to me they're a known quantity."

That their main accomplishment was, in fact, murder, albeit murder with carefully thought-out political and military goals—ethnic
cleansing was not just a war crime, it was a tactic for holding captured
territory without having to worry about a restive subject population—seemed, to the mounting frustration of the journalists covering
the fighting and the UN's role in relieving its effects but not interced-
ing in it, to matter not at all. To the average officer in UNPROFOR—
the acronym, much derided on the Bosnian side, where the word
"self" was added before "protection," stood for United Nations Protection Force—the atmosphere in the officers' mess in Pale was not,
making a few allowances for war conditions and Balkan peculiarities,
all that different from that of the mess halls in which he was accustomed to taking his meals or relaxing. In contrast, Bosnian government officers tended to be civilians learning on the job how to be
soldiers. They slouched in their chairs, walked with decidedly non-
military gaits, and gave the impression of being utterly innocent of
the various rituals and conventions that lie at the heart of the military
vocation in almost every country. Many if not most of them had been
civilians, the rest junior officers. Certainly, it was rare to meet a senior officer serving with Bosnia government forces who, before the
war, had held a commission above the rank of major in the JNA.

What the Bosnians did have was their illusions, particularly their
belief that what had been happening to them since the killing had

started was somehow a kind of ghastly category mistake. It was as if, in a kind of mirror image of Boutros-Ghali's dismissive sketch of their predicament, Bosnians imagined that the fact that they were Europeans would protect them from the horrors of war. Europe, for them, was a continent in which the cosmopolitan values they stood for had become the norm. In Sarajevo, in particular, up to almost the very moment the fighting broke out, the expectation had been that life in the future there would not be very different from life in other genteel, provincial European cities—Trieste, say, or Graz. Even when they realized they were cruelly mistaken about what the future held in store for them, few managed to entirely jettison these expectations. Wars were not supposed to take place in the hardwood forests of Europe in the 1990s, between people for whom the ownership of seaside cottages, second cars, and university educations had become commonplace. Wars occurred in the poor world. In a rich country such as the former Yugoslavia, its sanguinary history notwithstanding, a well-appointed, civilized peace was supposed to reign.

When war had come, the urban middle class of Bosnia, particularly in the cities of Sarajevo, Mostar, Tuzla, and Banja Luka, painfully came to realize that although they had listened to the speeches of Serb nationalists like Slobodan Milosevic, the President of Serbia, and Radovan Karadzic, the leader of the Bosnian Serbs, in truth they had heard nothing. Comparisons between Milosevic and Hitler are foolish and unworthy—the knee-jerk impulse of an age mired in rhetorical excess which has to insist that anything good is the greatest and anything bad the worst—but this Sarajevan inability to hear *is* reminiscent of the reaction of Karl Kraus, that paradigmatic Central European cosmopolitan of the interwar period, who wrote, "When I think of Hitler, nothing comes to mind." Even today so many cosmopolitan Sarajevans cannot quite take in what happened to them. It is this cognitive dissonance, this misunderstanding of their own historical situation, that has differentiated the Bosnian reaction to the war that engulfed them from that of Afghans or Angolans. In Bosnia, the universal pain that all wars engender has carried with it that tinge of surprise of those who believed that their material lives would always be happy. So much for the notion that the end of history, which was never anything more than the end of communism, would be followed by a dull and pacifying age of consumerism.

I think now that I believed it too, imagining that for white Europeans at least, the sanguinary epochs had ended definitively. I knew that, historically, Europe had not been an especially benign place and that in certain periods—like the first fifty years of the twentieth century, to name the one I should have been paying attention to—it had been a particularly *savage* place. But if I knew this, I did not believe it viscerally, whatever pieties I had been capable of uttering about Hiroshima and Auschwitz, the ruin of Africa and the Gulag archipelago. Those events might as well have taken place in another geological era. The crisis looming in Europe, I had thought before I started going to Bosnia, would revolve around the generalized global servant crisis that the rich world seemed to be going through.

In ever larger numbers, people from the poor, non-European world were successfully migrating to the countries of the European Union and North America, to do the jobs that the native-born were no longer willing to take on. It was the presence of these immigrants, and the challenges—cultural, racial, and linguistic—that they posed, which seemed to me the great, intractable dilemma that the future held in store for the rich world. That such a transformation was bound to create a crisis was self-evident. Europe had no tradition of immigration; unlike the United States, which was undergoing its own immigration-driven transformation, there was no powerful cognitive context for what was going on. But a crisis did not mean a war, although, in my bleaker moments, I found it easy to imagine a future Europe in which repression and radical de-democratization had become the norm. *That* Europe would be made up of citizens and immigrants. In other words, as a society it would be closer to slaveholding Athens than to the Social Democratic world of the post-1945, pre-1989 Western European consensus. But what I could not imagine was the sound of tank fire, and the ping of sniper's bullets resounding through the windows of high rises, across the neat parks, the supermarkets, and the gleaming cafes, the art galleries, auto-body repair shops, and historic centers, of a city like Sarajevo. I could not imagine these things any more than the Bosnians themselves could imagine them, before the unthinkable engulfed them.

II

I came to Bosnia almost by accident, with no real experience of war, persuaded that the fighting that was going on in Europe was no harbinger of the future but, rather, a dreadful, heartrending anachronism. Perhaps this is why even then, in the summer of 1992, the Bosnian slaughter remained little more than an abstraction to me, as it was, I think, to so many Western Europeans and North Americans. Despite the ample information that had already come out about what had been going on there, I could find no context out of which to react. I sympathized, almost on cue, by which I mean achingly when the televised images of the carnage were strongest, and almost not at all when the story was absent from the evening news broadcasts, but I didn't understand. That summer, with the Croatian war over and the destruction of Bosnia seemingly well under way, it had become common enough to hear decent, well-informed people on both sides of the Atlantic talk wonderingly of what was taking place and equally common to hear them qualify their expressions of moral solidarity with expressions of helplessness that were as much cognitive as practical. By and large, they seemed almost less shocked by the facts of "ethnic cleansing"—at that time still a relatively new phrase—or by the siege of Sarajevo than by the fact that these events were taking place in Europe in the early nineties.

The phrases I remember cropping up most frequently when the subject of Bosnia arose seemed to me to confirm that the dismay people felt when forced to confront any horrible event was joined, in the Bosnian case, by a genuine stupefaction that what was going on was occurring *in Europe*. People kept asking how it could be happening here (and, unsurprisingly, that "here" easily stretched to include Manhattan Island, Georgetown, and Cambridge, Massachusetts,

along with Frankfurt, Milan, and Paris), and shook their heads wonderingly at the thought of Sarajevo, *a European city,* being methodically reduced to rubble by the Serb gunners on the surrounding
heights. It should have come as no surprise that Europe, in this context, had become a moral category as well as a geographical one. For
all the supposed crisis of confidence in Europe, the knocks against
"Eurocentrism" that supposedly had led, in the phrase of the French
writer Pascal Bruckner, to the unwarranted "demoralization of the
Occident," the sense that Europe was a more civilized place morally
was far more entrenched than was often claimed. And if what was
taking place in the Balkans suggested that no such clear line of demarcation could be drawn between the values of Europe and those of
other parts of the world—between, as conservative pundits liked to
say, the West and the rest—that unwelcome news remained hard to
integrate into the daily experience of life in the West, to which the
idea of war remained almost wholly alien.

I had not come to Europe to go to a war. I was beginning work on
a book about the effect of the new and unwelcome constellations of
refugees and migrants who had arrived on the Old Continent both
from those areas of the globe most of us—despite our intellectual
bad consciences, since the term is so broad as to be in many ways
meaningless—still tend to call the Third World, and from that newly
visible, "blond" Third World made up of the devastated regions of
the former Soviet empire from which, until 1989, Western Europe
had been protected by barbed wire and totalitarianism. I have long
been drawn to borderlands, both actual and psychological. After
German reunification, the Oder became at least as compelling as the
Rio Grande or the Florida Strait. And perhaps because I am old
enough to have known many of the great European cities as they
were before the present age of mass immigration, I could not help
being more and more struck, each time I returned, by the increasing
resemblance between a Los Angeles, with its new majority made up
of immigrants from East Asia, Mexico, and Central America, and a
Brussels, which, in contrast to the relative ethnic and racial homo-
geneity that had characterized it only a generation ago, now had a
population more than a quarter made up of people from Turkey, the
Maghreb, and Africa. But it was one thing for Los Angeles to become a paradigm for twenty-first-century urban America. For Brus-

sels, the city that had become the administrative capital of the new European Union to be undergoing an analogous demographic transformation was far more extraordinary, and seemed to epitomize a Europe that, by dint of demography, would also soon be genuinely multicultural and multiracial.

And in Europe, such a transformation was far more difficult to make sense of. Fundamentally, the American norm was supposed to be change, however much, historically, each generation of "orthodox" Americans might resent and eventually have to accommodate to the successive waves of alien newcomers. Europe was supposed to be, if not immutable, then at least stable. That in the 1990s, Pershing Square in downtown Los Angeles would be unrecognizable to those who frequented it half a century ago was, for better or worse, the quintessential American predicament. But for the side streets off the Grand' Place to boast restaurants selling doner kebab, and for Turkish women in headscarves and long Anatolian dresses to walk about the city's historic center, with its fine boutiques catering to Belgian businessmen and Eurocrats, was another matter altogether. It was not only American tourists who imagined that the European identity was somehow more fixed and less contingent, that Europe, no matter how "American" it might have become in other ways since the end of the Second World War, had not become so Americanized as all that. As the Cold War receded, immigration was becoming the great subject over which Europeans were agonizing.

To an American, though, what was going on seemed so familiar, and it was in search of this "Americanization" of the European future, a project bred as much of wonder as of the more didactic conviction that in the twenty-first century we would all be polyglot or we would kill one another off, that I had come to Europe after long stints on the southeastern and southwestern borderlands of the United States. For months, I had been mooching around the neighborhoods that the immigrants had made their own in a number of the continent's big cities, but particularly in Germany, trying to get some purchase on what really was similar about the ways in which Europe and America were being affected by migration, and what was not. During these journeys, I also tried to visit as many of the new refugee camps and centers that various European national and local governments had set up as I could, all the while taking notes and hoping, as every writer tends to do at the outset of a new project, that eventually the form of the book I was writing would reveal itself to me.

The days were spent with asylum seekers, or skinheads, or social workers, but the war in Yugoslavia remained the stuff of evening newscasts wherever I traveled. But from the perspective of Rostock-Liechtenhagen, where neo-Nazis had torched an asylum seekers' hostel, or Mölln, where they had burned a Turkish family alive in their shop, or from the Polish side of the Oder River, where illegal workers from as near as Warsaw and as far as Somalia clustered each night to ford the waist-high water to the German side, Yugoslavia's collapse seemed to me like something of a sideshow, however tragic, not only compared to the theme on whose scent I had set out, but also compared to the collapse of the Soviet Union three years earlier. It was the Cold War that had defined my understanding of the world, and, if for no other reason, the end of the prospect of nuclear extinction that had seemed to accompany that conflict since the day I was born, made 1992 appear, though not as euphoric a time as 1989, nonetheless an era where any sensible person on balance would be reassured by the general course of events.

When all was said and done, what was the fall of Yugoslavia when compared to the final, overdue destruction of the Communist system? Yugoslavia was an interesting country, to be sure, and, if only because we had been lulled into a false sense of what Yugoslavia was becoming by so much pro-Tito propaganda that appeared in otherwise impeccably anti-Communist media in the West, outsiders like myself had never been as comfortable condemning it as we had a Bulgaria, a Poland, or even the more liberal "Goulash Communism" of Kadar's Hungary. And Tito himself had seemed, however wrong we may have been in retrospect, a far less reprehensible figure than anyone else in the East bloc—a tyrant obviously, but someone like Castro or Ho Chi Minh who had had the allure of being not only larger than life but also almost too large for the country he led, and unlike Castro or Ho, and more like Franco, a figure who would end up, perhaps despite himself, ushering in a far more democratic system than either his ideology or his history might have seemed to suggest as an outcome. Still, from the cold-eyed perspective of the world, did it matter? Sometimes perilously, sometimes fortuitously positioned between East and West, surviving on American subsidies in the late forties, then on the remittances of its guest workers in Western Europe in the era of the German economic miracle, then in the Middle East in the era of the petrodollar, and, at the end of Tito's rule, on ill-advised loans and credits from the International Monetary Fund and the World Bank—had not Yugoslavia always seemed like something of a sideshow?

In 1980, when the news of the genocide being carried out by the Pol Pot regime in Cambodia became known, no one claimed that the tragedy was important because Cambodia mattered geopolitically. If people concluded that the genocide there was unbearable, they did so on moral grounds, in the belief that there were certain extreme cases—cases of genocide in particular—where the world had a moral obligation, and, perhaps, even a legal one as well if one believed the Genocide Convention of 1949 to be binding on its signatories, to intervene to stop it from continuing. Even at the time of Cambodia, there were people who pointed to any number of other seemingly intractable calamities that were taking place all over the world at the same time. It might be, as the director of the United Nations Children's Fund, UNICEF, James Grant, told the British writer William Shawcross, "a noisy disaster," but viewed unsentimentally, it was only one of many and by no means the worst. Was what made Yugoslavia remarkable in 1992 the fact that it was taking place in Europe, in the one happy, favored continent where wars, as opposed to natural disasters or crimes, were not supposed to take place? Did that mean that what was going on there was specially worthy of concern? Why Bosnia? Why not . . . ? The list seemed to stretch on and on.

Perhaps this is why it was so much easier for people like Margaret Thatcher, and other conservatives who harbored no doubts about European civilization as not only conferring privileges but demanding a superior standard of political conduct for those within its orbit, to call for the defense first of Croatia, then of Bosnia. For them the Serb aggression, which they correctly identified—cutting through all the cant about civil wars, incipient Muslim fundamentalism, and the inherent violence of the Balkan character—was simply something wrong, something unacceptable, that had to be put right. But for liberals, who were already disillusioned with the idea of European civilization (however much, in their heart of hearts, they might subscribe to it still), the position was far more difficult. For a generation, these people had tried to purge themselves of their inherited Eurocentric self-absorption, and had tried to see the world not from the perspective of their own little corner of it, but in its totality. That made confronting Yugoslavia, and even caring about Yugoslavia, immeasurably harder, since they had grown accustomed to thinking that Europe was one of the few areas of the world about which one did not have to care quite so much, indeed, about which *it was wrong* to care quite so much. Those who did care could be sure that someone, whether it was Boutros Boutros-Ghali at the United Nations or the local left-wing columnist, would accuse them of being specially affected by the suffering of European whites. The Secretary General, after all, had felt free to make his celebrated remark about how much better off the Bosnians were than the victims of so many of the various other slaughters raging in the world during his visit to Sarajevo on New Year's Eve, 1992.

At the very least, the effect was inhibiting, a moral brake added to the confusion that the war had produced in so many people. Even among supporters of the Bosnian cause, it was common to hear rueful expressions of surprise over having to side with Mrs. Thatcher or with various former senior officials in the Reagan administration. To this, add the fact that throughout the Croatian war, no matter how appalled many liberals in France, Britain, and, particularly, North America might have been by what the Serbs were doing, they were also haunted by the memory of Croatian fascist atrocities during the Second World War. It was not only that they recalled that Croatia had been led by Ante Pavelic and his fascist Ustasha party, which had collaborated with the Nazis and had been responsible for the murders of hundreds of thousands of Serbs and Jews. It was that this memory led them to suspect, however irrationally, that all Croats remained, at heart, fascists and anti-Semites to this day. The fact that Germany and Austria were Croatia's greatest backers only served to confirm reservations harbored by people in the other NATO countries. And the Croats did nothing to help their own cause abroad. The President, Franjo Tudjman, who had been a Communist cadre and a general in the Yugoslav National Army before his conversion to nationalism, had written a book questioning the reality of the Jewish Holocaust, and though he strenuously denied being an anti-Semite, he tended to attach more importance to holding his governing coalition together than to denouncing those members of his own HDZ party (Hrvatska Demokratska Zajednica, the Croatian Democratic Union) who did have frankly pro-Ustasha leanings. More fundamentally, the Serbs, in the Western popular imagination, had been the good guys during the Second World War. To side with their enemies, about whom, in any case, well-meaning people could not help having reservations, did not come easily even after the destruction of the Croatian city of Vukovar. In France in particular, where pro-Serb feeling was especially strong, even to defend Croatia came hard, and one of the earliest French writers to do so, Alain Finkielkraut, acknowledged as much by entitling his polemical book *How Can One Be a Croat?*

With all these conflicting claims and inhibitions interfering with one's understanding, it is not surprising in retrospect that the news from the Balkans appearing on CNN, on Antenne 2, on Britain's Sky News and Germany's ZDF could at times both seem ubiquitous and simultaneously have an effect that was, if anything, far less compelling than that of events occurring at a far greater geographical remove. I do not think I was alone in watching the siege of Vukovar and, while marveling, when it ended and the Serbs had taken the town, at the Carthaginian completeness of its destruction, also wondering whether the Croats hadn't done something to deserve what had happened to them. Even in what was the clearest case of all, the seemingly senseless bombardment of historic Dubrovnik, I remember that while I winced seeing the television images that showed naval shells exploding on the walls of the old fort and setting the magnificent buildings of the Old City ablaze, I kept thinking that the Croat defenders of the town really should have surrendered and spared the city. For even as deracinated a Jew as myself, the idea that Croatian nationalism could be a cause worth dying for—something that now seems unexceptionable to me—in the wake of the shelling of Dubrovnik still remained hard to accept.

And Dubrovnik was easy, at least as it was presented on television. Its attempted destruction, even if the actual damage to the city turned out to have been exaggerated in the initial reports of the Croation authorities, was vandalism, not war. It was also emblematic of the way events in the former Yugoslavia were being received—largely without political analysis or historical context. The reporters on the scene knew better, of course, and tried to convey what they knew as best they could. In retrospect, I think that more often than not the forms in which they had to work defeated them. What came across, unless one had a context for placing the information one was being offered, were sentimental readings of what was going on: the martyred city; the refugee family; the ruthless militiaman. All of these types existed, of course. No one could have spent a week in Bosnia during the fighting without encountering them. And corny though it doubtless is to say so, I believe that the Serbs were the villains of the war even more now than I did when all I knew of "Chetniks" was their image on CNN and what reporters like Christiane Amanpour told me about their atrocities.

The televised spectacle of the war had made me credulous—I do not recall, for example, ever pondering whether there was *more* to the story than was being shown; and there was, even in so seemingly clear-cut a case as Dubrovnik—but, paradoxically, despite or perhaps because of the sentimentality of my reactions, and the shallowness of my judgments, it also made it easy for me to move on to other concerns, the great migration, the collapse of communism, the rise of a new, Confucian capitalism in East Asia, even though I knew that the killing was taking place so close by. Zagreb, the Croatian capital, was two hours away by plane from Frankfurt. Sarajevo was only forty-five minutes further, or would have been had Bosnian airspace not been closed to anything but United Nations relief flights and marauding Serb helicopters and fixed-wing military aircraft.

Knowledge, in any case, is not power. If the fall of Yugoslavia, televised down to the last detail, teaches anything, it is that simple fact. When I finally did go to Bosnia, I had lots of information, more perhaps than most people going to most wars have ever had. I even knew the lay of the land in places I had never been to. When I went to Sarajevo for the first time, I knew already that in order to get from the airport to the Holiday Inn, where the journalists stayed, I had first to wangle permission to ride an armored personnel carrier to the UN headquarters at the old telecommunications building in town, the PTT, since to ride in a "soft" car on the airport road was foolhardy because of all the snipers. I also knew that to get from the PTT to the Holiday Inn, I had to wangle a second ride, and that if I was riding soft, rather than in a UN armored vehicle or one of the correspondents' armored Land Rovers, it was safer to take the back road be-hind the PTT, rather than to go along the main avenue, as one might have done before the war, but which was known once the shooting started as Sniper Alley. And of course I knew all this because I had seen these roads on CNN. Sarajevo might have been full of surprises when I finally began to spend time there, but visually it was almost exactly as I had expected it to be. And yet I knew *nothing*.

People routinely speak of information and knowledge as if they were the same thing. Worse, they console themselves with the thought that once they have the relevant information, they will act. It is an old conceit. If the world had known about the Holocaust, peo-ple say, it would have done something—maybe not the "bad" Ger-mans, but the rest of the "decent" world. After two years in Bosnia, I am disposed to think that had there been cameras in Auschwitz, the world might very well have done as little as it did in that pretelevi-sion age, unless, of course, it had suited the people who have power in the world to act. It is true that the sight of sixty-eight dead and nearly two hundred wounded in the Central Market in Sarajevo did finally engender a response, and, in any case, I hope I am wrong. But there had been plenty of such images before, and there will be many again in the future. How long will people's sentimental interest last? A month? A year? Surely not much longer, whether in Bosnia or in any of the slaughters in the former Soviet empire to which Bosnia is only an overture.

Sentiment was a poor guide during the Croatian war, and it has been a poor guide during the slaughter in Bosnia. It was like a whip-saw. At one moment, decent people could shed tears for Vukovar and Dubrovnik, and, in Western Europe particularly, call upon their gov-ernments to quickly recognize secessionist Croatia and Slovenia. Al-most at the next, having discovered (or imagining that they had discovered) that this recognition had not led to an end to the slaughter and the devastation, but instead seemed to have brought about new fighting in previously peaceful Bosnia-Herzegovina, many were al-most as quick to throw up their hands in despair and accede to the idea being propagated by so many Western European and UN offi-cials that recognition had been a mistake all along. Only through the Yugoslav Federation, they insisted with perfect hindsight, had the eth-nic violence to which the South Slavs were so prone been containable.

They found the idea, which was a perennial one in European consciousness in any case, that the Balkans had always been a violent place suddenly far more reasonable. The Irish writer and politician Conor Cruise O'Brien was speaking for many when he wrote in 1992, "There are places where a lot of men prefer war, and the looting and raping and domineering that go with it, to any sort of peacetime occupation. One such place is Afghanistan. Another is Yugoslavia, after the collapse of the centralizing Communist regime." The historical lesson to be drawn from this view was that when all was said and done it was the tragic, historic fate of Serbs, Croats, and Bosnian Muslims to try to kill each other off once every generation or so. Its political corollary was to argue that Bosnia-Herzegovina could not be considered a state, outside the context of the Yugoslav Federation anyway. It might sit in the United Nations, but that had been Europe's mistake. Such legal recognition should not, whatever the Bosnians reasonably had imagined, confer real legitimacy.

The trouble with any response to a political event that is fundamentally sentimental—though easy to mobilize, sentiment is almost the antithesis of real conviction—is that it allows one to oscillate from view to view. People thought so many things about what had been going on in the Balkans since the beginning of the tragedy. Before the Serbo-Croat war began in 1991, most liberal Western Europeans and North Americans had sympathized with the Serbs. Then, after Vukovar and Dubrovnik, the Croats had become the heroes. Once the Bosnian war started, it was the great victims of the fighting, the Bosnian Muslims, who had claimed the sympathy of people throughout the world. Then, when Muslims and Croats fell out in early 1993, confusion reigned, until renewed Bosnian Serb violence gave the Bosnian Muslims back their status as those with whom one was supposed to sympathize.

With people knowing so little and feeling so much, it was hardly surprising that European and American politicians who wanted nothing done to reverse the Serbs' aggression were able to weather the storms of popular anger and sorrow that would occasionally erupt after some particularly well-publicized massacre. In any case, most politicians had been predisposed to inaction from the beginning. Bismarck's quip that the Balkans were "not worth the life of one single healthy Pomeranian grenadier" is only the most famous statement writing off the region that a celebrated European states-man has made. And what the Iron Chancellor had expressed offhandedly had, in a more expansive form, been at the root of several generations of European scholarship and political analysis. Most of it served to amplify the view that Yugoslavia, situated as it is on the border between the Orthodox and the Roman Catholic worlds, and, earlier, between the Ottoman and Hapsburg spheres, was inherently an unstable, perhaps even an unsalvageable place.

It did not seem to matter that, only a few years earlier, many of the same people one heard in Washington, Paris, and Frankfurt advancing these arguments about the innate ferocity of the South Slav character had themselves managed to enjoy holidays in these same intractable, barbaric badlands. And they had felt entirely at home while they did so, despite the fact that they now believed the people there to have been almost genetically bigoted. In 1985, going to the Dalmatian coast, say to Dubrovnik, had represented anything but an intrepid bit of tourism. It had been a generic European holiday, not all that different from spending time along the Italian coast around Ancona, which is almost directly across from the Dalmatian city of Split, a hundred miles away on the other side of the Adriatic.

In 1985, most people would have predicted that the Dalmatian coast, from Istria, on the Italian border, all the way down to Dubrovnik, would play the same role in the economic development of a Yugoslavia that seemed well on its way to integration with capitalist Western Europe that the Costa del Sol had played during the 1950s in the integration of fascist Spain into the mainstream of Western European development. With its caravan parks and its marinas, duty-free areas and resort hotels, and with a natural setting that was incomparably more beautiful than the Italian Adriatic coast (Italy might boast the most beautiful cities, the only competitors being Dubrovnik and Split, but Dalmatia had the islands) and more unspoiled than the Greek islands, it remained possible to believe, almost until the moment the guns began firing, that economic history really would repeat itself. The building boom along the Dalmatian coast, which actually extended into Bosnia-Herzegovina as far as the historic city of Mostar, testifies to the fact that even in the late 1980s investors were willing to back up their belief in Yugoslavia's integration into Europe with their money. Many of the hotels along the

Adriatic that now play host to refugees are less than five years old. And there are many half-finished residences, hotels, and marinas along the same stretches, their construction having, to all appearances, stopped from one day to the next.

Certainly the Yugoslavs themselves had believed that they would prosper and that they would do so through the tourist trade. Even today, it is common in Croatia to hear people say that if only the war could be stopped, assuming the Serbs would leave Croatia alone, all would be well. The tourists would return and the prosperity that accompanied them would soon return as well. In Dubrovnik, among the surviving graffiti there is one that is perfectly emblematic of that time and those heady, "Western" expectations. The words are mostly faded now, and hemmed in and overshadowed by other, intensely martial or political tags. Most of these offer scrawled support to the fascist Ustasha party, the NDH, memorialize the martyrs of Vukovar and Osijek, or call for fierce revenge against the Serbs. But there is one that recalls what Dalmatia's destiny might have been. It reads, "Sex, Deutschemarks, and Cevapi," the last being the national dish of Yugoslavia.

But whatever the peoples of the former Yugoslavia feel about themselves, whatever they do and do not recognize when they contrast their present with their former lives, and to whatever degree what has befallen them and what they have brought upon themselves over the course of the past three and a half years has changed the way they understand both their individual destinies and their identities as part of larger nations and ethnic groups, they have not expelled themselves from Europe. That delicate operation has been performed by the Western Europeans and North Americans themselves. As the fighting continued, they began once more, as they had intermittently since the age of Bismarck, to feel comfortable speaking and thinking about the Balkans as if the region were somewhere else than Europe just as it was something other than civilized. The real Europe, the Europe that remained a civilized place, was, of course, to be found on the territory of the European Union expanded to sixteen members, and Switzerland. In a pinch, perhaps, the Czech Republic (though not Slovakia) and Hungary might be thrown in. Summed up crudely, this approach could be stated as a syllogism: "Europeans could not do these things to one another, therefore the inhabitants of the former Yugoslavia could not be Europeans."

That European-ness had always been principally an ideology, modified by a geographical conception always subject to dramatic reformulation—how often during the Cold War, after all, did people speak of Prague, which is west of Vienna, as an "Eastern European" capital?—should have gone without saying. But what began to take place, at some point during the Bosnian slaughter, as both political understanding and humanitarian resolve were shredded by the horror of what was happening, was that an account arose that was based on the most old-fashioned, essentialist notions about the Balkan character, and came accompanied with much pseudohistorical guff about ancestral hatreds and a regional predisposition to violence. It was a story that effectively read all the South Slavs with the exception of the Slovenians out of Europe. Europeans didn't act that way—not real Europeans, anyway. And so one heard and still hears people who never would be comfortable speaking of the West African character or the Latin American character, proclaiming that what has taken place in the Balkans, tragic though it has been, was probably inevitable for these cultural and historical reasons.

Far from their white skins having given them more privileges, more claims on people's understanding, the fact that the Bosnians were Caucasian may have made it possible for many people in the West to dust off eugenicist cliches they never would have dreamed of using in non-European contexts. In the United States, politically correct types who cringe at even imagined verbal slights against ethnic minorities are actually rather comfortable with words like "redneck" and "white trash." And something of the same moral gymnastic was evident in the way that people talked about the former Yugoslavia. But if they took what the Yugoslav diplomat and historian Cvijeto Job once called the "fervent folk poetry of the Balkans" as expressing the essential natures of Serbs, Croats, and Bosnian Muslims, it was finally because it was easier to do so than to try to think in less reductive registers.

By now, these explanations based on the "nature" of the Balkans are almost the only ones that people seem to find palatable. In practical terms, such accounts have the effect of rationalizing why more was not done to stop the war in Croatia or to save Bosnia. They are, of course, particularly favored by diplomats from the United Nations who by and large can claim they have acted properly in the former Yugoslavia only if they can present their "peacekeeping" mission as having been hopeless from the start. One UN official who was involved throughout the UNPROFOR operation, a brilliant diplomat who in 1991 and 1992 had been intimately involved in trying to arrange the cease-fire in Croatia that finally took hold after the fall of Vukovar, smiled wearily during the first conversation I had with him—this was before I had set foot in Bosnia—and tried to answer my questions about the "senseless" shelling of the Old City of Dubrovnik with an analogy to Balkan marital jealousy. "You know," he said, "people tell you that in rural Yugoslavia, when a man lost the woman he fancied, he would sometimes disfigure her with a knife in the belief that if he couldn't have her, then no one else should fancy her either. Don't discount that impulse when you think about Dubrovnik. It was a beautiful city, a valuable tourist attraction. I'm not sure that some Serb soldiers didn't think, 'If we can't have it, then let's ruin it for the Croats as well.' "

I first encountered Bosnians, as opposed to reporting about Bosnia or hearing accounts of their essential nature as a people, in a refugee center on the eastern outskirts of Berlin in the summer of 1992. The camp was situated on a tree-lined drive whose drab residential expanses were punctuated, like so many postunification avenues in what had been the German Democratic Republic, by secondhand automobile dealerships and colorful posters affixed to linden trees advertising everything from newly available consumer products— "Test the West" was the slogan for the popular West brand of cigarettes—to newly opened venues for strip clubs, casinos, and, improbably, female wrestling.

I had been a number of times in Yugoslavia but the places I could claim to know, and then only passingly, were the federation's northernmost republic, Slovenia, and Croatia, particularly the resort areas between Zadar and Dubrovnik along the Dalmatian coast. That wasn't much. Even in the 1960s, when Tito's regime had so much more blatantly exhibited the style and repressive spirit (if not, of course, the foreign policy) of its East bloc neighbors, Slovenia had felt more like an outcropping of neighboring Austria—Austria *very* far south of the Enns River, as the joke went on both sides of the border, in Graz and in Ljubljana. I am not sure I even believed in that more ominous, more foreign-sounding entity known as "the Balkans," let alone ever having been to such a place. Of course, I knew it from books, from accounts of Tito's partisans, and even more basically from the history of the events leading up to the assassination of the Archduke Franz Ferdinand in Sarajevo in 1914, as well as from the great travel books of the interwar period like Rebecca West's *Black Lamb and Grey Falcon.*

About Bosnia, all I had in my head were the familiar shards and bits of half-truth, cliché, and misinformation that most reasonably well-educated people shared, or, for that matter, could be found in any conventional travel guide from the early 1960s through the 1980s and can still be found today in the tourist office in downtown Sarajevo, which has, improbably, remained open throughout the war. From the books on display there, the visitor might have learned— once he or she had assimilated the fact that the ethnic and national question in Yugoslavia had been definitively resolved by Tito and that "brotherhood and unity prevailed"—that Bosnia was full of Muslims, but that although Bosnia-Herzegovina, like Serbia, Montenegro, and Macedonia, had been part of the Ottoman Empire until the third quarter of the nineteenth century, the Muslims there were of Slav rather than of Turkish or Albanian origin; and that these Muslims had not immigrated to the region but rather had been converted, though not from Orthodox Christianity but from Bogomilism—a medieval heresy said to have flourished both in Bosnia proper and along the Dalmatian coast and the Herzegovinan littoral. The Bogomils' distinctive burial stones—how easy it is to write like a tourist brochure—were usually mentioned in the same breath as two of the country's other scenic attractions—the old Ottoman bridge over the Neretva River in Mostar, the Stari Most, and of course another bridge, the one called Princip in Sarajevo, having been renamed after the First World War to honor, local wags said, the man who had provoked it.

To know what tourists know, or what local residents like to tell tourists, is to have learned history as children learn it. When one tries to learn a language, one has to start with those basics familiar to a native speaker of four. New cultures make similar demands. Once I started spending time in Bosnia, I soon discovered the obvious: that even during the Tito period the national question had been anything but solved. Tito might have imposed the slogan "Brotherhood and Unity" on all peoples of the federation, but, as Cvijeto Job has pointed out, this "history lesson did not work out as expected. Nationalists from each group [Serbs, Croats, Muslims, Albanians] typically claimed that their own depredations had been exaggerated, while those of the enemy had been played down."

Unresolved quarrels, differing versions of even the most seemingly straightforward events were to be found everywhere. Not only the tragic was in question, as in the debate over how many Serbs had been murdered in the Ustasha concentration camp at Jasenovac. Even on the level of the archival, the truth was hard to find. In Bosnia, for example, there was the question of the origins of the heretical Bogomils. I had always assumed that the explanation for their conversion lay in their having been heretics who had accepted Islam in the hope of finding protection from the crusading armies of Christian orthodoxy, Greek and Roman alike. Not so, some said. Bogomilism had all but disappeared by the time the Ottomans arrived. To an outsider, even worrying about such questions only confirmed the comment on prewar Bosnia by the great Yugoslav writer Danilo Kis, who had other, far more interesting ideas about it. Bosnia, he wrote, was "that exotic country in the heart of Europe." And yet it was on the basis of readings of equally arcane events that had taken place hundreds of years earlier that people were killing and dying in Bosnia. The events themselves might have been forgotten, or the memory of them manipulated by contemporary nationalist rabble-rousers, but in Bosnia, to paraphrase the old joke about Northern Ireland, even when everything else disappeared one thing remained: the grudge.

I had not come to the refugee camp that day to argue Balkan history. What I hoped to see was the way in which immigrants from the nonwhite world and the former Soviet empire were dealing with one another, which, in the main, was not very well. The camp, like so many camps I had been in during the previous few months, had its own racial and geographic hierarchies. The Middle Easterners looked down on the Africans, the Eastern Europeans on the Middle Easterners, and both groups openly feared and despised the Gypsies and spoke bitterly of even having to share with them the surplus East German National People's Army barracks in which everyone was housed. Nonetheless, the officials who ran the camp reported that, wherever they were from, most of the residents soon learned to socialize fairly easily with one another in the evenings (people were free to leave during the day). They were quick to add that this fraternization did not extend to the Gypsies.

Only one non-Gypsy family did not conform to this general pattern, one of the camp's directors told me. He was a bluff East Berliner who in his gait and gesture resembled nothing so much as a small-town American high school football coach. Toward his charges, he exhibited that curious combination of distaste and solicitude that could have been said to mark his country's attitude toward their presence in Germany. He said the antisocial family in question were Muslims. Perhaps noticing my puzzled expression, he added quickly—letting the words hang in the air for a long moment—that they were Muslims from Europe, from Bosnia. "They're not the kind of Islamic people you and I normally imagine," he added. "They don't wear headscarves or pray all day. Actually, they really are Europeans, quite normal Europeans."

After we had completed our tour of the camp, he took me to see them. My visit had turned out to overlap with that of a party of schoolchildren from what had been one of the more prosperous neighborhoods in West Berlin in prereunification days, and the camp director had melded the two tours. The students had collected toys for the asylum seekers' children and carried them rather awkwardly as they were led through the dormitories. "It was all their idea," their teacher insisted, although her unwillingness to let me speak with her charges outside her presence made me wonder if the visit or the collection had been quite as elective as she pretended. Finally we extricated ourselves—the teacher was still lecturing her kids on the "beauty" of Gypsy culture as we moved out of earshot—and headed to the building where the Bosnian family was housed.

They were a family of seven, five adults and two children, ranging in age between eleven and forty-five, in a single room. All looked in reasonable shape both physically and psychologically, except for a young woman in her mid-twenties who was red-eyed and gaunt. Their dress was shabby, but certainly no shabbier than that of many people one saw in the part of East Berlin the camp abutted. Like refugees the world over, they all seemed to smoke constantly, with for me the interesting difference that unlike refugees in many parts of the Third World, the women smoked as much as if not more than the men.

Whatever his motives may have been, the camp director had been right to say in effect that as refugees these people behaved curiously. In contrast to the Sri Lankans, Kurds, and Somalis, and even some of the Poles and non-Gypsy Romanians I had talked with that day (none of the adult Gypsies I approached would speak to me), their entire bearing lacked the passivity so common among refugees in holding camps. And, to the obvious, barely concealed discomfort of the camp director, they exhibited none of the refugees' at least feigned deference either. They stared levelly back at us as we entered and, after motioning us to sit down and clearing a place, began voicing what seemed to be a large number of complaints—more in the tones of people complaining to a hotel manager or the superintendent in an apartment building than in those one customarily associates with people who have lost everything they owned and have fled for their lives from a war that consumed their country. "The heat did not work last night," the red-eyed young woman said. "Where can our daughter play safely here?" the oldest of the women asked, adding, "And when will the schooling start?"

The men said little, as is often the case when the figure in authority is also a man and, as a result, at least the distant possibility exists of any quarrel leading to physical violence. But they nodded emphatically as the women spoke. To listen to them was to get the sense that while these Bosnians were physically there in that shabby room in the camp, psychologically they had not yet made the journey from their homes into a precarious exile. It was their middle-class assurance that struck me most, a sense of entitlement that, while it might eventually be knocked out of them (I never saw this family again, though a year later I tried to recontact them), they had so far managed to preserve in the face of their material losses. It was by no means an asset. When one of the men asked, "How can we be expected to survive here?" it reminded me that a middle-class upbringing is anything but the best preparation for life as a refugee.

The camp director had been right, I thought looking at them. They seemed anomalous in the setting of the camp, to themselves as much as to the German official and to me. "We shouldn't be here, among these others," the older man said to me quietly, as if he had read my thoughts. To which, summoning up what for an ex-official of the German Democratic Republic must have been a newly minted familiarity with the rhetoric of racial tolerance and multiculturalism, the camp director interposed, "We are all human beings, you know." But the Bosnian was not to be moved by any sound bites from the "Ode to Joy." "I did not say all men were not brothers," he said with heavy irony. "And I do not say that I am against the other people here. I only say that I and my family do not belong in this camp. You must know"—his voice rose—"that what happened to us in Bosnia should not have happened. This is Europe. This is 1992. And we lived like you, not like the people who are here did before they came to Germany. These others"—he gestured, his arm tracing an arc encompassing the entire camp—"well, I feel very sorry for them. But what happened to them is another tragedy. What has happened to us . . ." He stared directly at the camp director and at me. "That is your tragedy as well as ours."

The camp director nodded sagely. "The loss of any home," he replied, "is a great tragedy." Then he quickly stepped out of the room, leaving me alone, as we had arranged, to speak with the Bosnians. The silence lasted a long time, as it often does in such situations. There is always something shaming about doing such interviews, the sense of being a voyeur, and of appropriating other people's losses. "When did you leave? What happened to your family? How many killed? Raped? Tortured?" It is all not quite on the level of the bitter joke of the British journalist arriving on some horrific scene and asking, "Anyone here been raped and speak English?" but it can come close. One notes the horrible story down, and, after the encounter has run its course—a self-serving way of saying after the refugees have spilled their guts to you, or at least as much as you need for your story—moves on to the next. Or one winds it up for the day and wanders off to a pub or hotel bar.

Such discomfort goes with the territory. What made the Bosnians seem different was certainly not their predicament—refugees are all too familiar at the cusp of the millennium—but, I came to realize uncomfortably, the fact I was addressing Europeans. At first, I was reluctant to admit this fact. Like the camp director, I too have my liberal pieties. I found myself unsure of what to say. The silence lengthened. In the end, it was the older of the Bosnian women who broke it. "Would you like something to eat?" she asked, in the tone of a hostess trying to draw an unsociable guest into the general conversation. I nodded, and she cut me a slice of hard sausage, a chunk of chalky white bread, and two orange sections, pausing before each operation to wipe off the blade of her small Swiss army knife on a corner of the wax paper in which the meat had been wrapped. After I took a first bite, she nodded happily. And then, first haltingly, then in a flood, the adults began to talk about what had happened in Bosnia to turn them into refugees. They used words like "ethnic cleansing," and spoke about facing snipers, artillery fire, and rocket-propelled grenades with a familiarity I had never expected to hear from any European who was not a soldier or an aid worker.

Two years later, their faces remain with me still. In my notebook, I read that they were Muslims who had been ethnically cleansed from the northern Bosnian town of Sanski Most; that they had then made their way to Germany circuitously; and that, if they blamed what had happened to them on the Bosnian Serbs, they attributed their survival to the fact that they had a family friend serving with these same Bosnian Serb forces. He, said the older woman, a fond expression crossing her features, had done what he could to protect them. As Bosnian stories go, this one is better than many. While they told *of* rapes and murders, they had not experienced them or even witnessed them directly. And they had had enough Deutschemarks to keep traveling toward Germany, rather than finding themselves stuck, like so many people from their part of northern Bosnia, as refugees in Croatia, where life was considerably harder than in the camps in Germany. They and their stories fascinated me in a way at the time I could not begin to account for. Shortly thereafter, with the strongest sense of compulsion I have ever known as a writer but with, otherwise, a very unclear sense of what I would do when I got there, I managed to secure a commission from an American magazine to write about Bosnia, and boarded a flight for Zagreb.

III

To a foreign visitor expecting to arrive in a city at war, the first surprise about Zagreb is how placidly Western European it looks. There are no sandbagged public buildings, no gun emplacements on the roofs of commercial buildings, and no fixed police checkpoints after one crosses the perimeter of the Zagreb airport. The only immediate giveaway that one has not arrived in some out-of-the-way corner of Western Europe is the fact that there are no nonwhite guest workers to be seen anywhere. Unlike France or Germany, Croatia, apart from its Gypsies, is racially homogeneous. Otherwise, the surprise is that there is no surprise. It is strange enough to arrive in Frankfurt or Zurich and realize how close one already is to the war in the former Yugoslavia. To arrive in Zagreb itself, which is less than thirty-five kilometers from the front line, and yet have no real sense of mobilization, let alone of war, is stranger still. The housing blocks on the outskirts of Zagreb look much like the working-class districts of any European city, while, before arriving in the city center, one crosses through a landscape punctuated by construction sites and new commercial buildings. The billboards along the way advertise the latest Western consumer goods—Benetton sweaters, German automobiles, and the like. They send the clear message that even if Western European levels of prosperity are not yet at hand, Croatians have every reason to expect to start moving toward them in the not-too-distant future.

In the historic center of Zagreb, the same message is driven home, though in a less consumerist way. In the shadow of the yellows, grays, and blues of the city's handsome nineteenth-century architecture, can the visitor really doubt the truth of that deepest of Croatian national conceits: its Western-ness? No matter how recently it was part of the country known as Yugoslavia, Zagrebers will tell you,

Croatia actually has less in common culturally with either the Balkans in general or Serbia in particular than it does with its Hapsburg past or with Western Europe's future. One of the most common decals one sees on cars speaks to this identification with the world of the European Union. The letters "HR," the abbreviation for Hrvatska (Croatia), are set on a blue background and surrounded by the twelve gold stars of the EU. Of course, the pervasiveness of this decal tells one far more about Croatian wishful thinking than about the country's actual situation. Nonetheless, it is common to hear even sophisticated people in Zagreb insist that if the fighting ended, the dream might become a reality.

In Zagreb they serve cappuccino, rather than Turkish coffee, in the cafes on Ban Jelacic Square. And, as is so often true in Austria, sitting down to a meal in Zagreb can seem largely like a long preamble to dessert. But these small details of life are not just facts of life; they carry with them a heavily ideologized quality. In the foam of a coffee cup, or the baker's whipped cream, there are symbolic resonances for many people that can appear out of proportion to their ostensible importance. One expects people to talk about Croatia's economic problems or the war, and instead, as often as not, they talk about their "normal lives," as exemplified by what kind of coffee they like to drink. And reminding one that the cafes serve cappuccino is not enough; Croatians also must make a point of telling one repeatedly that they do so "just like in a Viennese cafe."

This presentation of Croatia as belonging properly to Central Europe rather than the Balkans is as much a part of official propaganda as of popular conceit. "Today with over a million inhabitants," runs an article in Croatia Airlines' in-flight magazine, "Zagreb is in many ways a Mittel European city." Elsewhere in the same magazine, in a section entitled "Croatia is . . ." the visitor is instructed that "in the northern regions, the way of life is typically Central European, whereas the South is Mediterranean." The real message is as much concerned with what Croatia is not as with what it is, and that message, curious spellings and all, is that Croatia has nothing either historically or culturally to do with the Balkans.

Also implicit in such assertions, whether specifically they concern European Union membership, Sacher torte, tourism, or Zagreb architecture, is a deeper message redolent of far more than simple local pride or provincial defensiveness. Yugoslavia, for all its strains, was a big country; Croatia is not. Yugoslavia was an important country; Croatia is not. The realities of this are brought home to individual Croatians in obvious ways, from the ever mounting costs of goods in shops to the difficulty of traveling outside the country. They need visas to travel now (when they carried Yugoslav passports, most Western European countries admitted them without visas); and even if they can secure a visa, given the state of the economy few can afford to go abroad. And the tourism on which the economy of prewar Croatia was so largely dependent has all but disappeared. On the Dalmatian coast, from Zadar all the way down to Dubrovnik, paying customers probably couldn't get into even the best hotels anyway, because the Zagreb government has required hoteliers to take in tens of thousands of refugees both from Serb-occupied areas of Croatia and from Bosnia. In Zagreb itself, the city's largest hotel, the Intercontinental, a hideous tower block built over the protests of architectural-minded Zagrebers in the mid-1980s in anticipation of the city's future as a Western-looking commercial center, began to play host mainly to UN military and civilian officials in 1992. They get a hefty discount. The Intercon's doormen wear elaborate green-and-gold uniforms straight out of a Viennese farce, but there is nothing farcical about the French and British aircrews, or civilian officials from UNPROFOR and the Office of the United Nations High Commissioner for Refugees, as they move in and out of the lobby, often wearing flak jackets in light UN blue and cradling white Kevlar helmets under their arms

However nationalistic they may be, and however reluctant they are about discussing with a visitor what is really going on, most Croatians recognize the difficulties they face. Their attitude toward the past, however, can be almost as disconcerting as their attitude toward the present and the future. Contradictions abound. It is common to hear people talk about how impossible the current situation is for them economically. "Before the war," a senior Croatian academic who has been an unofficial adviser to the Tudjman government since 1991 told me over dinner on one of my first visits to Zagreb, "I had a house on the Dalmatian coast near Dubrovnik, two cars, and pretty substantial savings in Deutschemarks. Now, my house is partly destroyed by shelling, and the mines haven't been cleared from some of the land around it, and everyone's foreign bank accounts have been effectively frozen. I don't blame the government—Croatia is at war—but that's the way things are. It really is very, very hard for us."

A few moments later, though, he was insisting that his life had been even more desperate in Yugoslavia *before* the war. "We couldn't go on living the way we did," the professor told me. "Our lives were unbearable. The Serbs controlled everything. We weren't free, and what was more, it seemed we never would be free. Tito suppressed the historical longings of the Croatian people for independence. That was bad enough. But at least Tito gave us a little breathing room. When Milosevic came to power in Belgrade, and started transforming the Yugoslav Federation into a state that was centralized in Belgrade, the idea of Croatia's continuing to be part of Yugoslavia was inconceivable. Maybe it always was. I know that, to the end, some people here felt like Yugoslavs. I did, sometimes. But I also always felt like a Croat first and last."

If the past had been politically impossible, and the present was intolerable materially and economically, that left only the future. Most Croatians continued to hope for better times. There were moments when such optimism could seem to approach the level of fantasy. In January 1993, for example, President Tudjman had justified a Croatian military offensive in Dalmatia during which his forces had recaptured from the Krajina Serbs the Zadar airport and the site of the destroyed Maslenica Bridge—a vital link in the highway that before the war had linked Zagreb and Dubrovnik—by declaring that the attack had been necessary because of the upcoming summer tourist season. Without a rebuilt tourist bridge, he said, the foreigners would never come. As if Dubrovnik, whose outskirts were still heavily mined, remained a destination the average German or Dutch holidaymaker was yearning to revisit. Nonetheless, Tudjman asserted that the bridge would be rebuilt by summer. Warming to his theme, and making a prediction that unfortunately conjured up echoes of Hitler's "Thousand Year Reich," he went on to claim that the bridge would last for "a thousand years."

The rosy images of Croatia's future that Tudjman presented in his speeches hardly coincided with reality. Some areas of the country were relatively well-off. In Istria, the resort area in the northwest of

Croatia, between the town of Rijeka and the Slovenian border, tourists were beginning to return in substantial numbers. But Istria had been largely sheltered from the war, and had begun to see a revival of its prewar tourist trade as early as the spring of 1993. Things also remained relatively tolerable in Zagreb. But even in the capital, life in a time of neither peace nor war has been hard and is steadily becoming harder for most people. Supermarkets are well stocked, but the situation of many who shop in them could be discerned by bins full of loaves of white bread sold by the quarter-loaf. Cheaper still is black bread, which is heavily subsidized by the Croatian government, but is available in the bakeries only very early in the morning before regular store hours. The lines have formed by dawn and have disappeared by seven. A foreign businessman, out for an early-morning jog, might encounter these lines, as might someone coming home from a night in someone else's bed. Otherwise, it is possible to spend quite a lot of time in Zagreb, moving in one good Mercedes taxi after another between government buildings, office towers, and the first-rate Esplanade Hotel (the preferred haunt of the foreign journalists), without ever quite taking in the difficulties most people experience in their everyday lives, let alone the fact that the first front line begins some thirty-five kilometers away.

Some shortages are more noticeable. Pharmacies have not functioned properly for a long time, even in Zagreb. In 1993 and 1994, long after the Serbo-Croat war had ended, it was common to ask for something as ordinary as antidiarrheal pills only to be told that the shop had run out and that it was anybody's guess when more would be available. Still, Zagreb at its worst was never any shabbier than many other cities in Central and Eastern Europe, including most in the former East Germany. And the gap between rich and poor is far less noticeable than in, say, Moscow or even Warsaw. The streets are clean; most people are well dressed; and while native Zagrebers make much of the presence of beggars and panhandlers on their streets—"We are not used to this," the Croatian writer Slavenka Drakulic told me as she reached for a banknote to give to an elderly couple who were begging together and had approached us—even during the worst periods of economic austerity and mass unemployment, their number was low by Western European standards, let alone American ones.

For all of this, the anxieties of Zagreb remain not only hard to discern but internally somewhat contradictory. Croatia is not a police state, but it is scarcely an open democracy either. There is enormous pressure in the media and at the workplace to conform. And any opposition to the policies of the Tudjman government is likely to be denounced in the largely government-controlled press as near treasonous: playing into the hands of Croatia's enemies by sullying the nation's image abroad. This question of image is central; the debates in progovernment circles about how to improve it, endless. Before the Germans began to join the other great powers putting pressure on them, Croatians worried less. A rather triumphalist book that recounted German involvement in getting the EC to recognize Croatia summarized the mood of 1993 in official Zagreb. The title of the book, a bestseller, was *Bonn: Croatia's Second Front.* But as the degree to which the Croats as well as the Serbs were participating in the carving up of Bosnia became clear in Germany, and Bonn became increasingly unsympathetic to the Croat view, the mood in Zagreb became defensive and conspiracy-minded. There was more and more talk about Croatia's many enemies abroad. A senior government official spoke for many when he called upon Croatians to "work together to construct a positive image of Croatia in the world." The image he had in mind, of course, was of innocence, victimization, and virtue.

In this atmosphere of what amounted to a sort of linguistic martial law, vocal opposition, as opposed to a bit of grousing in the cafe or complaining to visitors, has carried real risks for Croatian citizens. Most of the independent media was closed down, or put into the hands of journalists loyal to Tudjman's party, the HDZ. Even at its freest, the Croatian press rarely came close to the kind of critical stance that was commonplace in much of the print media in supposedly totalitarian Belgrade. For Croatian males between eighteen and fifty, attacking the government too blatantly has led to suddenly being called up for military service. This happened to Victor Ivancic, the editor in chief of the one full-throatedly dissident publication, the satirical newsweekly *Feral Tribune,* in early January 1994. After completing three weeks of training, Ivancic was abruptly told he could go home, but warned that he could be called back and his colleagues on the paper mobilized at any moment.

The message was clear. Throughout the war, mobilization was understood by many urban Croatian professional men, and not only those involved in opposition activities, as the threat constantly hanging over their heads should they fail to toe the HDZ line. "Don't kid yourself," a young Zagreb doctor once remarked to me. "I may be riding high today, but one wrong move and I could wind up working at a field hospital in Central Bosnia. I don't worry about the secret police banging down the door in the middle of the night. It's the clerk knocking timidly in the late afternoon to present me with my mobilization papers. That's what persuades me to do my job and keep my mouth shut."

In previous eras in Croatia, emigration was always an option, but the war changed all that. It quickly became all but impossible for Croatians to secure the appropriate visas for their traditional destinations—Canada, Australia, the United States, and Germany. Tourist visas were hard enough to obtain. And if a Croatian were to receive permission to go abroad, it was by no means clear that he or she would be welcomed with quite the same enthusiasm as would have been the case before independence. In the large Croatian communities abroad, the mood was, as is so often the case with diasporas, far more extreme than it was at home. To leave Croatia for Melbourne or Chicago was more and more viewed as a kind of treason. In those places, the talk was all of returning home, not necessarily to fight, as exiled Croatians had done, savagely and effectively, in 1991 in eastern Slavonia, but to help build the country. As the professor had said, life in a free Croatia might be hard but Croatia was still free. That might not have been enough to banish the war from people's minds. But mostly people in Zagreb seemed to cope with their apprehensions by keeping them as much as they could under wraps, by living as much as possible as if Zagreb were a city at peace and they, its citizens, were just riding out some tough economic times.

In Zagreb, the streets around the main squares are full of soldiers, most apparently home on leave, but unlike, say, in Tel Aviv, Croatian soldiers do not carry their assault rifles with them as they window-shop or walk arm in arm with their girlfriends. Nor, as in Buenos Aires, do they stop what they are doing to salute a passing officer. The impression Zagreb gives is more like that of a Swiss city in which reservists on their way back home from a refresher course have stopped to have a little fun, than of the rear echelon of a country a third of whose territory remains under enemy occupation, and a place that is well within range of Serb long-range artillery and rockets. The most wrenching signs of the war, apart from the occasional military vehicle, with its telltale yellow license plates, which one sees being driven too fast and too imperiously through town, are the young men walking painfully with the help of crutches, or with long external metal fixators attached to their legs. Modern ammunition is so powerful that a negligible impact that formerly might have caused a flesh wound now will likely as not shatter bone because of the sheer velocity of the round. The press in general, and Croatia's appalling government-directed television in particular, might trumpet the latest war news. But on the streets few stop to pay attention to the memorials to the dead, or even to browse through the arrays of patriotic and neofascist trinkets—the red-and-white-checkerboard emblem of Croatia vying for space with Ustasha emblems, T-shirts, cassettes, and key rings—being hawked in the stalls that stand between Ban Jelacic Square and Zagreb's beautiful open-air market in the city's upper town.

Of course, however intent people may be, as Slavenka Drakulic put it, on "pretending to live in normality with all their might," after a while their masks are bound to begin to slip. Left to their own devices, though, most of the foreigners coming to Zagreb these days would be unlikely even to concern themselves with the city's state of mind, let alone its degree of genuine or affected "Western-ness." Most began coming to Zagreb at the time of the Serbo-Croat war, and returned once the fighting in Bosnia had started. Ironically, UNPROFOR had originally been based in Sarajevo, since, in 1991, the Bosnian capital had seemed like a safe, neutral place—Alia Izetbegovic's Bosnian government being viewed as neither pro-Serb nor pro-Croat. But once the siege of Sarajevo began in April 1992, the United Nations centralized the headquarters operations of UNPROFOR and the UNHCR in Zagreb. As a result, the city began to be the compulsory jumping-off point for relief workers, journalists in need of UN accreditation, and anyone else who wanted to get into Bosnia. Most foreigners used Croatia as a place for briefings and R&R. And the dirty secret, as Croatians kept discovering to their frustration, was that the foreigners didn't really care what was going on in Croatia once the cease-fire brokered by the former American Secretary of State, Cyrus Vance, took hold and UN forces were interposed between Serbs and Croats in early 1992.

If the Croatians kept listing all the various ways in which they were demonstrably a Western people, and comparing Zagreb with other cities to the north and west, more than anything they were talking to themselves, not to the foreigners who for the most part came from those cities. This is not to say that the national question, as it is called in the former Yugoslavia, has not been at the heart of both Croatian and Serbian politics and culture since at least the nineteenth century. The kind of rhetoric one heard in Zagreb in 1993 echoed that one would have heard around the time of the first Yugoslavia in the aftermath of World War I. In Croatia, the largely Hapsburg-derived legal and political codes were replaced by the laws and procedures that had governed life in Serbia before the "Kingdom of the Serbs, Croats, and Slovenes." And these differences were real enough. The year of the union was also the year when the relatively trivial though emblematic question of corporal punishment in the army had arisen. The lash had been abolished in Croatia in 1869 but was reinstated, according to Serb military norms, in 1918. The decision provoked many Croats vociferously to contrast their own civilized Western-ness with the barbaric Balkanness of their Serb fellow countrymen.

Nearly twenty years later, when Rebecca West arrived in Zagreb in 1937, at the beginning of her trip to what had become the Kingdom of Yugoslavia, her Serb guide, Constantine, cautioned her that most of the Croats she would meet could be depended upon to bring up the question of their own difference. They would tell her, he said, that "we are not as the Serbs in Belgrade, here we are businesslike, we do things as they are done in Vienna." West disliked the Croats almost as much as she admired the Serbs and hated the Germans, on the very grounds they advanced in their own favor, believing them to have been "weakened by Austrian influence as by a profound malady." "It was true," she writes. "So they had said to us constantly in the banks and hotels and museums."

For all her originality, West, in her famous book, was very much a writer of her times. However much she hated German "race thinking," she herself was unable to make sense of much of what she saw during her six weeks in Yugoslavia without appeal to explanations based on the array of supposedly immutable "national characteristics" that she believed to apply to the individual Serbs, Croats, Muslims, and Germans she encountered. Anyone arriving in Zagreb sixty years later from places to the north and west where such assumptions had fallen into disrepute soon discovered that whatever had been the fate of these habits of thought in the West, one way in which Croatia seemed very unlike the "advanced" Western societies to which it claimed kinship was people's uncritical adherence to the idea that every nation had a definable and unchanging national character.

Young Croatians might shop in the same boutiques as their opposite numbers in New York, have the same taste in popular music, or have adapted similar sexual mores, but this did not make them cosmopolitans in the "postnational" sense that characterized so many middle-class Western Europeans and North Americans. They spoke about themselves as Croats in much the way their grandparents had done when Rebecca West had visited Zagreb. In West's time, they had not looked the same as people in Britain or Germany, the gap between Western and Balkan thinking having been reflected in the alienness of their dress. But it turned out that having the same haircuts as people in Hamburg, or the same jogging shoes as people in Camden Town, had not altered these young Croatians' essentially nationalist and tribal understandings of themselves by one iota. Global village or no global village, it appeared one could become a fully vested member of the postnational, transnational consumer society—as so many Yugoslavs had done between 1970 and 1990—and yet remain a full-fledged tribalist at the same time. The mistake had been in imagining that acquiring new tastes and identities automatically meant shedding the old allegiances. In the Balkans, at least, it did not.

Moreover, the more carefully one listened, the more it seemed clear that the talk of Croatia being "Western" was as much, if not more, a negative proposition, a way of reading the Serbs out of Europe, out of "the West," as it was a positive claim meant to establish Croatia's bona fides for membership in the unified Europe of the twenty-first century. It was also a way of reconfirming the belief that Yugoslavia had been an impossible idea from the beginning, that

Croats were so different from Serbs that the two peoples had never had any business living together in the same country in the first place. Had the differences been only political—the function, say, of specific political decisions taken by Slobodan Milosevic after 1987 when he took over the Serbian Communist party—the possibility at least that one day they could have been resolved politically would have been hard to deny. But if the differences were based on two irreconcilable spiritual approaches to life, then the great slogan of the Tito regime, "Brotherhood and Unity," could safely be dismissed as little better than a sick joke. And those who argued otherwise in Croatia were denounced by followers of the regime as "Yugozombies," "Yugonostalgics," or "Hrbi" (a conflation of the words for Serb and Croat, *Srpski* and *Hrvati*), people who, for whatever reasons, had refused to learn the lessons of Vukovar and Dubrovnik.

It was so easy in Zagreb, no matter how far away it could seem from the war, to give in to these tribalizing ways of thinking. After three years of war, the spiritual and the political had become virtually indistinguishable almost everywhere in the former Yugoslavia. Everything that had happened in Croatia since 1991 or what had since happened in Bosnia was understood through the prism of concepts of civility and barbarism presented as being the innate national properties of the peoples involved. Too often, in Zagreb no less than in other parts of the former Yugoslavia, the proof of this virtue was to be found in the existence of some historic wrong, as if being a victim—as everyone in the Balkans had been at some point or another in their history—in and of itself made one a member of a "good" people. The corollary to this was that, as a victim people, the Croats could do no wrong themselves, while as a Western, civilized people, they could not behave barbarously. In other words, like all identity politics, the stories being told in Croatia, whether they concerned the nine-hundred-year-long struggle for statehood or the Croatian people's innate Western-ness, were a morality play, and not politics in the usual sense at all.

Inevitably, this degree of self-love, no matter how understandable it was historically as the Croatian response to the very real thwarting of national ambitions under the Hapsburgs and under both monarchist and Titoist Yugoslavia, carried with it an astonishing inability to imagine that anybody might not think well of Croatia. It also led many Croatians to gloss over even the most terrible periods of their own history and to become indignant when foreigners brought them up. In particular, while the overwhelming majority of Croatians were neither fascists nor fascist sympathizers, many viewed the Ustasha period quite differently than most non-Croats did. Where outsiders saw the era of the Nazi-supported state of Ante Pavelic as a descent into fascist barbarism, many Croats kept returning to the fact that, odious though his regime had been, for a brief period their country had been independent. Where outsiders reproached them—as had many local Serbs—for still using the checkerboard emblem, they retorted that the fact that it was used by Pavelic did not forever make this ancient symbol unusable. And where outsiders wondered why, when the Croatian authorities decided to abandon the Yugoslav currency unit, the dinar, they had insisted on adopting the kuna, the money that had been in use in Croatia during the Pavelic regime, Croatians insisted that an image of a *kuna* (the word means marten) had first appeared on a silver coin in 1256.

In each case, the Croatian reply was factually correct and morally obtuse at the same time. The checkerboard was an old symbol, and had been used by the Croatian cultural association, Naprednak, for more than a century. It is to be found on the facades of nineteenth-century buildings in many parts of Croatia and Bosnia, including the Hapsburg-era building on Marshal Tito Street in Sarajevo, where that branch of Naprednak is housed. But the checkerboard was undeniably a provocation, particularly to the Serbs in Croatia who lost family in wartime Ustasha massacres, or numbered relatives among the victims killed in the Jasenovac concentration camp, where, at a conservative estimate, several hundred thousand Serbs and Jews were slaughtered. And no learned references to medieval numismatics could mitigate the impression that in opting for the kuna, the Croatian authorities were also opting for a symbolic continuity between themselves and the Pavelic regime. More generally, for the Croatians to claim history's warrant for using such symbols, while denying to the Serbs and others the same history-based license to fear their use, was all too typical of the way people were absorbed by their own national pasts and quite indifferent to those of other nations.

By 1993, all over the former Yugoslavia, this understanding that all groups had of themselves as being the historical victims of other groups had reached a point where almost the only permissible stance was one of injured innocence. In this spirit, Croatians without an anti-Semitic bone in their bodies professed not to understand why outsiders had complained when President Tudjman, on the campaign trail in 1990 and defending himself against extreme-right hecklers who were questioning his Croatian-ness, had insisted that his wife was neither a Serb nor a Jew. Nor could they see why outsiders got so exercised over the renaming of streets after such figures from the Ustasha period as Pavelic's Minister of Religion and Education, Mile Budak. Croatians were civilized. To retort that the Serbs, too, spoke in such tones was to commit an intolerable affront. Serb martyrology was a self-serving, bogus creed that had led the Serbs to commit terrible crimes. But Croat martyrology wasn't this kind of bogus special pleading; it was an accurate appraisal of what had taken place. One bitter joke, told all over the former Yugoslavia, aptly summed up this lethal combination of injured innocence and bottomless pride. "Why should I be a minority in your country," it ran, "when you can be a minority in my country?"

I should declare that I have always found absurd the idea that any group of people is especially virtuous, or that a human identity can ever be other than fluid and contingent. I believed before arriving in the former Yugoslavia that there was nothing inevitable about the war there—that it was the result of political choices, not national character or ancient historical blood feuds—and I believe it after spending almost two years traveling in and out and seeing many people die and kill. And yet, when I first began to listen to the various accounts of just how fundamentally different Croats and Serbs were from each other, like so many other foreigners I found myself tempted to accept them at face value. All the blood that had been spilled and would go on being spilled, whatever the cost in material terms, whatever the sacrifices required, in the name of ethnic irreconcilability and ethnic pride seemed, during my first days in Croatia, to provide a definitive refutation of my cosmopolitan conceits.

Typically, the first day in Zagreb for a journalist must be devoted to securing accreditation. After an hour at the United Nations head-

quarters getting an UNPROFOR press card, I went over to the Intercontinental to get a Croatian press credential. As I was to find would
be so often the case in such offices, the staff was made up of young
Canadians of Croatian origin, some of whom had moved back for
good and others who had not yet decided where they would live. As
he obligingly filled out my ID card, I asked one rather sweet-looking
member of the staff, a public relations officer, when he had decided
to come to Zagreb. "I've always dreamed of it," he said, with a wide,
well-fluoridated smile. "Even when I was growing up in West Van, I
was waiting for the day. In my high school yearbook, I had them put,
'Jeff wants to return to a free and independent Croatia.' And now
I've done it, just like I knew I would."

"And do you feel at home?" I asked.

"Absolutely," he said, grinning. "It's like my parents—they came
to Canada after World War Two—always said. It's just great to be
home." All he would say about his parents' move was that they had
been "anti-Communists," and whether they were Ustasha or not I
could not get him to say. I do not think it matters particularly. Free
Croatia, the integrity of Bosnia, or the unity of all Serbs within or
outside the borders of Serbia and Montenegro proper, these were the
creeds that were causing people to kill and die, to give up the standard of living they had taken for granted before the fighting started,
to uproot themselves, and to live as they had never lived before.
"What about West Van?" I asked him. And he replied, "Well, I miss
the hockey—the Canucks—but it's better to finally be where you
belong."

"Could you have lived here when it was a part of Yugoslavia?" I
asked.

He laughed. "Not a chance. Even if I had been allowed to come
back, which I doubt, I wouldn't have wanted to. In those days, the
Serbs ran everything—the police, the government, the army—the
Serbs did, and the Communists. And I'm a Croat. I can get along a
whole lot better with an American like you or a Sikh in Vancouver
than I can with a Serb."

What people feel about belonging cannot be refuted by reason
alone, let alone by dogmatic theories—the Marxist idea of "false
consciousness" being only the most arrogant of these—that what
people think they feel is not what they actually feel. But I remember,

even that day, wondering if the young man's fervent assertions of difference really made sense. If Serbs, Croats, and Muslims were really so self-evidently different one from the other, then why did the examples people chose to illustrate this difference—one kind of coffee in Zagreb, another in Belgrade; a tendency among Croats toward promptness contrasted with the Serbs' more insouciant, "southern" sense of time; a certain Germanic obsession among Croats with cleanliness and order—not only seem comparatively trivial, but also seem almost generic recapitulations of all the clichés contrasting frugal, work-driven northerners with sexy, irresponsible southerners that can be found in almost every European country and in many East Asian ones as well?

After being told for the umpteenth time that Croats were really Westerners and the Serbs really Byzantines (at a certain moment after Croatia became independent, the term "Byzantine" had become a slur in nationalist circles; a prominent member of the HDZ had actually gotten up in Parliament, saying that he was pleased to announce that there had been "no Byzantine blood" in his family for three hundred years), I began, perversely perhaps, to wonder just how profound, despite all the blood that had been spilled, these differences really were. After all, the parliamentarian who rose to reassure his colleagues about his bloodlines would not have felt himself obliged to do so had he spoken a different language or been easy to distinguish visually from the hated Serbs—as hard-line Hutu in Rwanda claim, often wrongly, their Tutsi enemies to be, or as Nazis thought of Jews. Was it because he looked more or less the same, and sounded more or less the same, but genuinely felt himself or wanted to feel himself to be different—indeed, because he believed that his strength and salvation, both individually and as a Croat, lay in his sense of ethnic and national difference—that this Croat politician felt a particular obligation to trumpet his Croatian-ness as often as he could?

Mythmaking routinely accompanies the birth of new states. The historian Eric Hobsbawm gives as a classic example of this kind of thinking the references in Pakistani textbooks to five thousand years of Pakistani history. In reality, he notes, the notion of a separate Pakistani state was probably first bruited by Jinnah's nationalists in the 1930s, and any relationship between the Indus Valley civilization and the post-1948 government is purely mythological. But, as in Pakistan, in Croatia (and, of course, in Serbia as well) nationalist politicians were constantly fabricating continuities and imaginary communities where, historically, none had existed. The martyred city of Dubrovnik, for example, whose supposed destruction Croats used as the ultimate example of Serb barbarism, had not even been a part of the first Yugoslavia. Leaving aside the fact that it turned out that Dubrovnik had been much less badly shelled than was thought at first, historically the city had been Byzantine, Venetian, and Ottoman far longer than it had been Croatian.

The more essential task of the nationalists (claims in war are almost always exaggerated; this does not necessarily make them lies) seemed to be to create or amplify differences beyond those that already existed. Historical enmities had indeed separated Croats and Serbs as collectivities at various times in their histories. But when all was said and done, the only truly irreducible definition of what identified individual Croats, Serbs, and Muslims ethnically, and equally important, distinguished them from each other, was religion—more exactly, in many cases, religious origin, since most people in the former Yugoslavia were secular. They were all South Slavs, many bound more by region, class, and whether or not they lived in cities than by ethnicity in the conventional sense. That only this religious shorthand could adequately denote what in Yugoslavia was called a national group can be seen by what happened in 1974 when Tito established the Bosnian Muslims as one of the six "constituent nations" of Yugoslavia. To make this move, part of a complicated political calculus through which he intended to counterbalance both Serb and Croat claims, Tito had to fall back on the word "Muslims," which in all subsequent censuses in Yugoslavia was understood as designating only these Bosnian Muslims. The generally far more devout Muslim Albanians of Kossovo and Macedonia were listed as Albanians.

Certainly, for all the lip service nationalist politicians, particularly in Croatia, paid to the relevance of religious faith to the new countries being created—or, as the nationalists preferred to claim, restored—most Croats, like most Serbs and most Bosnian Muslims, remained almost as secular as they had during the Communist period. Religion mattered not so much in and of itself (although the

Serb church, historically, is not universal but national), but rather as the main vehicle of ethnic and national allegiance in new states that were bent on defining citizenship almost exclusively in terms of ethnic identity. Croatia, notoriously, had revised its old constitution in 1990, a decision that many critics of the Zagreb regime believed had made a revolt in the Serb-dominated Krajina all but inevitable. While, under the Communists, the Croatian Republic had been made up, constitutionally, of two constituent peoples—Croats and Serbs—as well as a number of other minorities, independent Croatia now defined itself as "the national state of the Croatian People and the state of other nations and national minorities, who are her citizens." The Serbs had thus been demoted to the status of a "national minority," and were grouped along with Jews, Muslims, Slovenes, Czechs, and others.

Strictly speaking, though, these were cultural rather than ethnic differences. What made someone a Croat was the fact that he or she was a Roman Catholic, just as what made someone a Serb was membership, however attenuated, in the Orthodox church. Not that actual religious devotion mattered all that much either in Croatia or in Serbia. What counted, once the nationalist mythmaking had been successful, was the way in which religion was put to use. When one went into a village where fighting had taken place, it was often easier to get a history lesson than a reliable account of what had occurred earlier the same day. It was not just in televised speeches and press releases that Serbs talked about their defeat at the hands of the Turks on the field of Kossovo in the late fourteenth century; Croats talked about a Croatian kingdom extinguished in the eleventh century; or Bosnian Muslims talked about the Bogomils. Some of them talked in this way on the battlefield. In a Bosnian Serb position near the northern town of Priejdor, I was once sent on my way with a handshake, a jerrican full of homemade slivovitz, the local plum brandy, and the word "1389"—the date of the Serb defeat at Kossovo. At the Zagreb offices of Merhamet, the Muslim equivalent of the Red Cross in the former Yugoslavia, a local notable listened to my account of conditions in northern Bosnia and replied with a long disquisition on Ottoman tolerance.

The actual value of these accounts as history was small. Whatever Croats might imagine, the notion that one could really draw a straight line between the Croatian state over which Tomislav the Great had reigned in the eleventh century and the one Franjo Tudjman had established in 1991 was all but indefensible. Dalmatia had belonged to Venice; eastern Slavonia to Hungary. But the drive to recast the past in the image of the present has been a powerful impulse everywhere. In the former Yugoslavia, for more than three years, hundreds of thousands have died to defend a sense of their own identity that, in many cases, they seemed to have all but willed into being. Sometimes the errors made in the course of all this enthusiastic fabricating could be comic. The British writer Mark Thompson cited the case of a series shown on Croatian television called *Croats Who Made the World*. The first of these was Pope Sixtus V, a medieval Pope who, as Thompson noted, there is no reason to suppose was a Croat. But more often the results were terrible, as when, throughout the war, the Bosnian Serb forces referred to Bosnian government troops as the Turkish army, and quite explicitly mobilized soldiers in the name of avenging their defeat in 1389 at Kossovo.

Afraid of the future as the Communist system unraveled, Croats and Serbs in particular began to spin ever more elaborate mythologies about their heroic, thwarted pasts, their epochal sufferings, and their bright future. Doubtless, before the killing had started, the rediscovery of one's Serb or Croat identity had been consoling to people who quite reasonably felt they were losing control of their individual lives and of the country they had grown up in. As Yugoslavia collapsed, so did real wages. A doctor in Sarajevo who had been making one thousand German marks monthly at the beginning of the 1980s was making a tenth of that by the time the war began. The fear was real enough. But however psychologically necessary all the mythmaking may have been, the real differences between the ways people moved or dressed or gesticulated in Zagreb, Belgrade, and Sarajevo should not be exaggerated. What motivated people to fight may indeed have been their half-baked notions of historical grandeur, and their secret grudges. But what divides them now are not ideas but the dead and the ethnically cleansed, the raped women and the mutilated children.

To attribute what has happened to the politics of identity taken to the ultimate extreme is too easy. People talk about the "tribalism" of the former Yugoslavia, and raise the specter of all those supposedly insuperable barriers of culture and ethnicity that divide Croats, Serbs, and Muslims. In doing this, they are in effect arguing—as, in this age in which ethnic nationalism has acquired authority in so many places, from South Central to Sarajevo, where people have lost hope or are in pain, it has become so easy to do—that, at least in the Balkans, people's communal identities are as fixed and permanent as their DNA. Whereas in fact, they should be pondering the fate of the South Slavs, a people who resemble each other more than they do not, and a political tragedy in which small cadres of politicized and power-hungry politicians, soldiers, and intellectuals have done everything they could to amplify and exaggerate the real differences that existed between Croats, Serbs, and Muslims in order to seize or to hold on to power. If the gulf between these groups seems as wide as it does after the long and brutalizing experience of communal violence and war, this does not mean that the violence was either culturally or historically inevitable. There was a South Slav culture that bound Croats, Serbs, and Bosnian Muslims together, just as there were Serb, Croat, or "Bosniak" cultures that separated them. And that South Slav culture—though not "Yugoslav" in the sense of either the pre–World War II monarchy or the Titoist dictatorship—at least at times transcended regional political forms, ethnic boundaries, and the specific gravity of history and place. The breakup of that culture, like the breakup of Yugoslavia, took a lot of work. So did the war in Croatia. And so did the genocide of the Bosnian Muslims.

For not only are Serbs, Croats, and Muslims all South Slavs; they also speak the same language, or at least commonly imagined that they did before the end of the Yugoslav Federation. As the political activist and writer Bogdan Denitch, himself an ethnic Serb from Croatia, has written bitterly, "eighty-three percent of the population of [the former] Yugoslavia speak one language . . . The differences between the literary versions are of an order resembling the differences between British and American versions of the English language." The proof of all this, Denitch adds, is that although Serbs use the Cyrillic alphabet and Croats and Muslims the Latin, each regional dialect of what before the war was called Serbo-Croatian tended to be spoken by everyone from the region in question, whatever their ethnic origin. Nonetheless, the visitor to Croatia quickly learns not to ask what the word for this or that is in Serbo-Croat, or even Croato-Serbian, but instead always to say "Croatian." The idea of an autochthonous Croatian language may be new to all but a few ultranationalists, but it has become the deepest of conceits. Official Zagreb has been bent on amplifying what distinctions do exist for some time, and on drawing more where possible. When I first started going to Zagreb, the sign at the airport read "Aerodrom," as it still does in Serbia. By the spring of 1993, "Aerodrom" had been Croatianized to "Zrackna Luka." Those words, at least, meant virtually the same thing. There were other new coinages, like one for "belt" that translated as "object that holds one's pants up," which were simply ludicrous. But ludicrous or not, the nationalists insisted that these words had to replace the Serb or Muslim words people had grown up using. After all, the new words had been invented in an independent Croatia—that state, as loyal members of the ruling HDZ sometimes liked to say, which all Croats had been dreaming of since the death of Tomislav the Great in 1109.

Nonetheless, if such distinctions seemed minor, especially when compared with so weighty a thing as a shared grammar, and what was still a nearly identical vocabulary and system of usage, many Croatians, reveling in their newly won independence, seemed quite unable to stop pointing them out. In a trench on an active front line near the Serb-controlled salient outside Zadar, I once drew a phrasebook out of the pocket of my flak jacket and began to page through it, looking, as it happened, for a way to say, "Has it been quiet?" The young officer I was with took the book from my hand, drew a pen from his pocket, and, as his men gathered round, ceremoniously drew a line across the word "Serbo-" on the cover so that it read "Croat Phrasebook." I remember saying weakly, "They'll have to reprint," and being astounded when the officer replied earnestly, "I should hope so." And yet the contents of the book had proved equally usable in Croatia, in Bosnia, and in Serbia as well. What divided people were their accents and two alphabets, not the words themselves.

I do not mean to say that people before the war had not identified themselves by their ethnicity, or to deny that the national question had been as much the fault line in Yugoslavian history—both the interwar monarchy and the Titoist republic—as race has been the fault line in American history. Nonetheless, throughout the war most people in Croatia and Serbia, and, as the war went on, on the Bosnian government side as well, have presented those things that divide them as if they were obvious and observable. "Why do you Westerners keep insisting that Serbs must live with Muslims?" Radovan Karadzic once asked a group of journalists, including myself, who had gone to interview him in his office in the Sarajevo suburb of Pale, which he had declared his war "capital." "Serbs and Muslims," he went on, looking, with his great unruly mane of hair and natty blue suit, like nothing so much as a slightly down-at-the-heel French pop singer, "are like cats and dogs. They cannot live together in peace. It is impossible."

In Karadzic's formulation, Serbian-ness, Croatian-ness, and Muslim-ness, were essences—unchanging and immutable. He spoke of ethnicity as a Jungian therapist might of archetypes, even though, as it happened, *Dr.* Karadzic had trained as a Freudian before joining the psychiatry department of Kosevo Hospital in Sarajevo. Whatever his particular formulation, though, he was not alone in using such language. The savagery of the war he had unleashed made what otherwise might have appeared to be his mad ideas convincing to people; and more than that, made them appear to have been confirmed by their experience. The fact that they had had these experiences because of plans conceived of by Karadzic, Milosevic, and their colleagues did not alter the fact that people were now likely to feel in their guts that they had been true all along. As Zdravko Grebo, a Sarajevo law professor and longtime political opponent of Karadzic, quipped, "Radovan Karadzic is the greatest genius Bosnia has ever produced. He says something that at the time is a complete lie. And two years later it becomes the truth."

Whatever Karadzic might claim, Serbs had not always believed that they could not get on with Muslims and Croats. They had been neighbors for generations. They had gone to school with one another, worked together, and, to a surprising extent, had intermarried—particularly in the urban areas of Bosnia-Herzegovina. It took a lot of propaganda to make them first begin to fear one another—the war started in fear and only ended in genocide—and then slaughter one another. And yet once the killing had begun, the violence was taken by many to confirm the justice of Karadzic's original diagnosis. This was often as true for many of the Bosnian Serb leader's bitterest adversaries as it was for those Serbs who had reluctantly begun to follow him. Many of the same people who considered the Serbs to have been the aggressors both in Croatia and in Bosnia, and viewed Karadzic as a war criminal, still reluctantly accepted one of the most important of his contentions—that it had been this immutable ethnic antagonism that fueled the war the Serbs had waged. Only Communism, one was told—this view quickly found favor among United Nations officials in the former Yugoslavia, who, as "peacekeepers" bound to dealing with all groups impartially, naturally were drawn to this "plague on all their houses" stance—had kept the nationalist demons at bay. Once the system had collapsed, the revival of ethnic antagonism had been inevitable, even if a more inspired international diplomatic effort or better leaders within the former Yugoslav republics might have mitigated the catastrophic form these clashes had taken.

A Russian officer serving with the UN once said to me, "You Americans are constitutionally unable to understand what is going on in the Balkans. You're nice boys and girls, so nice. You don't want to see that it's not politics here but blood and history. All you can do is ride out the cycles of killing and try to look after the wounded. For the rest, it's as unstoppable as an earthquake. You have to understand plate tectonics to see what is going on in Yugoslavia." He paused. "You'll see," he said, grimacing. "They'll kill each other until they're full up and then they'll stop. But not a minute before, whatever any of us do."

His friend, a Belgian paratroop major, had been listening quietly. "If it were up to me," he said suddenly, "I'd put a fence around this whole damn country and let the last survivor give the UN a call when it was all over. When you get down into Bosnia, you'll see what we mean."

The next morning, I was on my way to see for myself for the first time. Leaving Zagreb was the study in cognitive dissonance with which I would soon become familiar. To get to the Serb Krajina or to Serb-held northern Bosnia, one leaves one's hotel and drives through the streets of Zagreb toward the modern superhighway that used to take tourists all the way through Bosnia to the Dalmatian coast. Earlier, I had been complaining about the milk in the breakfast cappuccino not being warm enough, and one of the British journalists with whom I was traveling had asked the waitress in the dining room for some fresh croissants, since the ones on the buffet table were stale. Viewed out the car window, Zagreb could not, indeed, have seemed more European. And for a time, even after we crossed onto the highway, the only thing about the drive that was any different from a similar stretch of road in Austria or Italy was the absence of traffic.

The first sign of war was that the great gas stations–cum–travel emporia along the highway were closed or, when open, had only one or two functioning fuel pumps. Then we arrived at a toll booth that was unstaffed. There is something exhilarating about driving straight through a toll plaza at ninety kilometers an hour. Probably by now fifteen minutes of the journey had elapsed. Fifteen minutes on, the gas stations were not just closed, they had been blown up, the attendants' booths riddled with heavy machine-gun fire and the exit ramps dotted with mortar splashes. On the highway itself, the divider rail looked as if it had been run over by a tank, and one began to drive, no matter which way you were going, on only one side of the road. A few minutes later, you cross the last Croatian checkpoint, and a few minutes after that—you are driving on dirt track now, past bombed-out villages and exploded bridges, minefields, and artillery positions—you pass a barrier adorned with white, blue, and red stripes—the Serb flag—and enter the self-styled Serbian Republic of the Krajina. Twenty miles beyond is the Sava River, and, on the other side of that, Bosnia.

IV

The northern Bosnia I was entering in the late summer of 1992, especially that part of the region known as the Bosanska Krajina which abutted the frontier with Croatia, was already being physically transformed. It was not the fighting that had done this; unlike in central Bosnia, or in Sarajevo or Mostar, the battle damage in the north was comparatively slight. But in villages where mosques had stood, the foundations for Orthodox churches were being laid, and new people were moving into well-kept flats in the modern apartment buildings around the city of Banja Luka. According to officials of the United Nations High Commissioner for Refugees, many of the approximately sixty thousand Serbs who had fled their homes in Croatia during the Serbo-Croat war in 1991 were being resettled in the Bosanska Krajina, mostly in properties that belonged to the Muslim and Croat families who had lived in the region for generations. What was changing the face of northern Bosnia was not war but the process that the Serbs had undertaken to consolidate their victory. What was changing the face of northern Bosnia was the project of ethnic cleansing.

Here is one account of ethnic cleansing, an overview: "Houses and whole villages reduced to ashes, unarmed and innocent populations massacred *en masse,* incredible acts of violence, pillage and brutality of every kind—such were the means which were employed and are still being employed by the Serbo-Montenegrin soldiery, with a view to the entire transformation of the ethnic character of [these] regions." And after the fighting quieted down in any particular area, and the surviving local people had been driven away, Serbian and Montenegrin settlers were brought in, often from hundreds of kilometers away, to take their place, and were installed in the houses—those that were still standing, anyway—that had belonged to the people who had been forced to flee. The transformation of public spaces was equally radical. Mosques were destroyed with fire and explosives, to be transformed, in many cases, into building sites where the Serb militiamen started laying the foundations for the new Orthodox churches whose erection was almost as essential a measure of their victory as the murder or dispersal of the non-Serb population.

This account is not contemporary, although it could be. It is taken from the "Report of the International Commission to Inquire into the Causes and Conduct of the Balkan Wars," issued by the Carnegie Endowment for International Peace in 1914. What has taken place in Bosnia and Croatia since 1991 differs only very little in either ideology or method from what occurred early in the century in many of the same towns and villages, and occurred again during the Second World War. But there was a European conceit—born of wishful thinking and of the complacency that afflicted so much of Western Europe until the collapse of communism made everyone take a second look—that people on the Old Continent, even in the Balkans, would not go on slaughtering each other so regularly. Surely that chapter was finished. It wasn't, of course. The difference now is that to the outsider the catastrophe has a dissonant quality. It is as if Yugoslavia changed more than Yugoslavs did. This time, the war is being fought in a country that stopped counting as one of the "badlands" of Europe decades ago. It is carnage set in tourist country, whether in the Venetian towns of the Dalmatian coast, the ski resorts in the environs of Sarajevo, or the vineyards of western Herzegovina around Mostar.

On Mount Jahorina above the Bosnian capital, Bosnian Serb gun emplacements nestle in the shade of the pylons of destroyed ski lifts and alongside the great giant-slalom run built for the Winter Olympics of 1984 to which Sarajevo played host. Officers of the BSA, the Bosnian Serb Army, spend their off-duty hours in a former chalet-style tourist restaurant, playing chess and drinking slivovitz in rooms now decorated with propaganda posters—the map of Europe being covered by "Islamic"-green paint, and an image of a handshake between a man wearing a cuff link adorned with the Croatian checkerboard and another wearing a swastika, being typical examples of the form. And throughout Bosnia, across the garbage-strewn terrain of battle, amid bombed-out houses, gutted cars, burnt earth, and rotting livestock, one sees the signs reading "Bureau de Change" and "Zimmer Frei," "Albergo Turistico" and "Scenic View."

Despite everything that has gone on since the fighting began, there are in everyday life as well as in this detritus reminders of the old tourist Yugoslavia that drew millions of visitors each year before 1990. Nowadays, though, the motivation is likelier to be political legitimacy than profit, even at the *bureaux de change* that can sometimes be found in operation in some devastated town. Changing money makes no practical sense. The currencies of all the belligerents in Bosnia are virtually without value and anyone wanting to buy anything worth having, from a beer to gasoline, needs dollars or, better still, German marks—the new universal currency of the Balkans. But in towns and villages where there is rarely electricity or running water, it is often still possible, and sometimes a requirement of the local authorities, for visitors to change money. That such trips to the bank have no practical utility is beside the point. The message is, "You're in the Serbian Republic of the Krajina," or "the Serb Republic of Bosnia," or, until early in 1994, when the Bosnian government and the Bosnian Croat militia, the HVO, stopped fighting each other and accepted an American-brokered deal for a federative union, "the Croatian 'state' of Herceg-Bosna in western Herzegovina." It is the same message that causes hotelkeepers to ask journalists to fill in elaborate prewar registration forms (as if the local authorities were unaware of who passed through their towns), makes HVO fighters at checkpoints in central Bosnia who haven't bathed or shaved for a week wear clean white armbands complete with burnished metal symbols that identify them as customs officers, or made the Bosnian Serbs designate the checkpoint they erected between the UN-controlled airport and the Bosnian-held city of Sarajevo a "border crossing," and demand to know, when they want to be difficult, if the journalists have visas to enter or leave the "Srpska Republika," and show genuine, not just feigned indignation when they reply that they do not.

In most of the Bosanska Krajina, Serb control had been established early and in most areas was institutionalized by the late summer of 1992. Before the fighting started, the region's principal city, Banja Luka, was the second largest in Bosnia, a center of trade and light industry as well as the main agricultural market town of the area. Amply supplied with comfortable hotels and fine churches and mosques, it was a pleasant bourgeois place, with neither the tourist attractions of a Mostar nor the proletarian atmosphere of such centers of heavy industry as Zenica or Tuzla. In retrospect, some people in Banja Luka conceded, their city had been complacent, but, they stressed—and proudly, despite everything that had happened—in the way that so many small provincial European cities were. "We were a lot like people in Bergamo or Bristol. I don't know the right equivalent in America," a Muslim notable told me one evening, pausing every so often to look nervously toward the door of his apartment, or to lower his eyes when, as happened often in Banja Luka, a burst of fire from a Kalashnikov or a Heckler sounded nearby.

"We worried about our kids listening to too much rock and roll," he continued, looking up at the seventeenth-century "Bosnian-Oriental" decorative panel on his mantelpiece, "and losing their 'values' because of all their material privileges. We worried that they didn't study hard enough, that they spent too much time at the New York, a pool hall in town, and we pretended they weren't taking drugs. We were sometimes gloomy about what kind of futures they would have. But we did not really worry about ourselves. Our troubles were going to be personal—divorce, aging, mortality. But we did not think our society was mortal. Those years when everything had been cruel—the Second World War; the terror after the partisans took power—they seemed to us to be banished forever. I didn't even worry about growing old. I worried if I could afford to go to the coast, or even"—he shook his head wonderingly—"if I could afford to buy a piece of art that I coveted. Politics I never took seriously. People yelled and shouted, but I never thought any of us would be *stupid enough* to destroy what we had in Yugoslavia, whatever the motive. I never thought they would be stupid enough . . ." His voice trailed off.

Later, he told me at length about Banja Luka's well-known avant-garde puppet theater. "People came from all over Europe to see the work," he said. "We had Marcel Marceau, the Teatro Sperimentale di Parma, and the Berlin Schaubühne. My friend Sead was the director. He's a Muslim like me, but his company was completely mixed—

Serbs, Croats, Muslims, one half-Jewish guy. There was nothing strange about that. It was normal. We were all mixed anyway. My daughter married a Croat boy—they're in Zagreb with his parents, thank God. They say that our population was divided between almost equal numbers of Serbs and Muslims and a smaller group of Croats, but the intermarriage was so high that I believe these distinctions would have been meaningless in a couple of generations to anyone but a few old fanatics and people from the country." He paused. "But that will never happen now, will it? If we survive at all, we will survive in our respective ghettos—the Serbs here, the Muslims there, the Croats somewhere else. Karadzic says we are like cats and dogs. But we are not animals, we are human beings.

"At least I hope we are. Sometimes, I'm not sure. Sometimes, I think that what is going on now is human reality, and that the oddity is how we lived before all this started. Maybe Karadzic is a genius. Or at least maybe he's right. You know what happened to Sead's theater? Well, before the war, Sead, who for all his acerbic talk is a sentimental fellow, had a protégé, a young Serb actor. The theater was a collective and some of the actors didn't want to let him join, but Sead insisted. And the guy was good. Anyway, when the war started, he disappeared for a few days. Then he came back to the theater, only this time with a pistol in his belt and a piece of official paper in his hand. The paper authorized him to become director of the Banja Luka Puppet Theater. You can guess the rest. Sead was the first one to be fired."

The war had come suddenly to Banja Luka, and the city was taken by General Ratko Mladic's Bosnian Serb forces in April 1992, almost without a shot being fired. Mladic himself was a Bosnian Serb by birth. Throughout most of his career, he had shown no particular nationalist fervor. As a Belgrade lawyer who knew him remarked to me, "Mladic was an ordinary officer before the war. And nationalism was discouraged in the Yugoslav National Army. Its officers were linked to the system, to defending Yugoslavia, the economic system of self-management, blah, blah, blah. I don't think Mladic was a nationalist in Tito's time." And yet other people who knew Mladic, and the general himself, invariably pointed to the deaths of his father and mother at the hands of Croatian fascists during World War II. If he had not been a Serb nationalist before, it was because of his loyalty to the JNA and to the Yugoslav idea he and his fellow officers had sworn to defend. But once the state collapsed, Serbian nationalism took possession of him, and Mladic soon became one of its fiercest exponents.

In contrast to Mladic, whether Slobodan Milosevic himself was really a nationalist or simply a pragmatic and ruthless politician who came to believe from the late eighties on that in order to hold on to power he had to play on Serb nationalist feeling is something that will never be known for certain. What is sure is that having decided that if there was to be no Yugoslavia then there would be a Greater Serbia, Milosevic had found a perfect instrument when he passed over more senior Serb JNA generals (the officer corps was heavily Serb, but was not purged of its non-Serbs until 1992) and tapped Mladic to command the combined Yugoslav National Army and Serb separatist forces in Knin, a hundred and fifty kilometers to the southwest, during the Serbo-Croat war of 1991. The war that Mladic waged in Croatia, the goal of which was to carve an ethnically pure Serb territory out of the carcass of the Croatian state, succeeded in its aims almost completely. By the time a UN-brokered cease-fire had been arranged, Mladic had what he wanted. He also had the model for the war he would undertake in Bosnia in the late spring of 1992.

It was logical that one of the initial focal points of Mladic's operations would be northern Bosnia. All of Bosnia-Herzegovina had been a military and industrial center before the war. Both Croatia and Serbia were too close to the frontiers of Warsaw Pact nations. Tito, fearing a Russian invasion almost to the last, had determined that were the Russians to invade, Yugoslav forces would have to withdraw into the Bosnian mountains, and so he stockpiled arms and built bases there. The largest of these was the complex of military bases and underground airfields—said to be one of the largest and most modern such installations in Europe—near the town of Bihac, in the northwest. But Bihac was in an area that was ethnically over ninety percent Muslim. When it was clear that the fighting in Bosnia was about to begin, the JNA began to transfer most of the equipment from Bihac to Banja Luka (some went to an airbase near Knin) and destroyed what it couldn't move. Once the fighting in Bosnia did start in earnest, it made good military sense that Banja Luka would become one of Mladic's principal staging areas, the center of Serb power in northern Bosnia. It also followed that northern Bosnia, split almost equally between Serbs and Muslims, and lying next to the Serb areas of the Croatian Krajina, would become a proving ground for the campaign of ethnic cleansing that Bosnian Serb forces began almost from the moment Radovan Karadzic had left Sarajevo for Pale, the Serb provisional capital, with promises of war and Serb revenge fresh on his lips. Bihac was too Muslim to Serbianize, at least at the beginning. But Banja Luka, isolated from any possibility of Croatian or Bosnian government help, was ideal.

Shortly after the Serbs took Banja Luka, the civilian authorities they installed to run the city government established a "crisis committee." Some of its actions were quite mundane—you need water engineers and technicians at the gasworks to do their jobs, whatever else you have in mind for your citizens—but it also instituted a series of laws that effectively disenfranchised the non-Serbs in the city. No two genocides are alike, and General Mladic, who came to adulthood a victim of fascism, may be a butcher but he is not Hitler. And yet all genocides have something in common, and like the Final Solution, ethnic cleansing has been a relatively slow, legalistic, and deliberate process, an ever tightening noose around the collective neck of the subject population, more often than it has been a single, terrible event. It was one thing for Serb paramilitaries, like the Ustasha or the Einsatzgruppen fifty years before, to kill people quickly, an evening's work, in some out-of-the-way village. In the larger towns of northern Bosnia, where, if nothing else, the intermittent presence of a few journalists and international staff from the UNHCR made the mass killings the Serbs had gone in for in the Bosnian countryside too difficult to cover up, there were many stages to be gotten through, many bureaucratic hurdles to leap, before Muslim blood actually could begin to flow.

The incremental quality of the process played on the panic of Serb people living under martial law and exposed only to news they got from government-controlled media in Serbia or Bosnia. All other television networks' satellite transmissions were jammed, and, of course, the newspapers had been almost the first institutions to be subject to Bosnian Serb Army censorship and, often, control as well. In this atmosphere, Serbs in northern Bosnia, many of whom were recent arrivals from Croatia from which they, too, had been ethnically cleansed, genuinely believed that their Muslim neighbors were all terrorists, bent on destroying the Serbs. It was not as if Muslims were being shot in the streets, not often anyway. When they were, and it happened in Banja Luka, or Priejdor, or Sanski Most, as even the authorities were forced to admit, from time to time, city authorities would insist the crimes either were the acts of provocateurs—one more attempt of the world to blacken the reputation of innocent Serbs—or had been committed by "uncontrollable elements" who would be brought to justice.

They never were, of course, since the distinction between the "official" Serbs and the irregulars was all but meaningless in Banja Luka, as it was in most parts of Serb-held Bosnia throughout the fighting. Usually, it was a simple matter of a division of labor. The Serb irregulars, known generically as Chetniks, members of groups with names that sounded more like street gangs than an army—the White Eagles, the Tigers (their commander's nom de guerre was Major Mauser), and the like—did the dirty work that Radovan Karadzic's subordinates needed done but could not own up to. Then the "official" Serbs would claim they were doing their best to keep order in a difficult time.

Ordinary Serbs from northern Bosnia, who were not criminals themselves, understandably did not want to believe that their leaders were criminal. The Serbs who had fled Croatia during the fighting in 1991 or had themselves been ethnically cleansed by Croat forces—the Serbs might have perfected ethnic cleansing, but the Croats had been guilty of it as well—were in a different position. They could only think of themselves as victims, no matter how many Muslims they victimized or how innocent these Muslims were of what had gone on in Croatia in 1991. And the opaque, banal language of the Serb bureaucracy allowed people to pretend to themselves that the ethnic cleansing was not really going on. The concentration camps—Omarska, Trnopolje, and Manaca—were only a few kilometers away but deep in the countryside, and out of view. In wars, they told you, unpleasant things happen. And in civil wars, it was worse. Anyway, the Serbs were just defending themselves.

Had ethnic cleansing started in Banja Luka with a mass slaughter, perhaps decent Serbs would have rebelled. But it didn't, any more

than it had in Nazi Germany. In northern Bosnia, people's liveli-
hoods went first. The crisis committee began by barring any non-
Serb from retaining or securing employment as the manager of a
large concern. Soon after that, non-Serbs were excluded from all senior positions in which they might be called upon to make what the
authorities described as "independent decisions." In practice, this
meant that not only company directors and managers but also shop
foremen and accountants and bookkeepers—anyone, the committee
stipulated, who handled financial transactions—were to be dismissed or demoted to the most menial positions in their firms. By
this point, the only non-Serbs in Banja Luka whose earnings still
were unaffected by the committee's actions were those who had
never risen above menial employment in the first place. Even the
doctors, whose skills were desperately needed, were eventually dismissed from their positions. In a series of nonviolent steps, the Serb
authorities had eliminated the middle-class future of the Muslim and
Croat populations in a city where middle-class expectations had
been more and more the norm for the majority of the population.

Some of the committee's subsequent decrees were directed
specifically at non-Serb adult males, and concerned military service.
Here, too, the authorities' real goals were masked by an ostensible
procedural equality. Once it was clear that the Bosnian government's
resistance was going to be harder to overcome than Serb commanders had initially thought, the military authorities began to supple-
ment the forces they had begun the war with—mostly Yugoslav
National Army regulars who, the Belgrade authorities insisted
blandly, had not been seconded but had volunteered out of nationalist conviction for service in the new Bosnian Serb Army; "just to defend themselves," as Karadzic put it over and over again—through a
series of mobilizations. Every man from eighteen to sixty was eligi-
ble, and plenty of Serb men who were well past military age in any
normal army were happy enough to go into battle for Greater Serbia,
particularly since they completely outgunned the army the Bosnian
government was improvising, and were mostly occupied terrorizing
unarmed Muslim civilians in the villages. But, for obvious reasons,
most Muslims and Croats were terrified of being drafted into
Karadzic's army. There was one Muslim unit that fought alongside
Serb forces around the northern Bosnian town of Bosanski Brod, but

apart from that legion of the damned, few non-Serbs were suicidal enough to report for duty when they were called up. Thus, the mobilization served a dual purpose—raising much-needed troops for an army whose Achilles' heel, throughout the fighting, was a shortage of men, and disenfranchising the captive non-Serb population at the same time.

For the consequences of refusing to serve in this army that, in reality, wanted absolutely no part of them were incredibly severe for the non-Serbs of northern Bosnia. Those who failed to report would discover within days that their nonappearance had cost them their jobs. "We're at war," the Mayor of Banja Luka told me blandly in October 1992. "Every citizen has a duty to fight." But only Serb officials obliged to speak to outsiders on the record even tried to pretend that these firings were anything but deliberate. When the Mayor talked to me, he could barely keep a straight face. "I must insist that you believe me," he said with a faint smile. "Everyone in Banja Luka can live together, if only Muslims stop attacking the Serbian people. We do not want war, but since a war has been imposed upon us, every loyal person must help. If Muslims want to live with us, they must prove that they are loyal. Instead, what do they do? They refuse to be our brothers. If they will not fight alongside us, why should we have to work alongside them?"

In fact, the orchestration had been perfect. In a part of the world that had never been known for Teutonic efficiency, people's dismissal notices tended to be in synch with the dates on their mobilization papers. It was an open secret. In the restaurant of the Bosna, the city's main hotel, I met a young Serb fighter, just back from the front line near the town of Bosanska Krupa. He and his comrades were drunk on slivovitz but also drunk on the success of their arms. They were perfectly happy to explain the game to me. "It's the same either way," the fighter said. "The Muslims report to the army, we have them dig trenches in the first line right away. That is bad for their health." He laughed, and one of his friends poured him another drink. I remember thinking, incongruously, that in a region not exactly celebrated for its dental care he had beautiful teeth, and I remember wondering, as had happened a few nights earlier, whether when they all got a bit drunker they would start to threaten me, or buy me dinner, or both. "But if they will not come to the army," he continued, clapping me on the back—it turned out to be dinner and friendship; they were likable guys, though I wish it were otherwise—"then we give the jobs their Turk bastard ancestors stole from us long ago to good, honest Serb people here in Banja Luka."

"That's right," his friends choroused.

The fighter leaned across the table toward me. "You know," he said, "before the Second World War, Banja Luka was a Serbian town. If there hadn't been so many massacres, if the Muslims and the Ustasha hadn't tried to exterminate the Serb people in Bosnia, we would still be in majority here, instead of having to always defend ourselves against them every fifty years."

His comrade interrupted. "Why do you Americans hate the Serb people now? We were allies in two world wars, fighting together. Why do you side with the fascists? It is bad. We should be friends." He paused. "Many of my comrades say America has become a bad country. I do not think so. I think you do not understand what has happened here. Do you know about the battle of Kossovo in 1389?" I must have grimaced, for he shook his head and grabbed my wrist. "No, really, it is important. You Americans care nothing for history, but you should care. Serbs only have history. For five hundred years we Serbs have been defending Western civilization against the Turks. Vuk Karadzic did it in the nineteenth century, our leader, Radovan Karadzic, does it now. We all do. *All!* And yet you make us the enemy. It is wrong." He let go of my wrist, then patted me on the shoulder, in a gesture that started as a manly clap and ended almost as a caress. "It doesn't matter," he said. "Let's not waste time talking about the damned Turks. We'll just quarrel. Let's have another drink." He turned to gesture for the waitress. "But I tell you," he said over his shoulder, "after what I have seen, I do not think it is so terrible if someone loses his job."

The fighters would say no more about the "Turks"—neither those they had been fighting on the front line near the city of Bosanski Brod, nor the ones I had been asking them about in Banja Luka. And the fighter was right in a way. Life for Muslims in Banja Luka was not nearly so bad as it was in the villages or in the combat zones. But even leaving aside the fact that depriving people of their jobs was only a step along a continuum of ethnic cleansing that, in the end, led to murder, the loss of work was far graver than it appeared at first sight. It was not simply a question, as it would have been in a Western European country, of losing one's job in a place and at a time when jobs were hard to come by. People in the West changed jobs all the time, but in the former Yugoslavia, only entrepreneurs and professionals had moved through the job market freely. This was changing, of course, as Yugoslavia became less and less communist, even in this institutional sense. But most people still expected to work in the same place for life, and had grown accustomed to looking to the workplace for all kinds of accompanying benefits. Being fired meant losing a great deal more than a paycheck. Money was worth less and less, anyway, and, as the war dragged on, almost everything except newspapers and basic foodstuffs was sold for Deutschemarks. But what were indispensable were the health insurance and other state benefits that were immediately revoked when a person was fired.

People were even made insecure in their lodgings, since many had acquired their apartments through their unions or professional organizations, which, technically, were still the owners. In Serbia proper, people's fear of being fired (as opposed to laid off or simply not paid, which in an era of hyperinflation and scarcity actually didn't always matter that much) from a state enterprise and losing a flat owned by that enterprise was one of the ways the Milosevic regime compelled consent. Better support the regime than be out in the street homeless. In Banja Luka, this legacy of the Titoist period provided the Serb authorities with the next move in the process of ethnically cleansing the urban non-Serb population. The firing itself was only a beginning. For once someone's dismissal had been made known officially, the next step was for a letter to be sent demanding that the person vacate the apartment in which he or she had been living.

Thus, to be deprived of a job was almost to stop being a citizen, to be forcibly moved from the status of non-Serb to the status of nonperson in only a couple of official decrees. This expulsion of non-Serbs from the workplace also coincided with the elevation of the workplace into the principal context in which people got access to increasingly scarce commodities. As supplies of medicine dried up, for example, workplace pharmacies replaced many of the ones that had operated in town. The workplace, too, was where fuel rations would be made available, although this became far less of a concern as the war dragged on and almost all fuel had to be bought for hard currency on the black market. People could buy other things they needed for hard currency on the black market, of course, but before long most Muslim and Croat families in Banja Luka had exhausted their Deutschemark-denominated savings. That, too, was of benefit to the new Serb overlords of Banja Luka, since non-Serbs were, in effect, transferring their foreign currency holdings to Serb black marketeers. And, not surprisingly, since the gun and the black market work hand in hand in war, these people tended to be not just ordinary criminals out for a fast buck but uniformed criminals, members of the most extreme and murderous Chetnik paramilitary groups. It was beyond irony that many of the same fighters who got drunk at the Hotel Bosna and then would career through the streets of Banja Luka, lobbing the occasional grenade through the front window of a Muslim home, were those the Muslims had to pay to get the things they needed in order to survive. But here again, a comparison to the Jewish Holocaust came ineluctably to mind. The Muslims were paying their tormentors, but hadn't the Jews of Holland and France been charged by the Germans for the trainfares to Auschwitz?

Repeated efforts by the United Nations High Commissioner for Refugees in Zagreb to organize humanitarian relief convoys to Banja Luka did little in material terms to improve the situation of non-Serbs. Once they became aware in general terms of what was going on in the city, UNHCR officials had managed to persuade the Serb authorities after prolonged negotiations to let in several convoys per week. The idea, of course, was to provide help for what in humanitarian bureaucratese were known as "populations at risk," in other words, for the most part the non-Serbs of the Bosanska Krajina. But the Serb authorities were masters of this situation as well. In giving in to the UNHCR's request, they had attached a stipulation. The Serb population had to receive as big a share as the Muslims and Croats. That was the pattern throughout Bosnia. The Serbs would first refuse to allow aid through, then demand that they get a share. The UN would first refuse, insisting that distribution had to be on the basis of need, then temporize, then, more often than not, faced with the choice of getting some aid through or no aid through, give in to Serb demands.

The policy of the United Nations High Commissioner for Refugees was entirely defensible given that the Serbs controlled the roads, and that aid would get through either on these terms or not at all. The problem was that this arrangement could be made to work when convoys had to cross areas controlled by Serb forces in order to get to areas controlled by Bosnian government forces—the Serbs took their cut and, with luck, allowed the convoys to move on—but Banja Luka was different. There the Serbs controlled everyone's rations, Serb and non-Serb alike. Serb paramilitaries guarded the gate and the perimeter of the warehouse in which the convoys went to be unloaded when they reached Banja Luka. And it was the same Bosnian Serb bureaucrats from the Mayor's office and the Serb Red Cross who had been so inventive is disenfranchising non-Serbs in Banja who oversaw the distribution of the UNHCR supplies after the Danish volunteer drivers had turned around their white-painted Mercedes trucks with the letters "UNHCR," the United Nations logo, and the Serbo-Croatian words "Humanitarna Pomoc" (Humanitarian Aid) painted in blue on the cab doors, and headed back north, through the Bosanska Krajina, toward the Sava and Croatia.

If there was little the UNHCR could do to succor, let alone rescue, the Muslims and Croats of Banja Luka—there was even a period in late 1992 and early 1993 when it was barred from the city altogether—the non-Serbs themselves already had begun to despair of their situation in the city by the fall of 1992, only half a year into the fighting. With neither jobs nor future, their lives involved a round of scavenging and bartering for daily necessities, of regular humiliations at the hands of the Banja Luka authorities and violence at the hands of the paramilitaries, and, in the evenings, of talking about whether or not to try to bribe their way out of the Bosanska Krajina and into Croatia. The fee the Serb paramilitaries charged was one thousand Deutschemarks, but for most it was a moot point anyway, since the Croats were loath to take in any more Bosnian Muslim refugees (ethnic Croats were allowed in if they could make it through the Krajina). Muslim notables and leaders of what before the fighting started had been the local branch of the governing party in Sarajevo, Alia Izetbegovic's SDA, tried to negotiate with the Serb authorities, but they did so from a position of abject weakness, and, as the months went by, a few managed to flee and many more were killed. No responsibility for any of the deaths was ever established. My friend the notable was one of these "disappeared." He was alive in October 1992. When I returned to Banja Luka in February 1993, he was nowhere to be found. A Serb family occupied his apartment. They professed never to have heard of him.

Wars are no simpler than individuals. In Banja Luka, many Serbs behaved loyally and honorably toward their Muslim and Croat friends. Only a few non-Serbs dismissed from their jobs in Banja Luka ever managed to find lowlier work, and those who did owed it to the good offices of Serb friends. But even those jobs could be dangerous. A Muslim woman who had been a doctor before the war now worked selling men's clothing. Although the Serb owner of the shop had, she said, probably not expected her to come to work, and only hired her to provide her with some money and access to health care, she had taken the job seriously. Dressed in the clothes of her former station in life, she dutifully sat behind the counter every day. One morning, a Serb irregular walked into the store, an assault rifle on his shoulder. He leveled the weapon at her, pointed to a shirt in the window, and said, "I want that shirt, and I'm not paying for it." Without demur, she rose, got the shirt from the display, and handed it to him. The militiaman put it over one shoulder and lowered his weapon. Before he left, he looked her up and down, taking in her proper if threadbare skirt, jacket, and blouse, and said in ringing, satisfied tones, "*I* haven't had a bath in fifty days."

A trivial event by Banja Luka standards, since the woman was neither killed nor hurt, though she cried quietly, behind her dark glasses, as she told me the story. Even during the day, from the modern housing developments at the edge of the city to the town hall in the main square—once the office of a Wehrmacht lieutenant named Kurt Waldheim, active in the ethnic cleansing of his time—Banja Luka is a sullen and frightening place. At night the city is terrifying. Not only does the Balkan darkness allow the easy settling of scores, but tempers flare for no particular reason, and nonpolitical mayhem also takes its toll. I have never spent a night in Banja Luka without hearing gunfire and the sound of shouts and broken glass. But coming downstairs from my room in the Hotel Bosna, I have also never been able to get a straight answer from anyone about what happened. The hotel staff would play dumb; the gunmen having an early drink or finishing breakfast would smirk. Once, one looked up from his eggs and said, "*Strani novinar* [foreign journalist], you ask too many questions."

Sometimes, what had gone on the night before was impossible to cover up. In late September 1992, the Bosna lost most of its glass frontage, as well as its marble reception area, from one day to the next. This was less than a week before Cyrus Vance and David Owen were due to travel to Banja Luka for the first time and hold yet another of their meetings with Karadzic. Some people, mostly Serbs in uniform, explained that there had been an attack on the hotel that was intended to prevent the negotiators from coming to Banja Luka. It was the work of Muslim mujahedin, they said. (Referring to Bosnian government soldiers as if they were Shiite truck bombers was almost as common among Bosnian Serbs as referring to them as Turkish soldiers or "Janissaries.") Others, usually Muslims or Croats, whispered that the attack had been a Serb provocation, designed to foment a new round of retaliatory violence against non-Serbs.

A few days later, I ran into one of the friendly Bosnian Serb soldiers with whom I had spent an evening drinking a few days earlier. He smiled ruefully and shook his head. "A horrible night, man," he said. It turned out that what had actually happened was that another Serb irregular, slivoed to the gills, had been drinking in the Bosna. Suddenly, he had stood up, pulled the pins on two grenades and sprayed the place with his AK-47. "I don't know why he went crazy," the soldier said. "Crazy bastard." Three people had been killed and several more wounded—their blood was to stain the cheap brown marble for a week before the charwomen managed to get the last of it out—before other irregulars, only slightly less sodden themselves, managed to grab their own weapons and shoot him dead. "I would rather be back on the first line," the Serb soldier said. "At least there you know where the bullets are coming from. That night, they were shooting from all directions. I thought I would get hit in the crossfire for sure."

For non-Serbs, of course, Banja Luka was a front line from the day the Bosnian Serb Army rolled in. Almost all of them were in mourning for a family member who had been killed or "disappeared," and in shock, as people were and are in shock all over Bosnia, at the way in which their lives had been turned upside down. But in Banja Luka, where the consolation of resistance was unavailable from the start, and even the adrenaline rush of fear that sustained many Sarajevans during the siege was missing, non-Serbs often give the impression of being in mourning for themselves, rehearsing their own deaths in a mood of detached, musing wonder. "I sometimes speculate," the notable had said to me toward the end of the last evening I spent with him, "whether I will be shot, or butchered in a camp, or if I will die in some unexpected way. I'm sure my death warrant has already been issued. I have a friend, a Serb I went to school with—he's a very nice man; you'd like him—in the Mayor's office. And he told me I'm on a list of SDA members they plan to kill. He's seen it, he says."

I found myself insisting that although they certainly looked bleak at the moment, perhaps things would improve. UNPROFOR might finally succeed in deploying the Canadian battalion they kept trying to get to Banja Luka to monitor things in the region. And maybe the United Nations High Commissioner for Refugees could help. The new American head of the office, Robyn Ziebert, was said to be very good. She'd been an aid worker in Central America—very brave, very dedicated. She knew her job was to protect people like him, whatever UNHCR officials were supposed to do. Besides, the UNHCR people in Zagreb were trying to make Banja Luka a priority. It was for that reason they had pushed Vance and Owen to come to Banja Luka: to send a message to Karadzic and Mladic that the world's attention was focused now on what was going on; to raise the alarm about ethnic cleansing.

Of course, the only thing that was going on and on was me. I was talking complete nonsense, and both the notable and I knew it. The truth was that I would leave Banja Luka in a few days, and the notable would be killed. Whether his death occurred in a few days, a few weeks, or a few months was irrelevant. The fact that he could say it did not make him a hero but it was, perhaps, the only way he had left of being a free man. His colleague Dr. Muharem Krzic, who had been the leading veterinarian in Banja Luka and was now the regional head of the SDA, Izetbegovic's Party of Democratic Action, had exhibited some of the same fatalism when he appeared at the

Hotel Bosna, met privately with Vance and Owen, and then gave a press conference in the hotel dining room to the international press during which he explained the process of ethnic cleansing in great detail. As he rose to leave, he had said, "Make it a good story." Then, after pausing to contemplate his slightly trembling hands, he had added quietly, "I've probably just written my own obituary."

Robyn Ziebert did manage to keep Krzic alive for a long time, sending UNHCR cars to his house at times in defiance of the curfew, and expressing her concern for his safety at practically every meeting she had with the Banja Luka authorities. He may, in fact, be alive still, although I have never been able to find out for certain. It's a common enough problem. I can no longer count the number of conversations I have had in Bosnia that began, "You remember X? Is he still alive?" Or the number of replies that have taken the form "I'm not sure. I've heard nothing." When you tell someone in Sarajevo you are going to Banja Luka, they sometimes give you names of relatives there, hoping you can clear up their doubts. Rightly, they have learned to assume the worst. But about the notable's death, sadly, I am in no doubt whatsoever. He'd told me he could never leave Banja Luka, that being away from his art and his carpets would be too painful to him. "You know what collectors are like," he said. "They don't believe there's a difference between themselves and their treasures."

"But you've told me you have a house on the coast," I'd remonstrated. "You must have put some of your treasures there, too." But he had only smiled and shaken his head. "It simply isn't possible for me, you know," he had replied sadly. "I got my family out and that's enough. My place is here. Whether I'm resting above ground, or under it, I have to stay in Banja Luka."

The notable was rehearsing his own death. It is taking nothing away from him to add that he could afford to, since the people he loved were safe. Other non-Serbs in Banja Luka were still trying to come to terms with the deaths of those they had loved. It was one of these who told me a story that I still feel can stand for the tragedy of the Bosnian Muslims, the Bosniaks, as he called them. "My half brother," he said, "was one of the first to be killed. He was a teacher in an elementary school in a small village. The attack was not a surprise. Neighbors came and told him, 'You're educated and the Chet-

niks are killing all the Muslim notables. You have to flee. Go to the
Sava. The current is not too strong. You should be able to swim
across to safety.' But my brother refused. He said, 'I'm not leaving. I
haven't done anything to anyone. I'm not even a real Muslim. I drink
and eat pork.' And so he stayed, and the soldiers came, and they
killed him, just as the villagers had warned would happen.

"And now I keep thinking about his death, and I can't hate. I just
can't generate the hatred. Sometimes I pray to God, atheist Muslim
that I am, that He will come and make these pigs who murdered my
brother disappear from the face of the earth, but I realize that I
couldn't lift a finger to help make them disappear. I wonder about
this all the time. Am I right not to hate? Am I right to try to hold on
to my cosmopolitan feelings? I think so, but I'm not sure. In the
schools, when I was a boy, they taught us about the Nazi persecu-
tions of the Jews. It seemed like ancient history, an artifact from a
museum, something you read about. I remember looking at the pic-
tures of the Jews lining up to board the trains for Auschwitz, and
somehow never entirely believing in them. I don't mean that I didn't
believe six millions of Jews died, only that it wasn't real. Maybe it
was because the photos were in black and white. And now we're the
Jews, we Muslims of Banja Luka. I see my friends lining up in front
of the bus station here when there is a rumor that it is possible to
leave, and I think sometimes, 'That's the way it was in the forties.'
But it's in color now, and it's not the Jews, it's us.

"I try not to hate," he repeated. "I try not to let in my ignoble
thoughts." In other words, morally at least, the man continued to try
to be a hero—which, in the context of northern Bosnia, meant that
he could only be one thing: a victim. I met him in the fall of 1992. A
year and a half later, things had only gotten worse. He did escape
Banja Luka, as did many others. For non-Serbs, hoping against hope
gave way to the realization that all was lost. Instead of clinging to
their homes and to their civic identity in Banja Luka, as the notable
had done, and with great courage resisting all the pressures coming
from the Serb authorities to leave, people were begging to be evacu-
ated. They crowded the UNHCR offices and pleaded with visiting
representatives of the ICRC, the International Committee of the Red
Cross, to assist their departure.

In February 1994, after a particularly vicious series of killings and bombings around the town of Priejdor ("They're all bastards in that area," an aid worker warned me, "but the Priejdor bunch are the worst of the worst"), the UNHCR tried to organize the evacuation of the ten thousand remaining Muslims in the Bosanska Krajina. Given the Serb war aims, one might have thought that the local authorities would have leapt at the chance to get rid of them. And they did agree to the deal. But then Radovan Karadzic intervened, saying that everything was fine, that there would be no further killings—what had happened, he said, had been at most an isolated incident—and that he was sending investigators from Pale to find out what was really going on. "If anyone is killing Muslims, or taking away their human rights, they shall be punished," he said from his headquarters. Unable to *compel* the Serbs to allow the evacuations, the UNHCR backed down. The evacuation was first put on hold, then canceled. There then followed a brief pause during which the media attention died down. Then the killings and bombings resumed. Naturally, nothing further was heard of Karadzic's investigation. The victims were to remain victims, whatever the threat they posed, however diminished their numbers. Whether the world watched or averted its gaze, whether aid agencies and the United Nations acted or were silent, the genocide went on. And the Bosnian Muslims waited for death or displacement.

V

Ethnic cleansing in Bosnia has been as much about methodically humiliating a people and destroying their culture as it has been about killing them. The Serb assault on the Ottoman and Islamic architectural legacy throughout the country was not a by-product of the fighting—collateral damage, as soldiers say—but an important war aim. For the Bosnian Serb leadership, the Serbianization of areas of Bosnia that had been ethnically mixed before the fighting started could not be accomplished simply by driving out many of the non-Serbs who lived in villages. Even after two years of fighting, it still was commonplace to encounter people in refugee camps who would ask when "all this" would be over, when they could go back to living as they had before. As long as middle-class Muslims could continue their professional lives in the towns, and as long as Muslim refugees could imagine that one day, when the political balance shifted, they could return to the homes they had been expelled from, ethnic cleansing would not be a success. The massacres at the beginning of the fighting in the spring of 1992 had only been the start. The process and program that was ethnic cleansing of necessity involved the rewriting of the Bosnian past as well.

In the town of Zvornik, which before the outbreak of the conflict had had a Muslim majority despite its proximity to Serbia proper, the Bosnian Serb authorities liked to boast to visiting reporters about their plans to rename the town. The old Serb name, they insisted, had been Zvonik. The Turks had add the *r*. That, they would tell you, was part of the cultural genocide the Ottomans had perpetrated on the Serb people. Now, the wrong could finally be righted. And if you suggested to Bosnian Serb officials in the town that, after all, Muslims had been in the majority in Zvornik for a long time, they usually responded with counterfactuals. If so many Serbs had not been killed by the fascists in the Second World War, they said, Zvornik would still have a Serb majority. Serbs had been the majority in Bosnia before 1939, they would add. This was one of the most familiar tropes in Serb nationalist thinking. Even in the Serbian province of Kossovo, where the population in 1994 was ninety percent Albanian, Serb nationalists often remarked, as if the fact were of great significance, that there had been no Albanian presence in the region before the fourteenth century. By comparison, the attempt to delegitimize the Bosnian Muslims seemed a much easier undertaking.

Before the beginning of the fighting, there had been approximately a thousand mosques in the Bosanska Krajina. By the winter of 1994, there were certainly no more than a hundred and probably far fewer. Even the great Ferhabed mosque of Banja Luka, perhaps the finest example of sixteenth-century Islamic architecture in the Balkans, was not spared. Throughout the first year of the fighting, it had stood, not far from the city's main square, a monument to both the Islamic past and the Muslim present of Banja Luka. On one side of its facade, it had been defaced with a scrawled cross into whose four quadrants had been inscribed four *C*'s (the *S*'s of the Cyrillic alphabet), standing for the slogan "*Samo Sloga Srbina Spasava*"— "Only Unity Can Save the Serb." There was nothing remarkable about this. Any non-Serb dwelling or handy space on a wall in towns or villages the Chetniks seized were daubed with that Orthodox cross and those four *C*'s, often accompanied by the letters "JNA" (for the Yugoslav National Army) and a boastful phrase or the first names of individual soldiers. But neither most people in Banja Luka—Serb and non-Serb alike—nor visiting journalists and aid workers worried much about the Great Mosque. Unlike the Muslims themselves, it seemed safe.

During Cyrus Vance and David Owen's visit to Banja Luka in September 1992, Radovan Karadzic had even boasted publicly about the continued existence of the mosque. He had greeted the United Nations and European Community negotiators as their motorcade came to a halt in the main square of Bosanska Gradiska, on the south bank of the Sava. Waving his arm toward a nearby steeple, Karadzic had said, "You see, that's a Catholic church. It hasn't been destroyed, any more than the mosque. We all live in peace here and all over the parts of Bosnia where we control and where the Muslims do not attack us. We cannot live in the same state with Muslims, but if they live with us and do not attack us, we will not harm them and we will respect their religion. In Banja Luka it is the same."

In Bosanska Gradiska, the Catholic church in question turned out to have been bolted shut. The mosque in Banja Luka was open, though empty, and defaced, as I have mentioned. Two jokes were making the rounds among non-Serbs in Banja Luka at the time. The first went, "What's the definition of Serbian pacifism?" To which the answer ran, "Greater Serbia all the way to the Pacific." The second asked how one could tell the difference between an Orthodox and a Catholic church. The reply was, "The Orthodox church is the one that is still standing." But when I heard the joke for the first time, no one I knew—foreigner or Bosnian—really imagined that six months later, in one evening, after cordoning off the main square, Serb fighters would blow up all five mosques in the northeastern Bosnian city of Bijeljina (the destruction might not have been revealed for months had not an ITN reporter named Gaby Rado managed to smuggle out film of what had happened), or that six months after that, the main mosque of Banja Luka would be dynamited. We had seen how bad things were in the countryside, but we consoled ourselves with the thought that in towns like Bijeljina, or Zvornik, or Banja Luka, places that the Serb forces had taken in the first days of the fighting, the worst was over. After all, didn't the Serbs have everything they wanted? Even wasting troops on persecuting the non-Serb population or explosives on blowing up churches and mosques was foolish militarily while the fighting was still going on.

Or so we thought, anyway. In retrospect, the destruction of the mosques of the Bosanska Krajina was only an emblem of our naïveté in believing that the fact that there was no practical reason for the Serbs to do something meant that they would not do it. What many of us missed, I think, is that they considered themselves to be the injured parties, engaged in a defensive war. In interview after interview, Karadzic would make this point with varying degrees of eloquence and hyperbole. "We Serbs are only defending ourselves against Muslim attacks," was one of his catchphrases. A fallback was to use the horrors of the war—"It is civil war," he once said, "what do you expect?"—to prove that Serbs and Muslims could not live together in Bosnia, and that, in fact, what the Serbs were trying to accomplish was in the interests of the Muslims as well, whether they realized it or not.

Whether Karadzic himself believed any of this is open to question. In trying to come to terms with what happened in Bosnia, it is important not to take the claims of the Serb leadership at face value. In any case, wars have more often been about money than about ideology. Karadzic himself had followed a number of political tunes before he became a Serb nationalist, including a brief stint as one of the founders of the Green movement in Bosnia. And the Serbian president, Slobodan Milosevic, an economist by training, had presented himself as an *antinationalist,* a pragmatic Titoist, before opting to play the nationalist card in Serbia. While still in his former ideological guise, he had gone so far as to denounce the 1985 memorandum of the Serbian Academy of Arts and Sciences—which many viewed as a sort of ideological blueprint for the Serb nationalism that would follow in the late 1980s—as unacceptably corrosive of Yugoslavia's unity.

On the other hand, in war General Mladic did seem to have become a convinced Serb nationalist, while a few officials in Pale gave ample evidence of having taken leave of their senses altogether. Biljana Plavcic, who, in fairness, was far and away the weirdest of the lot, once received Jose Maria Mendiluce, the head of the UNHCR for the former Yugoslavia, with the complaint that "live Serb babies are being fed to the zoo animals in Sarajevo." She said this at precisely the moment when the city's zookeepers were risking their lives to go to the zoo to feed the animals—a vain act of heroism, since all the animals eventually starved to death. Even Mendiluce, skilled diplomat though he was, could not keep his composure. "Mrs. Plavcic," he exploded in his heavily accented English, "if the Bosnians are feeding live Serbs to the zoo animals, then why are the zoo animals starving?"

There were people like Biljana Plavcic to be found among ordinary Serbs, for whom, in any case, outlandish declarations of the sort she had made to Mendiluce were the common currency of the television they watched and the radio they listened to. But far less farfetched ideas influenced what they were doing as well. In particular, the Serbs who came from as far away as Belgrade or Novi Sad to settle themselves and their families into houses in Banja Luka, or Bi-jeljina, or Foca, vacated by Muslims and Croats might have been seized by the fever of ethnic nationalism, but they were also getting something for nothing. Karadzic might claim that before 1992, Bosnian Serbs had controlled sixty percent of the land ("Muslims prefer to huddle in cities; it is not their way to work on the land," he once said), but not only were his figures doubtful but, unlike in the Krajina region of Croatia, few areas of Bosnia had been all Serb and most villages and towns had been mixed. Ethnic cleansing, which was both the military strategy and the war aim of the Bosnian Serb forces, was a way of reversing this. In this sense, the Serb war on Bosnia was not a civil war or the uncontrollable eruption of a people driven mad by fear and ideology so much as it was a crude land grab—a straightforward case of which group would own the land, profit from it, and eventually get to pass it on to their children.

Trying to make sense of what was going on in Bosnia by talking to Karadzic was, as the successive waves of United Nations officials both civilian and military who were sent to deal with him all learned eventually, a hopeless exercise. Karadzic was a liar, and not in the sense that all politicians lie but in that of the florid schizophrenics he had treated in the psychiatry department of Kosevo Hospital in Sarajevo in a former incarnation. Whether it was claiming, before the imposition of NATO's so-called "No Fly" zone over Bosnia-Herzegovina, that no Bosnian Serb Army aircraft were conducting bombing raids or transporting troops; or denying that the Serb shells raining down on Sarajevo were coming from his positions—"It is the Muslims," he said over and over again, "who shell themselves. They hope to gain the sympathy of the world"—or even claiming that there was no such thing as ethnic cleansing, a term Karadzic himself had resuscitated, there appeared to be no limits to how far he was willing to go. And why not? What Karadzic and the other Serb leaders learned over the course of the two years in which they conquered Bosnia was that whatever they did, the United Nations and the great powers were not going to lift a finger to stop them. And if their deeds brought no retaliation down on their heads, why should their words have any consequences?

A BBC film crew following Karadzic around in the summer of 1992 even recorded a conversation between himself, General

Mladic, and Biljana Plavcic about complaints from UNPROFOR concerning Serb air activity. It is a surreal scene. Karadzic reports the protest. Plavcic then says flatly, "The planes weren't flying." Even Karadzic can't quite swallow that. "Of course they were, Biljana," he says exasperatedly. "We were flying like crazy that day." Mladic's impulse is just to tell UNPROFOR to fuck off. He is shown drumming his fingers, increasingly exasperated by the whole conversation. In the end, though, it is decided that Karadzic will tell the UN that the planes were up in the air because it was the commemoration of Serb "Air Day." The question of what they will do if the United Nations does not accept this explanation never comes up. And rightly. For Karadzic, Mladic, and Plavcic assume that the UN will have to accept *any* explanation they provide. As it happened, they were wrong about air activities—the No Fly zone was eventually put in place—but whether it was in Banja Luka in 1992, in Sarajevo all the way up to February 1994, or in the Gorazde pocket two months after that, events were to prove just how right they were to bank on their being able to act with impunity and say what they liked.

After two mortar shells landed next to a breadline in the center of Sarajevo in August 1992, killing sixteen and wounding many more, Karadzic was quick to issue the claim that the Bosnian government had planted land mines under the site. The fact that a mine leaves a hole in the ground and a mortar that distinctive splash that looks like a slightly abstract animal paw made no difference. Pressure from a great power might have led Karadzic to change his story, even if only by laying off the blame on some rogue element within the Bosnian Serb Army or on the fact, as he once put it when conceding that perhaps "a few cases of rape" had occurred, that "every war produces a few psychopaths." As things stood, in any case, hectoring from foreign reporters and toothless reproaches from the United Nations were not what the Bosnian Serbs feared. At times, the UN could even act as the Serbs' ally, most notoriously in the case of the breadline massacre itself. There, many UNPROFOR officials actually supported Karadzic's ascription of blame at first.

Its anti–Bosnian government Canadian commander, Major General Lewis Mackenzie, never actually visited the site on Vase Miskina Street, but at the time, and, later, in his memoir, *Peace-*

keeper, stuck to the view that it was impossible to know which side was to blame or even to know whether the destruction had been caused by mortar fire, as the Bosnians claimed, or explosives, as the Serbs claimed. And yet the distinctive "mortar splash" was and remains there for anyone to see. More often, though, it was simply a question of the Serb leaders knowing that, with the world community supine, the only propaganda war they had to win was among their own people. In this, they had been astonishingly successful. Traveling through Bosnian Serb–controlled territory, it was common enough to meet Serbs who were sick of the war, and horrified by the way in which Bosnia had been shattered. But it was all but impossible to find anyone who believed the Serb side had started the conflict, or that the Serbs were anything but misunderstood victims. Ordinary Serbs spoke with genuine bewilderment about the attitude of the Western powers. "I used to love America," a high school teacher told me in the Sarajevo suburb of Ilidza during the summer of 1993, the tears welling up in her eyes. "For a while, I told myself that you American people had been duped, but now I realize that you are all our enemies, and that I must learn to think of you that way—even though I don't want to. I see what you write about us, the lies, and I just don't understand."

I asked her why, if the Serbs were the true victims of the war, they continued to shell Sarajevo pitilessly, and why Sarajevan children had to die at the hands of Serb snipers. She just sighed and shook her head. "It is not true," she said, softly reproving. "If we shell the city, it is only because the Muslims shoot at us first. Don't we have the right to defend ourselves? Don't you think that every human being has that right, even we evil, evil Serbs? I am sure that if they would stop firing, we would stop too, right away. Nobody wants war."

"And the sniper fire?" I asked, the memories of the maimed children of the Kosevo pediatrics ward coming, terrible and unbidden, to mind.

She looked at me coldly. "I think you are mistaken," she said. "Sniping is a coward's weapon. Serbs are incapable of behaving in this dishonorable way. I come from Sarajevo. I was thrown out of my home by Muslims. Our soldiers, many of them, come from the city also. They would not kill children. If kids are being killed, it must be the Muslims who are doing this to blame the Serbian people."

Anyone who had spent time in the bowl of Sarajevo, where the snipers can see and pick out their victims, and where, throughout the siege, even to stand at your window was to risk your life, might have been tempted to question her sanity. But her sincerity was beyond question. Perhaps it should not have been surprising. The only information about the fighting this woman had received in more than a year, except through chance encounters with foreign journalists and aid workers whom she already had written off as being pro-Muslim, was what was dished out each night on Bosnian Serb television and radio. Her only other source was what the fighters returning from the front chose to tell her. Not that the fighters themselves were always without similar leaps of faith and fancy. In a sandbagged revetment on a hill above Sarajevo, not too far from the no-man's-land of the city's Jewish cemetery, a bearded Serb fighter said to me, "Before this summer ends we will have driven the Turkish army out of the city, just as they drove us from the field of Kossovo in 1389. That was the beginning of Turkish domination of our lands. This will be the end of it, after all these cruel centuries."

He was, compared to those of his comrades that I met—their tastes seemed to tend toward *Penthouse*-style pinups and images of Saint Sava, patron saint of Bosnian Serbs—an educated man. Like the woman I had met in Ilidza, he too had been a high school teacher in a Sarajevo suburb, and later that evening he would ask me what I thought of the novels of John Updike. But when this man looked down at the city of Sarajevo, into which he had been shooting his fifty-caliber machine gun for the better part of a year, he did not see what had once been a rich city by world standards, the Balkan capital of rock and roll, but rather the campsite of the Turkish army that had conquered the Balkans in the fourteenth and fifteenth centuries. Somewhere he must have known that the people he was shooting at were civilians—already, after a year of the siege, thirty-five hundred of the dead were children—but imaginatively he could not see anyone in that urban bowl below except armed invaders. His job was not to murder them. One cannot murder invaders; one defends oneself against them, repels them. "We Serbs are saving Europe," he boasted, "even if Europe does not appreciate our efforts, even if it condemns them."

A Polish king had saved Vienna when the armies of the Ottomans had been on the point of capturing it in the seventeenth century. Now, the Bosnian Serb fighter said proudly, it was up to the Serbians to sacrifice themselves for the cause of Europe in the Old Continent's eternal war against Islam and the Turks. Then there would be peace; only then. "But you must understand," he told me wearily, "that the only language that Turks ever understand is force. Europeans used to understand that. They used to understand what we are facing and have always faced here in the Balkans. France helped Serbia in 1911 and 1915. There is a statue to the French erected in gratitude by the people of Belgrade after the war. And the USA and Serbia have been allies in two world wars. I don't how you have forgotten what your grandfathers understood so well. But it makes no difference. We have to fight."

I asked him if he had always believed in a Greater Serbia. "No," he replied. "Before the war started, I thought we could all live together peacefully here in Bosnia. I had Muslim friends, and, of course, many students. Even after the end of Communism, I thought it would be okay. But the Turks are duplicitous and cunning. Izetbegovic said one thing on television, but when he was talking to members of his party, he talked about making an Islamic state here in Bosnia. You can read his book. He says that Islam and Christianity are incompatible. 'There can be neither peace nor coexistence' were his words. Look them up. Or look up the SDA party magazine. I'm sure there are copies in Sarajevo. You will find stories about building mosques all over Bosnia, in Serb towns. At their party conference in 1991, Izetbegovic swore he would restore Bosnia's 'true' Muslim identity. What did you expect Serbs to do? Let Izetbegovic and Silajdzic put a mosque in the anteroom next to the hall of Parliament? We tried to live peacefully with them, but in the end we realized that we had to fight them." And with that he nodded approvingly, then nodded once more as, from the next firing position, one of his comrades began to fire long bursts down into Sarajevo.

When the teacher spoke of the Serbs who remained in Sarajevo, the overwhelming majority of whom had remained loyal to the Izetbegovic government, it was in terms of fifty thousand Serb hostages, held against their will by the Muslims. "They would all leave if they could," he told me. Even in the summer of 1993, he was right, but not for the reasons he imagined. By then a majority of

Sarajevans would have fled the city if they could have. But the reality was, no one wanted to let people out: not the Serb besiegers; not the UN, which took the view that the agreement it had signed with the Serbs to open the Sarajevo airport obliged it to prevent Bosnians from fleeing across the airport runway to the Bosnian government–controlled territory beyond; and not the Bosnian government itself, which felt it could not afford to lose any more people. But for the teacher, the belief that fellow Serbs were being held against their will allowed him to think about himself not only as a Christian warrior but, once again, as a victim. If he was firing down at Sarajevo, it was to prevent the Muslims from doing to the Serbs of Pale and Ilidza what they had already done, or planned to do, to the Serbs they held in the capital.

This sense of being the injured party helped explain one of the more curious minor experiences of life in Sarajevo. It was the habit, when the phones were working, of Serbs in the hills to occasionally call Muslim and Croat friends in the city below. People on the receiving end of these calls tended to be dumbstruck by them, particularly when it became clear that those making the calls were not at all ashamed of what they were doing, had not called to apologize or explain themselves, but were only concerned, and on a strictly private basis, for their Muslim friends' welfare, and nostalgic for contact with people from whom they had been separated. As a friend of mine put it, "I can accept that my old schoolmates are shooting at me, but how dare Vlado ring up just to say hello? I couldn't believe it. It was as if he had no responsibility at all for what was happening. He asked about my family. He even asked if I remembered a holiday we all took on the coast in the early eighties. It was completely bizarre."

But what seemed incomprehensible to a Sarajevan under siege made perfect sense from the Bosnian Serb perspective. Serbs had nothing to apologize for. If they initiated the calls, it was because it was easier to call Sarajevo than to call out of the city. The fact that one of the first things the Serb gunners had targeted was the telephone company building, knocking out most people's phones right away, went unmentioned. The Muslims had brought what was happening down on themselves, and while an individual Serb might feel sorry for his Muslim friend, such solicitude did nothing to alter his conviction that, as a collectivity, the Muslims of Sarajevo were getting what was coming to them. If anything, Serbs I talked to who occasionally made such calls seemed to feel that it was they who were conceding a lot by initiating a conversation that magnanimously tried to ignore the current situation and somehow recapture personal relations as they had been before the siege began.

These distorted perceptions at least were a little easier to understand in Sarajevo, where former friends had had no opportunity to meet face-to-face since the fighting started, than they were in a place like Banja Luka where no such enforced separation had taken place. Even by the standards of Pale and Belgrade, the anti-Muslim propaganda in the Bosanska Krajina was extreme. Unlike in Belgrade, where dissident voices still managed to make themselves heard, there were no oppositional voices in Banja Luka, any more than there were in Pale. More startlingly, because the Bosnian Serb leadership was not monolithic, there seemed to be no moderate Serb nationalist voices in the Bosanska Krajina either. This ideological overdrive in which Serbs operated in Banja Luka made sense. It was bound to take a lot of work for ordinary Serbs' perceptions of non-Serb neighbors whom they had known all their lives to be so transformed that, when they encountered them, they could only discern alien beings whose very presence posed a threat.

Getting individuals to kill is not that difficult. There is savagery in every civil war, and rarely any moral bottom. (Paradoxical though it may appear, the Bosnian conflict has been *both* a civil war and a war of aggression; it has been as ruthless as the former and as one-sided as the latter.) Once the blood has flowed, the individual fighter thirsts as much for revenge as for victory. And since in the former Yugoslavia atrocities have been committed by all sides, the desire for vengeance has taken the form of further atrocities. But, from the beginning, such excesses were also a Serb war aim. The more terrified the Muslims could be made to feel, the more likely they were not simply to flee but to resist ever returning to lands the Serbs had taken. And tales of terror and torture are the common currency of talk among Bosnian refugees who languish either in Bosnian government–controlled towns and villages or in refugee camps and cramped apartments outside the country.

Westerners found these tales hard to believe at first, and Serb apologists have consistently dismissed them out of hand. And yet a majority of even the most lurid tales the Bosnian Muslims told from the beginning of the fighting about the process of ethnic cleansing—stories that were initially dismissed as exaggerations—eventually turned out to be true. The numbers have been questioned. Were fifty thousand Muslim women raped, and many thousands of these forced to carry the offspring of the rapes to term (the implications of this last step being clear, since for Serbs as well as Muslims, and unlike Jews, the ethnicity of the father is decisive), or was the number "only" fifteen thousand? Were there dozens of secret camps in which Muslims were slaughtered or "just" a dozen? But the genocide itself is not open to question, nor are the atrocities. When it came out that a Muslim refugee from Bosanski Petrovac had told a field officer from the UNHCR that he had been forced by his captors to bite off the penis of a fellow captive, my first response, and that of everyone I knew—this despite the press's reputation for being uncritically anti-Serb—was disbelief. Then the UNHCR official who had taken the man's testimony cabled that he would stake his reputation on the man's truthfulness.

And, on reflection, atrocities like this one were one logical consequence of ethnic cleansing. If you keep repeating on television and radio and in every address to your troops, as the Serbs have done, that the enemy is not human; that you may have grown up with the man, and you may think you know him, but in reality you don't; in short, that you are confronting a devil, then the results are all but foreordained. It is no longer a question of whether there will be killing, only of how long the bloodletting will go on. And not just killing; mutilation as well. Muslim men are circumcised and Serb men are not, and the easiest way for Serb fighters to find out whether a prisoner they had taken was Muslim was to make him drop his trousers. From there, it was too often only a short step, psychologically, to cutting off his prick. That, too, was predictable. From the Armenians to the Jews to the Bosnian Muslims, there has never been a campaign of ethnic cleansing from which sexual sadism has gone missing.

And just as those who have carried out the ethnic cleansing almost invariably behave as if the atrocities they have perpetrated are somehow justified, so it was not only propagandists who insisted that the Muslims were less than human. The aggrieved innocence so commonly and unaffectedly displayed by individual fighters made it clear that they felt themselves and not those they were killing or displacing to be the real victims of the war. And like victims everywhere, they thirsted for what they usually called justice but were sometimes willing to categorize as revenge. When Serb forces took possession of conquered lands, houses, and farm animals, they were as likely to burn the houses and slaughter the livestock, even though they obviously realized that their actions made it impossible for their fellow Serbs to start farming them themselves. But they thought the price worth paying, so deep-seated was the Serb feeling of being the injured party.

It made no more sense to wonder at the lack of economic calculus in this "village war" than it did to wonder at the destruction of the National Library in Sarajevo, which had no military value but was specifically targeted for destruction by the Bosnian Serb gunners in the hills above the city during the first days of the fighting. To be puzzled, to imagine that there was some kind of mistake, was to miss the point, just as wondering why Hitler had diverted critical rolling stock needed to resupply his forces on the eastern front to transport the Jews to the concentration camps was to miss the point of the Nazi enterprise. Ethnic cleansing was undertaken to eliminate the Muslim presence in much of Bosnia. And it was the Muslim past as well as the living, ethnically mixed population of the city that was being targeted in Sarajevo. Indeed, it was hard to say which target was more important. Serbs in Sarajevo had to be relieved of the burden of the School of Oriental Studies, of the National Library, of the capital's grand mosques. Serbs could not live with the presence of these oppressive monuments. And if individual Serbs in the city were killed or injured, or even if Orthodox monuments like the cathedral off Vase Miskina Street were hit, well, that was what happened in a war. The Serb gunners did their best. The small cemetery in Sarajevo where Gavrilo Princip and his colleagues in the Young Bosnia movement lie buried was not hit once in two years of the siege, even though targets all around were devastated. But if necessary, the Serbs would target their own without compunction.

In the villages, radical military operations were often accompanied by equally radical cognitive ones. "We've liberated Radovac," a

Serb fighter in Banja Luka told me one afternoon. We were in a pool hall in the town's youth center, trying to communicate in fractured German—a process made no easier by the boom of U2's music in the background. That in itself was ironic. The Irish band was well known for its passionate support for the Bosnian government side. But that did little to inhibit the Serb soldiers I was drinking with from playing their U2 tapes. Radical-chic Western academic theorists of rock music might divert themselves with the conceit that popular music is inherently emancipatory and subversive, but in Banja Luka young people were quite capable of distinguishing between their taste in music and their politics. The international youthquake was the international youthquake—United Colors of Benetton and all—and war was war; neither got in the other's way. The young Serb fighter standing in his sub-Benetton civilian clothes, swaying to the music and trying to carry on a conversation with me and still maintain his proprietary, corralling hold on his girlfriend's haunch might be visually indistinguishable from any gawky teenager from San Francisco to Bremen, but his adherence to this universal style did nothing to rein in his conviction that it was his duty as a Serb to kill and to risk his own death in northern Bosnia that season.

"We've liberated Radovac," he repeated, practically bellowing at me, apparently believing that I hadn't heard him the first time. He then flashed a thumbs-up. I nodded. "It was a hard fight," he shouted, "but we got it back." Only later would I learn from a French UNHCR protection officer in Banja Luka named Pierre Ollier—one of the many brave people I have met in Bosnia who did not survive the war—that Radovac had always been an entirely Muslim village. The Serb fighter was a local, Ollier had remarked with a shrug, he must have known this. For the Serb, though, such considerations were secondary. For him, the Muslims of Radovac were not and could not be the village's real inhabitants. However long their tenancy, it could never be long enough in the Bosnian Serb version of history. It was a variant of the same story each time the Serbs attacked somewhere. If the area in question was not full of Serbs being oppressed or killed by Muslims, the Serbs were only trying to protect Serb parts of the area. This was how Karadzic justified the shelling of Sarajevo throughout the war, when, with a straight face, he insisted that there was no siege, only Serb forces trying to protect

Serbs who just happened to live in all the neighborhoods that ringed the city. Karadzic said more or less the same thing when Gorazde became a major target in April 1994. And when neither of these claims would do, the Serbs would fall back on history, and insist that the area in question had once been Serb, until some Muslim or Croat massacre had upset its proper demographic future. Radovac was an example of this last approach. The Muslims were interlopers. They should not have been in the village to begin with.

The Bosnian Serb forces tailored their tactics to the kind of area in which they were operating. It was one thing to lay siege to Sarajevo, but in the ethnically mixed villages of Bosnia, the fighters could not pursue ethnic cleansing successfully on their own. They had to transform those local Serbs who were either still undecided about joining the fight or frankly opposed to it into their accomplices. The natural impulse for self-preservation was the fighters' greatest ally, providing they could summon up the necessary ruthlessness. One common method used was for a group of Serb fighters to enter a village, go to a Serb house, and order the man living there to come with them to the house of his Muslim neighbor. As the other villagers watched, he was marched over and the Muslim brought out. Then the Serb would be handed a Kalashnikov assault rifle or a knife—knives were better—and ordered to kill the Muslim. If he did so, he had taken that step across the line the Chetniks had been aiming for. But if he refused, as many did, the solution was simple. You shot him on the spot. Then you repeated the process with the next Serb householder. If he refused, you shot him. The Chetniks rarely had to kill a third Serb. As a fighter in Bosanska Krupa, who, to my astonishment, boasted of the tactic, informed me gleefully, "By the third house, they're shitting themselves and asking you where you want the Muslim shot, and how many times."

But in most places, this kind of raw terror was not enough. More than killing or making people accomplices to murder, it was the engendering of a deep fear that was required. From the start, fear had lain at the heart of the Bosnian catastrophe. The fear of the future that the collapse of the Yugoslav economy in the late eighties began to produce in ordinary people had made them lose faith in each other. Only the old atavistic notions of identity seemed to offer any sanctuary from this fear. It was not that people had only felt themselves to be Serbs, or Croats, or Muslims before—or that Tito's slogan, "Brotherhood and Unity," had been only an imposed sham—but rather that the failure of cosmopolitanism, of Yugoslavism, or, more properly, its murder at the hands of political leaders like Slobodan Milosevic, had breathed such new energy into the old national feelings and national grievances. Ethnic nationalism was no more inevitable in the former Yugoslavia than Hitlerism had been inevitable in Germany in the 1930s. It was one possibility—inevitable only in the sense that everything that happens is inevitable in hindsight.

After a year of war, the young Serb fighter might be able to construe his identity only as that. But when I asked him whether he had thought as he did now before the fighting started, he smiled and shook his head. "No," he said, almost wonderingly, "I had many Muslim friends. The guy who owns this place is a Muslim." He paused. "Well, I mean the guy who used to own it. He's working for the UN here in Banja Luka. Sometimes I tell him, 'Frantzie, get the fuck out of this place.' He was a good guy, before. You can see that it's a nice place. When I came here, I never thought about a Muslim guy owning it. We were friends." Then his face darkened. "But I didn't understand many things in that time. I thought the Muslims were okay. I was just another naive Serb bastard. You know, you foreigners say we're killers and that's a lie. But I'll give you this much, we are a trusting bunch of fools. We trusted the Americans, the Europeans, and we trusted the Muslims, too. Now we have to fight." His tone softened. "It's terrible," he said.

Of course, he meant what had happened to the Serbs was terrible. He had no sympathy to waste on Muslims or Croats, although he did tell me that the Croats would one day realize the Serbs had been right about the Muslims, and the two groups would join together to fight Islamic fundamentalism. But what animated him was fear, and what made him able to respect himself was the belief that everything he had done had been in self-defense. Outsiders and, for that matter, Balkan intellectuals talked a lot about an almost innate Balkan proclivity for violence. But for all this loose, essentialist talk, in the past Bosnia was not a particularly violent place—at least by the violent standards of European history. The twentieth century was something of a tragic exception, but no more in Bosnia than in Poland, and people do not harbor similarly extreme fantasies about the Polish national character. Nevertheless, few ideas or allegiances die out completely in the space of one or two generations. Ethnic nationalism was one such idea, and it triumphed in Bosnia in 1994. The multiculturalism of Sarajevo—an idea that had been around at least since the era when the city became a haven for Sephardic Jews—was another. It was murdered in Bosnia that same year.

This does not mean that the victory of the ethnic nationalists was inevitable. They won in Serbia because of what they did, and because of what others did not do—particularly in the West—not because history was on their side. They won because Slobodan Milosevic was far and away the ablest politician in the former Yugoslavia, because the idea of Greater Serbia was coherent in a way that the idea of the Bosnian state never succeeded in becoming, and because General Mladic had a hundred heavy guns for every one the Bosnian side had. And the Bosnian Serbs won because they knew how to take old fears and old complaints, repackage them, and cause otherwise decent Serbs, people from a national community with no more of an innate predilection for murder than any other national community, to commit genocide. And then there was that terrible Serb fear. As Herbert Okun, the American diplomat who became Cyrus Vance's deputy in both the Croatian and the Bosnian peace negotiations, warned Radovan Karadzic before the fighting started: "If you continue to talk about the mortal danger that Serbs are under in Bosnia, you will end up committing preemptive genocide."

Once that genocide began, however, the fear had to be fed. Had the Bosnian Serb leadership not put a particular effort into propaganda, it is at least possible that ordinary Serbs, having defeated the Bosnian government forces and seized most of the territory they had been taught to covet in the first half-year of the fighting, might have been less eager subsequently to go along with the seemingly endless further rounds of killings and displacements. But if every living Muslim remained a threat, then the ethnic cleansing had to go on. What began as a tactic of pure massacre and terror in villages had evolved within six months into a sophisticated system for the destruction of a people. In northern Bosnia, in 1992, Muslim men who were taken, either in the course of fighting or during an episode of ethnic cleansing in a particular district, were then divided into three groups. Professional people, local notables, and young, able-bodied men were usually separated out and killed by Serb fighters who believed themselves to be retaliating for the Muslim atrocities that were the staple of the radio and TV reports they had been exposed to. If you are told over and over again that your comrades are being castrated, roasted alive on spits, and drowned in their own blood, and you have no sources of information from which you might learn a different story, it is a foregone conclusion that before too long you will, as you imagine it anyway, reply in kind.

For their part, the Serb leaders were not acting out of blood lust. By ordering the deaths of as many educated Muslims as possible, they wanted to ensure that, whatever else happened, any future Bosnian Muslim state would be as bereft as possible of people who could make it work efficiently. The success of this campaign—of what the British journalist Michael Nicholson called "elitocide"—can be inferred from the fact that apart from a few thousand middle-class refugees who made their way to Zagreb, and the small number who got to Bosnian government–controlled areas, the Muslim professional classes of the Bosanska Krajina all but disappeared. Those who were not killed in this malign triage were then divided into two groups. The first, about whom the Serbs were still undecided, were held in what at the time were known as "intelligence camps." Some prisoners were later killed; others were released. The remaining group, made up mostly of peasants and poor townspeople, were marked for release from the start, and were housed in what the Serbs sometimes called "open centers," which in practical terms designated camps that representatives of the International Committee of the Red Cross were allowed to visit.

In these camps, all but a few remaining Muslim diehards seemed resigned to the idea that they would have to leave Bosnia for good. Far from constituting, as so many Serbs imagined, a prospective fifth column, the prisoners we journalists encountered were concerned with finding out whether any country might grant them asylum. They knew Croatia was all but closed to them, and many now pinned their hopes on the Western European states where there were Bosnian guest workers. In the Trnopolje camp, the men I met penned up behind the wire could practically see their own farms. But what they dreamed about was flight. "I have a brother in Germany!" one tough-looking middle-aged man shouted to a group of foreign journalists with whom I was traveling. "Here's his address. Do you think you could get a message to him?" As we made our way through the camp, we heard the same story repeated, in broken German, broken French, broken Dutch, broken Italian, and imprecations launched at the guards in the same languages. The war in Bosnia, and in Croatia before it, had been a war between former guest workers, exiles, immigrants. But mostly, the men neither cursed nor pleaded, but simply stood around, as prisoners do.

But to our Serbian escort, these three thousand filthy, demoralized prisoners were the vanguard of a Muslim horde that had almost overrun a Serb nation whose only fault, as he told us repeatedly during the drive from Banja Luka to the camp, was that it had been too indulgent, too willing to allow other national communities to prosper at the Serbs' expense. Just outside a village along the narrow road approaching the camp, this young man—he had been a cub reporter on the main Banja Luka daily newspaper before being mobilized—assured us that we would see that the mosque in this village had been left intact, even though there had been fighting. "Any Muslim house that displayed the white flag of loyalty," he said, "was untouched by our soldiers. There was fighting only because we were attacked by the mujahedin." Surely the white flag had the same meaning in Bosnia that it did everywhere else in Europe—surrender—but he continued with his longish disquisition on the particular animalistic savagery of the Muslim fighters. "The worst," he said grimly, "are the Handzar"—a word that the interpreter, who was mystified by it at first, eventually explained as "a kind of Muslim knife."

The word *handzar* means scimitar. In using it, the Serb propagandists not only were playing on the current wave of anti-Muslim hysteria among Bosnian Serbs, but were attempting to rip off the scabs of wounds of the Second World War. If they had heard it at all, young Bosnian Serbs would have heard the term from their grandfathers. "Handzar" was a reference to the battle of Kossovo, of course, but it was also an allusion to the Handzar Division, an SS unit that the Grand Mufti of Jerusalem helped recruit for the Germans in Bosnia in 1943. Even though many Bosnian Muslims had fought with Tito's partisans, and, proportionally to their population, had suffered the greatest losses of any national group in Bosnia during the war—

mostly at the hands of General Mihailovic's Serb monarchist Chetnik forces—this bitter memory endured among the Serbs. It was now being fed to gullible boys, a generation off the land, like our guide that day in Trnopolje.

When we entered the village, there were white flags on the houses, and even on a pile of logs stacked high in a nearby field. As in so many Bosnian towns where, before the war, Serbs and Muslims had lived in peace for a generation at least and, more commonly, for as long as anyone could remember, it was the Muslim houses that had been rocked by shellfire and penetrated by tracer bullets, and the Serb houses that stood untouched: Muslim houses that had, it seemed, been burned after they were shot up, and Serb houses that would not have looked out of place in a prosperous peasant commune somewhere in Austria or Switzerland. It was common in Yugoslavia for guest workers to return to their villages every summer and build a little more of the house they had gone abroad to raise money to pay for. These unfinished homes, often surrounded by scaffolding and piles of bricks, stood interspersed between finished houses. We reached the mosque. It had been destroyed: the roof was gone, the minaret demolished. Without missing a beat, our escort said, "Yes, this is the village where there was a sniper in the minaret. The tankers had to fire, of course. Otherwise our boys would have been killed."

I will go to my grave believing that this Serb soldier had no idea that he had said something entirely different to us a few minutes before. With Karadzic, the chances were that when one asked him a question, his response would be a lie. Most journalists assumed this, and assumed as well that, most of the time at least, Karadzic knew he was lying. Our escort was something else. His whole world was an illusion, the product of the Serb leadership's carefully orchestrated propaganda campaign. It was as if the message "Only Unity Can Save the Serb" blocked out contradictory information. The Serbs were good; therefore they would not destroy a mosque. If it turned out that the mosque had been destroyed, there had to be a reason, and since the Serbs were good, the reason had to be that the Serbs had been fired upon. Otherwise why was the minaret in ruins? Serb minds as well as Muslim bodies have been cleansed in Bosnia.

In the Trnopolje camp, the prisoners just laughed when we asked them whether there had been resistance in the village. "The village was sleeping, not sniping," one gray-haired farmer told me in serviceable French. "The Serbs came into the village and started firing. We tried to surrender—those are the white flags you probably saw—but a lot of shooting went on first. Then they went house to house, dragging people out. Some of the Serbs doing this were our neighbors, people we'd known all our lives. Who knows? Maybe they were forced to help the soldiers. Then they dragged some of us away. I think most of those people are dead, and the rest of us they have been holding around here. First at Omarska, and, for the last month, here in Trnopolje. So I'm back where I started, except my house is gone, and I don't know where my sons are."

I asked him if he would go back to his home if he was allowed to.

"Never," he said. "Bosnia is a dead country, at least for Muslims. This is Serbia now . . . I'm perfectly willing to sign my land over to the Chetniks. Because what is the point of holding on to something that is already lost?"

VI

As David Owen once remarked, "In Bosnia-Herzegovina, time does not move on, it deteriorates." At the end of every stay in Bosnia, I would leave thinking things could not get any worse. But each time I returned, usually after an absence of no more than a month or six weeks, I would discover that they had. To go to the Bosnian war was like arriving at the deathbed of a country. *Everything* seemed to get worse *all* the time. There were times when the experience resembled that of visiting a friend with AIDS. For even in periods of relative calm, one knew where things were leading: that over the long term there was absolutely no hope.

It was not only outsiders who felt this slide into the abyss. The story of Bosnia has been largely one of settling for less and less. On a political level, there was the spectacle of the international actors in the crisis first insisting that Bosnia was a legitimate state whose territorial integrity had to be preserved in more or less the form it had existed in when the fighting started. But once General Mladic began to make it clear to everyone that he was not impressed with UN resolutions, the toothless indignation of the world community, the bluster of the Americans, or the pleas of the negotiators, the tone in Washington, Paris, London, and Brussels began to change. The negotiators began to reveal just how altered their expectations were for the deal they were trying to get in Bosnia. Privately, they made it clear that they had assumed all along that putting Bosnia back together again would be impossible without some sort of Western military pressure on the Serbs. But in public they went on insisting that there was still a Bosnia to be saved, long after it had become clear that what was in fact being discussed was the partition of Bosnia into three ethnic ministates rather than its preservation.

In early 1993, at what was a fairly advanced point in the fighting,

David Owen insisted categorically that "there will be no Srpska Republika." If all sides could bring themselves to what Vance and Owen conceded was an unappetizing solution—a map in which Bosnia-Herzegovina was divided into a series of cantons, delineated according to their ethnic majorities, that would be subject to the authority of a weak central government in Sarajevo—the country could still be preserved. It was by no means ideal, the negotiators conceded privately—"a peace from hell," Owen said—but it offered a measure of justice. The Bosnian government balked though, at first unable to accept a division that legitimized ethnic cleansing, and still under the false and tragic impression that there would be an American intervention. And the Americans, though they had no intention of intervening, were unwilling to be seen publicly sanctioning a Bosnian defeat by throwing their weight behind the Vance-Owen plan, which, whatever else it did, sacrificed the principle of the right of Bosnia, a legal government, to assert itself as a state, in favor of an autonomy for ethnic cantons. The Bosnians were willing to die for their state and their principles, and the Clinton administration preferred to let them do so—and never to really make clear what the limits of its involvement were—rather than be seen as abetting ethnic cleansing or, initially, climbing down from the stirring promises of help for Bosnia that candidate Clinton had made during the 1992 presidential campaign to embarrass George Bush.

Whether the Vance-Owen plan could have succeeded is debatable. The great powers would have had to show a willingness to commit huge numbers of troops—fifty thousand by the most conservative estimates, reinforced by enormous numbers of civil police, judicial officials, and technicians—and would have had to be willing to use them to face down the Bosnian Serbs. In light of their subsequent irresolution, the chances they would have acted in so decisive a way seem slight. Certainly, there were many in Belgrade who believed that it was safe for the Bosnian Serbs to sign the plan *because* the Western troops actually would never be sent to Bosnia. One of the principal ideologists of the Milosevic regime, Mihailo Markovic, once told me that the Serbian President had assured him in May 1993 that the Americans would not deploy the twenty-five to thirty thousand peacekeepers Clinton had promised. "I was skeptical at the time," Markovic said, "but given what I have seen of the Clinton administration's behavior, I am inclined to think that Milosevic was right."

In any case, Vance and Owen were unable to persuade the US government to prod the Bosnians into a quick acceptance. The negotiators believed that the best chance came in late January 1993, but it foundered when Secretary of State Warren Christopher, having assured Vance of American support in a meeting on February 1, promptly withdrew it the following day. The plan was revived in the early spring, and, in part for the reasons given by Mihailo Markovic, was even finally endorsed by Milosevic. But in May 1993, when the plan came before the Bosnian Serb parliament in Pale, General Mladic more or less ordered the deputies to reject it. This they duly did, and their act ended any hope of the Vance-Owen plan being adopted. To their credit, Vance and his able deputy, Herbert Okun, resigned soon after, unwilling to negotiate another agreement that they knew would be morally unjustifiable. Owen, for his part, did not resign. The joke about him in Bosnia was that "Dr. Death," as he was called, was now responsible for the destruction of two British political parties and a small Balkan country. In the aftermath of the collapse of the Vance-Owen plan, he seemed to many of us to live up to his nickname and his reputation. Of course, Owen described his motivation as "realism," but whether unwittingly or because he saw no other option, what he ended up advancing was the granting of more and more concessions to the Bosnian Serbs. The strange thing was that Owen saw clearly what he was doing. "There won't be a lot of honor, and there won't be anywhere near the settlement I would have liked," he said at the time. To which the obvious question was, "Why don't you resign?"

Most critics of the Vance-Owen plan, including, myself, thought that there was not a lot of honor even there. But as subsequent plans for Bosnia took for granted that the country would be partitioned and only a rump Bosnia would survive, the Vance-Owen plan, however unjust it may have been, came to look preferable to the best Bosnia would now get. Holding out for intervention, the Bosnian government and their foreign supporters like myself got partition. By 1994, the only question was which map and with what temporary constitutional arrangements. That within a short period of time Radovan Karadzic would bring the Srpska Republika into union with Slobodan Milosevic's Yugoslavia was a foregone conclusion unless Milosevic himself decided otherwise. What remained to be seen was whether any Bosnian state that could be economically or socially viable would be allowed to survive, or whether the whole country would become a larger version of eastern enclaves like Srebrenica and Gorazde—a Gaza Strip writ large, unable to sustain itself economically or militarily, dependent on international assistance for everything, and at the mercy of Serbia and Croatia.

The disaster revealed itself in stages. It was not a question, as in Rwanda in the spring of 1994, of nearly a million people being killed and millions made refugees in a few weeks—a genocide in fast forward. In Bosnia, the slaughter took place as if in slow motion and under the cover of a negotiating effort and a United Nations relief effort whose officials kept insisting that progress was being made on both the humanitarian and the political level. The little successes of this effort—whether the success of a UNHCR convoy in getting through to some previously cut-off area of Bosnia or the success of UNPROFOR in arranging a cease-fire somewhere—obscured the fact that no real progress was being made. Some of the suffering was being alleviated thanks to heroic efforts on the part of the United Nations military and UNHCR personnel, but in Bosnia the humanitarian disaster was only a symptom of the political disaster. It was a vicious cycle. The UN fed people and allowed them to be shelled; the Security Council declared "Safe Havens" whose safety UNPROFOR was neither disposed nor militarily capable of guaranteeing; and UNHCR sent protection officers into the field knowing they could not protect. They were, as the bitter Zagreb joke went, "eunuchs at the orgy." UNPROFOR and the UNHCR only got more resentful and more exhausted at having to carry out a mission most of its best officials had long before concluded was hopeless.

When the men in the Trnopolje camp talked resignedly in the fall of 1992 about the Bosanska Krajina being part of Serbia, there were still eighty thousand non-Serbs in the regions and more mosques were standing than lying in ruins. Two years later, the Bosanska Krajina had been cleansed to the point where the possibility that any Muslim communal life there could ever be reestablished except by force of arms was delusion. When most of the Srebrenica pocket fell to the Serbs in April 1993—the event that led to the Security Council's adoption of the "Safe Havens" resolutions—few people imagined that almost exactly a year later the Gorazde pocket would be allowed to fall in almost exactly the same way.

With each Serb crime, the nadir was supposed to have been reached. The ethnic cleansing of eastern Bosnian towns like Zvornik in May 1992 had been the low point, but then journalists revealed the existence of the camps and the ethnic cleansing of the Bosanska Krajina that summer and early fall. The discovery of the rape camps near the town of Foca near Sarajevo in early 1993 seemed unthinkable. Then it turned out that the Serbs had used rape as a weapon of war all over Bosnia, a way of terrorizing the Muslim population into flight and thus fulfilling the Serb war aim of ethnic cleansing. Not only did the UN Protection Force commanders insist that it was not part of their mandate to help the women, but they categorically refused to investigate repeated allegations that certain UNPROFOR soldiers had had sex with some of the captive Bosnian Muslim women. The fact that, if true, the likeliest explanation for this was that the soldiers were under the mistaken impression that their Serb opposite numbers were simply standing them to an hour in a military brothel might have excused the behavior of the individual soldiers, but it did not excuse their commanders.

It soon became clear that the refusal of the United Nations to take seriously the possibility of malfeasance in its own ranks was a systemic flaw. A law unto itself in Bosnia, responsible, as its officials constantly pointed out, only to the mandate of the Security Council in New York, UNPROFOR could do more or less as it pleased. There was no accountability and, more serious, no acceptance by United Nations officials that they could ever be at fault. They spoke of themselves as if they were instruments, not human beings. If a soldier behaved badly, that, senior UN people said, was the responsibility of the national government in question. If a policy was immoral, that was the fault of—the word was repeated like a mantra—"the mandate." And when abuses came to light, the United Nations moved quickly to exonerate itself of *every charge* of human rights abuses or systematic corruption on the part of its personnel anywhere in the entire Bosnian mission. An Austrian major general named Gunthei Greindl was sent to help Yasushi Akashi, the newly arrived Special Representative of the Secretary General, investigate the corruption charges. Until a few months earlier, Akashi had been running the United Nations operation in Cambodia. What he knew about the UN in the former Yugoslavia, he knew from briefings. For his part, Greindl, a former commander of UN forces in Cyprus, was an old peacekeeping hand. Most outsiders considered him utterly devoid of the kind of objectivity needed to look into the matter dispassionately. It was like a police shooting on a city street being judged by a review board made up entirely of policemen. To no one's surprise, Greindl appeared to talk to no journalists, and few locals, even though in Sarajevo savvy locals used to say, "Red wine and condoms from the French; caviar and diesel from the Ukrainians." He ignored the prostitution that was visible around most of the UN barracks in the city, and he seemed unaware that most journalists, including myself, bought black market gasoline from complaisant UN Protection Force soldiers of various nationalities. And yet in his report, Greindl insisted that he had looked into the charges against UNPROFOR fully and could state categorically that, although there were some isolated instances of abuse, there was no systematic corruption within any command of UNPROFOR, including Sarajevo.

But UN corruption was the least of it. If the soldiers of an occupation army only behave corruptly (and, for all its pretensions to merely being in Bosnia to escort humanitarian aid, UN Protection Force troops, particularly in Sarajevo, were an army of occupation, albeit a relatively benign one), the civilian population can count itself lucky. At least in Bosnia, UNPROFOR soldiers didn't massacre civilians, as members of a number of United Nations contingents in Somalia had been accused of doing by several international human rights organizations. It was the war crimes, the privations, and the endless degradation of the political situation that spiraled relentlessly downward. Again and again in Bosnia, people living in terrible times would tell you, if only as an afterthought, "Well, at least we've seen the worst." And yet the one thing one could depend on in Bosnia was that the worst was always still to come. If the catastrophe did not grow sharper materially—there were, after all, times when the fighting ebbed, or when more humanitarian aid got through to a particular area—it was sure to do so morally and psychologically. To travel through Bosnia was immediately to come face-to-face with the reality that was statistically measurable and newsworthy: corpses; destroyed villages and towns; flushed, triumphant Serb irregulars; and, everywhere, refugees and would-be refugees.

But to make sense of what was occurring in Bosnia meant confronting the moral disaster that had accompanied the material and political one. As time went on, this catastrophe had grown worse. Prewar Bosnia had been a comparatively cash-rich country, if only because there was not all that much beyond a house and a car for ordinary people to spend their money on. When the fighting started, a great many Bosnians had some foreign currency, and it cushioned them to some extent during the first months of the fighting. But after six months, a year, two years, however long it took, the money eventually ran out. The implications of this were not just hardship for individual families, but the collapse of life as people were accustomed to living it. Civilian life continued in Bosnia, of course. People married and got divorced; they sued each other and had children; they signed leases and played guitars. But in an industrial society like Bosnia, the kind of white-collar work that the majority of city and town dwellers had done ceased to have any sense. Office workers might brave the sniper fire in Sarajevo; or factory workers might show up at the plant in Zenica. But when they got there, they rarely had anything real to do. For the most part, they sat around for a while, often in spaces newly ventilated by shellfire, collected the rations that turning up at work entitled them to, and went home.

Many people I met in Bosnia told me that they found living through the shelling and the sniping easier to bear than trying to cope with the feral new society they found themselves inhabiting. It was not simply that they had nothing real to do, but that they didn't know their role anymore. This sense was particularly sharp in Bosnian government–controlled areas, where the struggle to simply survive was most acute, although people in Croatian or Bosnian Serb areas often voiced many of the same complaints. And, for obvious reasons, it was strongest of all in besieged Sarajevo, where people's difficulties in fending for themselves were gravest. Sarajevans were as dependent on elevators, gas pipelines, automobiles, tram lines, supermarkets, and electricity as any other population of a modern, developed country. Suddenly, they had been deprived of all these things and yet, because they were besieged, they were unable to flee to areas where they might not have to climb fifteen flights of stairs with two jerricans of water, or walk three kilometers to a food distribution center. On the psychological level, the degree to which the environment in which they had grown up was suddenly not just dysfunctional but dangerous added to people's difficulty in coming to terms with what had happened to them. Their own modernity had betrayed them.

In central Bosnia, in the Bihac pocket, or in Tuzla in the northeast, environments that were often as modern as Sarajevo, there was at least no siege. Supplies, however meager, could sometimes be gotten from the adjacent countryside, particularly for those with relatives in the villages. In Bosnia, where urbanization was largely a postwar phenomenon, this included a great many townspeople. And because these places were not surrounded, and did not have to depend almost wholly on humanitarian aid or on the black market, the sense of being inside a killing jar, no matter how acute people's justified apprehensions might be, was not nearly so acute in the rest of "free Bosnia" as it was in Sarajevo. Some of the most isolated areas were the most self-sufficient. Before Bosnian Serb forces began their attack on Gorazde in April 1994, eventually reducing a pocket of about thirty square kilometers, and including numerous villages, to the three-kilometer radius of the town center, the sixty thousand people in the enclave not only had had enough to eat but had been able to send some supplies to the other Drina Valley enclaves, Srebrenica and Zepa.

But often it was not just a question of what depriving people of their material self-sufficiency did to their morale. That did not always work out the way one might have expected. Srebrenica, after the Serbs reduced it to a glorified holding pen for Muslims, became a place where morale had been shattered and where girls offered themselves to outsiders for a few cigarettes. But there were other places in Bosnia, notably Bosnian government–controlled East Mostar and the Sarajevo suburb of Dobrinja—which, cut off from the city proper, was undergoing a siege within the siege—where scarcity and extreme danger had produced not corruption but organization and a steely resolution. In East Mostar, for example, everything was rationed down to the last gram of flour. And there was even a period in 1993 in Sarajevo—when elements of the Bosnian

army were running amok, terrorizing the people they were supposedly protecting—when quite a few city residents seriously considered moving to what they only half jokingly called "the People's
Republic of Dobrinja" to get away from the gangsters and the profi-
teers who ruled in most of the capital. "I may be more likely to get
killed by a Chetnik bullet there," a friend said to me at the time, "but
at least I won't risk getting robbed by some young kid with a Kalashnikov every time I walk out my door."

The truth was that one way or the other, few could escape the corruption that had accompanied the Bosnian catastrophe. The black
market and the gangs were only the most visible emblems of the
problem. There was also the intellectual corruption that the transformation of the media on all sides into vehicles for agitprop had en-
gendered. Even so heroic a symbol of Bosnian resistance as the
newspaper *Oslobodjenje* (Liberation) was not immune. As the
killing went on, the editors of the paper came to see themselves as
more and more duty-bound to support the Izetbegovic government
uncritically. That *Oslobodjenje* appeared at all was a miracle. Its
modern high-rise headquarters, fifty meters from the Bosnian Serb
front line, had been systematically destroyed, and its reporters and
production people worked out of the atomic bomb shelter in the
basement of these ruins. Under the circumstances, it was hardly surprising that even though the Izetbegovic regime had tried to destroy
the paper's political independence in the year before the fighting
started, its editors felt that doing nothing to undermine the war effort
had to come first. If that meant impoverishing the language in which
correspondents wrote—in *Oslobodjenje* stories, the Serbs were always the "fascist aggressors," the Bosnian government side invariably "heroic"—it seemed not only a small price to pay but a duty for
what was, after all, the only daily newspaper published in Sarajevo.

And, in a sense, the editors of *Oslobodjenje* were even factually
correct. The Chetniks *were* fascist aggressors in the strictest sense of
the term, and the defense of Sarajevo *was* heroic. And yet what
struggling, often against impossible odds, to keep the newspaper going throughout the siege had been about, as *Oslobodjenje*'s editors
rightly kept insisting, was keeping faith with the kind of independent
journalism that they had tried to practice before. And yet, the newspaper could not help reflecting, particularly as the fighting dragged

on, the exhaustion, despair, and paranoia of its readers. Catastrophes always provide fertile ground for conspiracy theorists, and Bosnia had its share in abundance. By the end of 1993, *Oslobodjenje* was running opinion pieces which elaborated further explanations for why the West was not helping Bosnia. In one, Sadako Ogata, the head of the UNHCR, was accused by an irate citizen of not being willing to help Bosnia because she was a Freemason and connected to lodges in Serbia. More commonly and damagingly, it was becoming normal in Sarajevo to assume, as the art critic Nermina Kuspahic, the half sister of *Oslobodjenje*'s editor in chief, Kemal Kuspahic, said to me one afternoon, that "Europe hates Muslims. What they really think is that the Serbs are doing their work for them."

In this atmosphere, for the paper to support the Izetbegovic government, glorify the soldiers' struggle, and give some ventilation to the more paranoid or embittered strains of thinking in Bosnia was only to be expected. In hewing to much of the SDA's line, *Oslobodjenje*'s editors were also trying to preserve their paper from attacks by an Izetbegovic government. In this, they were increasingly unsuccessful. By the fall of 1994, the paper was being regularly attacked by SDA militants close to the government for the independence of its editorial line.

If there is one thing that a catastrophe engenders, it is self-absorption. Bosnians did not want to be reminded that the world had stood by just as complacently when the Yugoslav National Army had reduced the Christian city of Vukovar to rubble, and, if it came to that, that the Izetbegovic government, for understandable but hardly admirable prudential reasons, had itself taken no stand on the fighting in Croatia in 1991. Nor had individual Sarajevans been all that disturbed by what had gone on in Croatia at that time. Many explained this by saying they were already too frightened. Others were more self-deprecating, recalling wonderingly that they simply had not believed anything similar could happen in Bosnia. "I used to turn the channel when the footage from Vukovar began to run," a friend told me. "I should have paid more attention, shouldn't I? But you know, Sarajevo was such a nice, civilized place. I thought there might be fighting in the countryside, but that here we all got along too well for that sort of thing to develop."

To note all of this is not to say that Bosnians were wrong after April 1992 to think of themselves or of their own predicament. The fact that most Bosnians could not muster the rarefied altruism to preface their own complaints with sympathetic remarks about Angola, Liberia, or Afghanistan, and that, on occasion, some expressed this self-absorption in offensive or hyperbolic ways—comparing Sarajevo to Auschwitz; protesting that they were Europeans, not Somalis; or insisting, as a military commander in Mostar once put it, that the war in Bosnia was the cruelest war in world history—might have been offensive to Boutros-Ghali and his aides, but always seemed simply human to me. I remember riding into Sarajevo with a UN official and passing, along a shattered building on one bombed-out stretch of the airport road, the famous Sarajevo graffito that reads, "Welcome to Hell." The official pointed to it and snorted. "That's the problem here," he said. "It's bad, of course, but everyone is always exaggerating. That's why you can't get a peace agreement."

When I said to him that what he meant by a peace agreement was a Bosnian surrender, he only shrugged. His attitude was typical of a certain strain of thinking within the United Nations which held that the Bosnian government was the real problem. The Serbs had committed great crimes, of course; everyone conceded that. But now they were, UN officials kept insisting, ready to sit around the table and make peace. Why wouldn't the Bosnians go along? And to point out that what the United Nations was asking was for the Bosnians to surrender cut no ice. The UN was interested in peace, not in justice. UNPROFOR's mandate, senior officials kept reminding one, was not to protect Bosnians but to protect the humanitarian relief effort, whatever misconceptions its name might have given rise to. General Mackenzie had remarked after leaving Bosnia that he thought the name, United Nations Protection Force, had been a big part of the UN's problem there. And he was right. Bosnians could not understand why all these soldiers had been sent if they were going to do nothing to protect Sarajevans, or Tuzlans, or Banja Lukans.

In fact, the first name for the UN force the Department of Peace-keeping Operations came up with was United Nations Interim Force in Former Yugoslavia. But the acronym for that was UNIFFY—too close to the word *unify* to be acceptable to anyone. But under whatever name UN troops were deployed, Bosnians soon learned that not only would the United Nations not protect them, but in the main they didn't even sympathize with them. UNPROFOR had a peacekeeping mandate, and the Bosnians, by 1993, had become the principal obstacle to completing that mission.

Small wonder then that, feeling themselves abandoned, the Bosnians fell back on fantasies of their own essential virtue and harped on the uniqueness of their suffering. When the influential Muslim religious scholar Enes Karic, who would later become Minister of Education, much to the discomfiture of "multicultural" Sarajevo, wrote in his fictional "Extract from a Sufi Chronicle of 2092" that "before the Bosnian calamity of 1992, offensives against the honor and integrity of women were unknown," he was expressing the feeling, shared generally in Bosnia, that the outside world still refused to take in the enormity of what was taking place. He was not, as a UN official to whom I showed the piece had remarked to me (inadvertently confirming everything people like Karic suspected), "conveniently forgetting what the Pakistani army did in Bangladesh, the way Bosnians always forget that there are and have been other tragedies in this awful world we live in than their own."

To defend Bosnian sorrow and Bosnian self-absorption against facile dismissals like the one this bureaucrat had advanced was the easy part. Harder to accept was that this general mobilization of feeling, however understandable it was, had exacted its own terrible price on the Bosnians themselves. The question of whether a war effort based on mass mobilization (even though, in practice, it was never imposed systematically by the Bosnian government which might have been expected to have done so) and an ideological consensus required citizens never to stray from a united front, or whether people had an obligation to go on saying what they thought whatever the practical consequences seemed to demand, had been contested at least since republican Barcelona during the Spanish Civil War. It was this debate that Orwell had anatomized in *Homage to Catalonia*. And there probably was no good answer, except the most contingent one, to the problem of what to do when truth and justice came into conflict during an emergency. The more friendless the Bosnians perceived themselves to be—and the blow the UN's barely concealed enmity represented was a grave one—the more they tended toward the belief that internal disagreement could not be risked.

As Gordana Knesevic, the Serb deputy editor of *Oslobodjenje*, who had been one of its animating spirits throughout the fighting, and whose husband, Ivo, a Croat, was the Bosnian government Minister of Information, put it, "Before the war the paper supported none of the three national parties in Bosnia. But once the war started, Kemal went to President Izetbegovic and said, 'In war, we will support the legal authorities of Bosnia-Herzegovina as part of the defense in wartime. But after the war, the moment this war ends, we will go back into opposition. In the meantime, we will do nothing to undermine the state at a time when democratic political change is impossible.' "

Nonetheless, when even the most independent-minded Bosnian media people saw it as their regrettable duty to propound a great amount of agitprop alongside the news, the corrupting effect on thinking of reader and purveyor alike was bound to be considerable—no matter how virtuous or understandable the motivation. Gordana Knesevic was committed both biographically and intellectually to the multicultural Bosnian ideal that, before the fighting, the SDA party leadership had viewed with suspicion. And yet she said she had no doubt that the course *Oslobodjenje* was pursuing was the correct one. The agitprop on the Bosnian side, she pointed out, assuming that was even the right term for it, was nothing when compared to what was coming out of Pale, Belgrade, and, depending on which way the Croatian government was listing, Zagreb. And it was altogether unjust to compare Bosnian attempts at solidarity with the merciless world of feeling encapsulated in the slogan "Only Unity Can Save the Serb" that had given rise to so much suffering and death.

What Knesevic was unwilling to confront was the possibility that any corruption of thought, even in a good cause and however human and understandable, is hard to undo once it is assented to. Most wars have ended long before the mentalities that they give rise to fade away. Still, had this psychological war footing been the only way in which Bosnian society had been transformed by the fighting, the mental damage so many people talked about experiencing would probably have not been nearly as extreme as it was. For if any people in recent memory have had the right to oversimplify their own situation, extol their own virtues, ignore their own responsibilities for the ruin of their country, and demonize their enemies and the international community that was unwilling to lift a finger to help them, it has been the sinned-against people of Bosnia-Herzegovina—the Muslims in particular. But everywhere in Bosnia, there were not just the rhetorical oversimplifications of war to contend with—these were, after all, hardly peculiar to Bosnia or particularly extreme there—but a corruption of daily life as well that was extreme.

One of the earliest, deepest, and most pervasive effects of the fighting had been to turn the social pyramid on its head. The bourgeoisie had been ruined and demoralized by the war. With every passing month its material situation worsened. For those who had had little before the fighting started, the situation was reversed. Simple boys from the countryside and tough kids from the towns found that their guns made them the ones who could start amassing the Deutschemarks and the privileges, sexual and otherwise. It often really was a question of the first being last and the last first. Whether it was in Sarajevo, or Tuzla, or Mostar, young men dressed in Rambo-like gear could be found lounging in the cafes, or be seen driving their girls around in the few civilian vehicles left in any particular area. The degree to which they had styled themselves on characters they had seen in films like *Rambo* and *Road Warrior* led the Sarajevan theater director Haris Pasovic to once confide to me that after peace returned, he hoped there could be a war crimes trial. When I told him that he should not imagine the UN was really serious about this, that the people negotiating with Karadzic and General Mladic were not going to try to lock them up later, he shook his head impatiently. "No, no," he said, laughing. "I don't mean them. I mean Sylvester Stallone. He's responsible for a lot that has gone on here!"

It was not simply a question, as it was, say, in Israel, of the privileges and coddling willingly accorded to the men who do the fighting and the dying. On the Bosnian side, so many of the fighters tended to be young men raised on violent Hollywood films, who dressed and acted as if they really did think they were Stallone or Mel Gibson. The way they swaggered around off duty, wearing their ammunition in great pouches on their chests—they would have broken their sternums had they had to suddenly dive for cover—and carrying as many weapons as they could hold, was pure Hollywood. Of course, on the

Serb and Bosnian Croat side, it was far more extreme. The Bosnians were short of weapons and ammunition. But the attitude was not so different. It was not surprising, given who was doing the fighting, that in Bosnia war and the black market went hand in hand.

Part of the reason for this was historical. On the Serb side, the most extreme Chetnik paramilitaries had been drawn from the old prewar Mafias of Belgrade. When the fighters of an Arkan or a Seselj—two leading commanders of Chetnik militias who had themselves been underworld figures before the breakup of Yugoslavia—entered a Muslim town, they were after loot as well as blood. But the Bosnian government had found itself relying on its criminals too. Hoping to stave off war in 1992, the Izetbegovic government had not created its own territorial army, as had been done in Croatia and Slovenia. "It takes two sides to have a war," Izetbegovic had said, "and we will not fight." But of course, it does not take two sides to have a slaughter, and that had come anyway, despite Izetbegovic's effort not to appear too bellicose. Had it been left to the SDA politicians and the urban middle class, Sarajevo probably would have fallen to the Serbs almost as easily as Banja Luka did. In fact, before the fighting Izetbegovic had asked UN officials to deploy peacekeeping troops. They refused, saying that they had no mandate to station troops in a province of a country in order to facilitate that province's secession.

The fighting did come and, almost spontaneously, a ragtag force made up mostly of gangsters and Muslim townspeople had risen up to defend the city. They were an odd lot. Some had belonged to a Muslim paramilitary group called the Patriotic Leagues. More were drawn from the Sarajevo underworld. With pistols and Kalashnikovs, they pushed the Yugoslav National Army back into the hills, broke into their barracks, and finally, to the fury of United Nations mediators, ambushed a column of JNA troops who were in the process of withdrawing from the city under a brokered cease-fire. As the fighting intensified, they moved through the neighborhoods in which they had grown up, cajoling, inspiring, or intimidating their erstwhile schoolmates into joining the fight. One of their leaders had been a respectable leather goods manufacturer; another was a twenty-nine-year-old club musician called Musan Topalovic, known as Caco; a third, known as Celo, was a career criminal with a bodybuilder's physique who had just come out of prison after serving eight years for rape. It was only after this first spasm of fighting had ended that the Bosnian army had begun to organize itself, and more than a year before the small dedicated cadre of ex–JNA regular officers who remained on the Bosnian side—among whose senior ranks were a number of Serbs and Croats—could even begin to reshape it and give it some of the aspects of a disciplined regular force.

The defense of Sarajevo was an inspiring story, the stuff Balkan folk songs from previous centuries had been made of. But as the fighting wore on, the involvement of gangsters on all sides meant not only that the fighting took on a more and more lawless, brutal character, but also that the political aims of the war became hopelessly intertwined on a day-to-day level with profiteering and black market activities. The same courage that allowed a Caco to fight the Yugoslav National Army no matter how hopelessly outgunned he was, made him the likeliest candidate to smuggle into Sarajevo the supplies the city needed and to make a tremendous profit out of doing so. What Caco, Celo, and the others (the story was much the same among the Bosnian Serbs and the HVO fighters) brought in, they had no plans to give out for free. Nor, since fighters who were loyal to them individually defended key areas of the front line, was the Sarajevo government in a position to order that these activities cease. Not until Haris Silajdzic accepted the Bosnian premiership in the late fall of 1993, and made a condition for doing so the elimination of these gangs, was the hold of the gangster guerrillas over Sarajevo broken. In other parts of Bosnia, the situation was very much the same: a fragile society, at once militarized and increasingly lawless, trying to maintain its ideals in the face of the ruthless war being waged against it, the indifference of the world, and the bargains it had been obliged to make internally in order to survive.

Given the fragility of the Bosnian state, it is unlikely that very much could have been done to avoid many of these contradictions. But the blind eye the Sarajevo government had turned for so long to the activities of men like Caco and Celo nonetheless made many ordinary Bosnians even more cynical sooner than probably would have been the case otherwise. As the fighting dragged on, the seeming hopelessness of the military situation led many of them to suspect—a view that became particularly entrenched in Sarajevo and

Tuzla—that the real purpose of the war was no longer victory, but profit. Rolling up Celo's and Caco's private fiefdoms did not help all that much. If anything, once they were dead, many who had been terrified by them in their lifetimes looked back at them as the only fighters with real guts. And many suspected that their elimination represented little more than a falling out between thieves, and there were many who, once he was dead (shot, the government said blandly, while trying to escape), recalled Caco's heroism at the beginning of the fighting. By the summer of 1994, average soldiers on the front line said bitterly that they were not defending their homes but the black market. The fact that the families of most of the senior members of the Bosnian government were abroad did not help morale. "Silajdzic has his family in Pakistan; the others are just the same," one fighter in East Mostar told me. "It's easy for them. They don't care if this shit goes on forever."

True or not, such sentiments had already become pervasive by the end of 1993. In the real world, suffering is not ennobling, it is corrupting. Every day of the war in Bosnia, ordinary people found themselves facing circumstances which nothing in their education or past experience had given them any basis for coping with. Having been used to living comfortably, they had to adjust to the most radical discomfort. People who had never been cold except on the ski slope were suddenly cold for months at a time. People who had bathed twice a day had to get used to taking cold cat baths a few times a month. People who had traveled had to get used to being cooped up. People who had prided themselves on their honesty found themselves cutting corners to get by. The shelling might have been an affront to their sanity—it was estimated that well over a third of the children in Sarajevo were suffering to some degree from posttraumatic stress syndrome; what used to be known as shell shock—but the conditions in which they had to live were an affront to their sense of themselves as existential beings.

The petty details were almost worse than anything else, and it seemed that the more self-sufficient a person had been, the harder it was for him or her to learn to depend on others, to wheedle favors, to plead for special treatment. Country people and working-class people tended to be more resilient. They had lived with these necessities before the fighting started. But for the urban middle class, the accommodation with this new reality was traumatic. "I am so tired of saying thank you," a woman named Amela Simic told me one evening in Sarajevo. "I think what I look forward to most in peacetime is never having to say thank you again. What a terrible expression. I think I will send my friends envelopes with money in them and boxes of chocolates. I will give them gifts. I will be myself again."

And as Simic, a distinguished translator and Sarajevo literary figure, was herself the first to admit, she and her Serb poet husband, Goran, were relatively privileged people by Sarajevo standards. They had friends abroad who tried to send them things. They were on good terms with many foreign journalists in Sarajevo who usually could be relied on to try to help. But the psychological pressure of being recipients of charity, and, more acutely, the humiliation of it, became more and more unbearable as the siege dragged on. I grew accustomed to visiting Amela and having to struggle *not* to accept from her a book, a treasured opera recording, a scarf, or some small household item. "I don't need these," she would always say. But of course, what she was really saying was that she wanted some normal balance restored, and some release from the oppression that her indebtedness to foreign visitors had produced in her. She wanted her autonomy back, the dignity that two years of the siege had taken away from her.

And, quite correctly, Amela questioned the motives of visitors to Sarajevo. "I have been trying to find out," she wrote a friend abroad, "what makes us so interesting to the people coming here. Why do they admire, give compliments, swear that it is an eternal friendship? . . . This is how I imagine it might be. A journalist (humanitarian worker, etc.) comes here expecting a jungle (most of them are not very educated) and finds out that there are some people in that jungle who are decently dressed, relatively clean, and they can even speak a foreign language . . . It will be very interesting to see if those friendships will last on the other side of the border when there is no Sarajevo 'halo.' I don't think so. And that is why I fight against our being declared victims, heroes, etc."

At the end of the letter, she added resignedly that "we have to be happy for the opportunity to 'use our heroism.' " Because, as she knew perfectly well, as the siege continued, the situation in Sarajevo was becoming one of utter dependency. More than that, it *was* becoming a jungle. What Amela Simic was referring to, of course, was the way Sarajevans were treated by both the press and the United Nations as a colonial people. Even the UNHCR had garnered most of its experience in the Third World. It had the ingrained habit of feeling that it knew what was best, and "the locals," as UN officials so often referred to them—a term that, to the untutored ear, sounded like nothing so much as an updated and not particularly improved version of "the natives"—should do what they were told. Whether even in Africa in the 1990s people were all that pliable was open to question. But in Bosnia, particularly in the cities, the local staff member of the UNHCR or the International Committee of the Red Cross was likely to be better qualified at his or her job than the international staffer who had been sent in from Geneva. This was galling to Sarajevans, as Amela Simic's letter, with its reference to the foreigners' lack of culture, amply demonstrated. And it was puzzling to most of the foreigners.

And yet in the end it didn't matter if Sarajevans had better degrees or had read more than the foreigners who had come to help and, in the case of UNPROFOR, for all intents and purposes to rule over them. The skills that Bosnians had learned in their civilized, middle-class society no longer made much sense. Others, less proud than Amela Simic, or perhaps just more practical, simply gave in to the situation in which they found themselves, cultivated foreign reporters whom any acute observer would have realized they couldn't stand, in the hope of getting a few cups of coffee, a drink, or simply the chance to ride in a car, out of the interaction. But whether a Bosnian found it relatively cost-free psychologically to adapt to this situation of dependency or found it intensely painful and demoralizing, no one escaped from the situation unscathed. The price of such few privileges as were available in places like Sarajevo and Tuzla— and even for foreigners life was Spartan; we didn't have all that much to give—was dependency on the foreigners. The price of rejecting such contacts, unless, instead, one was in a position to curry favor with the local Mafias, the army, or the political *nomenklatura,* or was already part of it, or had something to trade on, as so many young girls traded on their bodies, was a life of cold, darkness, and want.

"Do you know the way we lived before? Can you imagine it as you look at the ruins of what we were?" a woman who had once been a judge asked me at a reception in a makeshift art gallery given by the then newly arrived French Ambassador in Sarajevo. "We lived better than you. I know about New York. Such crime. So many poor people. We did not have that in Bosnia. In Sarajevo, you could walk the streets as late as you pleased." Her eyes filled with tears. "That wonderful life," she said. "I want it back so desperately. When you see me now, it is not as I really am. I am not this dirty, poor woman, in dirty, smelly clothes, that all my perfume cannot cover. I am the person I was, you see." Then she smiled, and after a pause repeated, "To myself I will always be that person that I was before all of this."

Many Sarajevans felt that way. They hated what they had to do in order to survive. "I never envied anyone before the war," the woman continued. "And now I am consumed, eaten by envy. I think of something my neighbor has, and sometimes I think, 'Tomorrow, when she goes out to fetch water, I'll sneak in and steal it.' It's worst when a visitor comes. I wonder, 'What has he brought her?' And then I think, 'For God's sake, you were a judge before you became a pathetic refugee. Has this war really turned you into one of the criminals you used to lecture before you locked them up?' " She looked away. A French officer was passing a flask to the Bosnian couple to whom he was speaking. Then she shook her head. "You see? I wondered just then why I was talking to you. You didn't give me a drink. That's what I have been reduced to, what all of us have been reduced to in Bosnia. We have become a nation of beggars."

As she spoke, a Bosnian writer I knew slightly had wandered over. It was cold and he was dressed in several layers of threadbare sweaters under his brown leather jacket. He listened intently, too intently for a man who wasn't already quite drunk. "Yes, beggars," he said suddenly, interrupting her, as Bosnian men, drunk or sober, tend to do to Bosnian women. "It's a moral catastrophe. A moral catastrophe. Tell me, please, what is morality. What am I to believe if there is no God, no democracy, no United States principles? I loved those things. Now, how am I to live if these things are not real? What is to stop me from killing you, or killing her, or doing whatever I fucking well please? That wasn't the way she was brought up or I was, or the way we brought up our children to behave.

"I knew Karadzic," he said. "We were colleagues in the Writers' Union. He was a nice guy. I always liked him, even though I always thought he was a better doctor than a poet. Now he is a madman, a murderer. So where does that leave me? I believe in poetry, not politics. Am I supposed to become a madman too? It's easy, you know. You just . . ." He paused, and said, enunciating the words very slowly and deliberately, ". . . do . . . exactly . . . what . . . you . . . want." Then, his speech speeding up, he began to ask the question that was all but the common currency of conversations between foreigners and Bosnians: "What is the United Nations on the East River? What is it doing? Today, they are in New York talking as they always are. Here a four-year-old child died near a factory in Velika Kava. Why? I just don't have any sense of why."

The judge had drifted away and we were alone.

"Can you help me?" he said.

Trying to be surreptitious, I reached into an inside pocket, drew out a hundred-Deutschemark note, and handed it to him. "Thank you," he said, kissed me on both cheeks, and moved off. The judge returned. She had seen the whole thing, and her tone was now surer than it had been when she had first spoken to me. "I'm not quite certain which is worse," she said, "the undignified way in which he asked you for money, or the understanding, knowing expression you had on your face when you gave it to him. You see, we are beggars. And you foreigners, you are tourists. I don't say this with any ill will toward you. It is simply the nature of the situation. This war has corrupted all of us. I'm not sure we will ever recover. The buildings can be rebuilt. Europeans will probably feel so guilty that they will send us some money. And the Arabs will want to rebuild the mosques, I suppose. But we have become damaged goods—a generation of shell-shocked beggars."

She stared across at the French Ambassador, who, followed at a discreet distance by his security detail, was now saying his goodbyes to the Bosnian notables still in attendance. The exhibition, which consisted of works by French artists intended to express their "solidarity" with Sarajevo, and forming part of a pan-European project to create an "art bridge" to the Bosnian capital, was full of affirmations that Sarajevo would live. The judge eyed it equably. "Very nice," she said. "It's too bad the French didn't send soldiers here to protect us at the same time. They could have, you know; they have had the power all along. It would have been so simple for them. Instead, they left us to die."

VII

No matter how long the dying and the ethnic cleansing dragged on, and how often United Nations officials reiterated publicly and privately that UNPROFOR troops were in Bosnia to intervene only, as Marrack Goulding, the former head of the UN's Department of Peacekeeping Operations had put it, "to protect humanitarian activities during wartime," ordinary Bosnians could never quite get it into their heads that the United Nations really meant it. The UN was supposed to be more moral than the most enlightened government, and yet what was going on in Bosnia was so patently immoral. The UN was supposed to stand for peace; its officials insisted that it did. In the 1990s, even peacekeepers had public relations slogans. In Bosnia the UN had printed thousands of bumper stickers and pins that read, "UNPROFOR: Working for Peace." In every UN office in Bosnia, there was a stack of leaflets. One, addressed to children, was entitled "What the United Nations Does for Peace." In the ideal world of this brochure, there was no talk of mandates or limitations. "UNPROFOR," it claimed, "is a big group of people from a lot of different countries who have come to the former Yugoslavia to try to stop the war. UNPROFOR stands for United Nations Protection Force. It tries to protect people from getting hurt in the fighting, just like a teacher who stops bullies from hitting you at school."

The tragedy was that the world described in that brochure was the world many Bosnians imagined they lived in at the beginning of the fighting. The words of the UN leaflet might be childishly simple, but so was the Bosnian situation. Only they were not being bullied, they were being murdered. But instead of doing what was necessary to protect the Bosnians, by hewing to the task of delivering humanitarian aid the United Nations seemed not just to be failing to prevent murder but implicitly to be sanctioning it. That, at least, was the way it looked from the ground in Bosnia. And even when UN officials did not appear, as to both Bosnians and the foreign journalists they so often did, to be taking their vaunted impartiality to the point where they seemed to be actively collaborating with the Bosnian Serbs, their inaction was a source of frustration and bewilderment.

It was as if most United Nations officials wanted to deny the fundamental reality of what had gone on in Bosnia. As time went on, many, particularly within UNPROFOR—officials of the UN High Commissioner for Refugees tended to remain more pro-Bosnian—grew increasingly frustrated by what they saw as the Bosnian government's refusal to accept its own defeat. Their thinking was not mysterious. UNPROFOR's job was to facilitate the UNHCR's delivery of humanitarian assistance. What was getting in the way? The fighting. And who was keeping the fighting going? The Bosnian government side, which was not prepared to accept the dismemberment of the country. To many in the UN, the Bosnians thus became the ones "getting in the way" of the aid effort by continuing their resistance.

It was not surprising, under these circumstances, that many United Nations officials seemed almost to delight in pointing out that the Serbs were by no means the only villains in the Bosnian tragedy. "There are two black hats and one very gray hat in this war," was the way an American colonel assigned to UNPROFOR in Sarajevo put it to me, referring to the Serb, Croat, and Bosnian government sides. But when they could leave their personal animosities toward the Bosnians for prolonging the fighting to one side, most UN officials were willing to admit that what had befallen the Bosnian Muslims was a genocide. When Bosnians heard this, but then also heard that the United Nations had no "mandate" to do anything about it, they took the acknowledgment of the crime more seriously than the institutional caveat and drew the conclusion that sooner or later the United Nations would come to its senses.

Surely stopping a genocide had to be more important to people who actually saw what was happening than hewing to a directive from the Security Council, far away in New York. And surely any future moral authority the United Nations could hope to exercise depended on its doing something to help in Bosnia. If all the United Nations intended to do was to bring in food and medicine, didn't this just amount to keeping people alive longer so the Serbs would have more chances to kill them? Wasn't it incongruous that UN soldiers and UNHCR convoy drivers risked and sometimes lost their lives to bring in food to isolated areas, but steadfastly refused to silence the guns that were causing the emergency? It seemed unimaginable that the United Nations would be content to go on in this way indefinitely.

Had more Bosnians paid attention to the quip of Fred Cuny, a brilliant American aid worker with vast military and humanitarian experience who had been commissioned by the Hungarian-American financier George Soros to construct a new water supply system for Sarajevo, they might have realized that they were wrong. "If the UN had been around in 1939," Cuny liked to say in his soft Texas accent, "we'd all be speaking German."

There is a Talmudic expression that goes, "It is your obligation to tell people things they can hear; it is your obligation not to tell people things they cannot hear." That they should stop believing in the UN, as so many foreigners told them, was something many Bosnians were not prepared to listen to, even after two years of slaughter. Many could not listen because it would have meant saying that their futures were hopeless. Many others could not because in the Tito period they had so idealized the West that they could not imagine that it would betray them. For them, and in this their diagnosis was not wrong even if the conclusion they drew from it was, the United Nations was a Western instrument.

As Gordana Knesevic once put it, "You cannot have any idea of the degree to which people in Sarajevo exaggerated the West's virtues. They assumed that the West's prosperity was a testimony to its virtue, just as Communism's poverty went hand in hand with its tyranny. Many people I knew genuinely believed that in the West you had created an empire of justice. That is why people who, I will admit, probably should have known better were so surprised when there was no intervention. They felt as you would feel if you were mugged in full view of a policeman and he did nothing to rescue you. Now you and I know that the West does not actually want to be a policeman—not on behalf of Bosnian Muslims, anyway—but people in Bosnia didn't. And when the world sent something called UNPROFOR—the UN *Protection* Force—it was normal that people imagined that it had been sent to protect them, not just to protect the humanitarian workers and the relief supplies."

These expectations were hard to avoid in Sarajevo. Occasionally, they took on the frankly racist overtones of Europeans who expected special treatment from history. "I can't understand why you don't do anything for us," a Sarajevo businessman once said to me in anguished tones. "We're not Africans, we're civilized Europeans just like you!" His words had been provoked by attending a slide show organized in Sarajevo at the Obala Gallery, an avant-garde arts space that, against all odds, had continued to operate throughout the siege. The show had presented the work of a young British photographer, Paul Lowe, who had worked in both Somalia and Bosnia. To put it on at all had required considerable courage, since mentioning the two tragedies in the same breath was hardly a popular thing to do in Sarajevo. And, in fairness, it was not that the businessman was indifferent to the tragedy of the Horn of Africa. But he rejected the analogy that Lowe and the Obala director, Miro Purivatra, had been trying to establish between the two situations.

Self-absorption is often a by-product of great suffering, and the businessman's unexamined attitude toward other people's tragedies was not just typical of Sarajevo, it was typical of people everywhere who don't know if they are going to survive the week. If the Bosnians were as "Eurocentric," which in their case only meant self-absorbed, as UN officials often liked to say sneeringly, there was a kind of reverse racism inherent in expecting them to constantly preface their own complaints with expressions of sympathy for the Somalis, the Afghans, or the Rwandese. It was, after all, not the case that people in Kigali in May 1994 wanted to hear about Bosnia either. What did distinguish the response of many Bosnians was surprise that what was happening was happening to them. Like other citizens of the rich world, they imagined they would witness such tragedies on television, not suffer them in the flesh. A young woman who worked for one of the international news agencies summed up this slightly aggrieved bewilderment when she announced one summer afternoon that she intended to spend the rest of the day working on her tan. "Since the UN doesn't treat us as white people," she remarked, "I think I need to get brown."

On the deepest level, however, what was at stake for Bosnians was not their status as white Europeans but their faith in the world as a moral place. After two years of fighting, events in other places had become something of an abstraction anyway. Ordinary Bosnians worried about getting food and water, dodging snipers and shells, staying warm, staying sane. Middle-class people might listen to the BBC or the Voice of America on their shortwave radios, or ask visitors about what was "going on" in Paris, London, or New York, but while they missed their lives as consumers of things and information, most of the time they really could only focus on what was happening to them: on their pain and on their wonder. They kept asking why, as Jews in the aftermath of the Holocaust had asked why the skies had not darkened, as victims everywhere ask why.

Doubtless there were propagandistic reasons for Bosnian government officials to talk in terms of the slaughter in their country representing a moral "crossroads" for the West. But whatever the cynics might imagine, their wonder was genuine, too. One of the sad ironies of the Bosnian situation was that before the war Izetbegovic's SDA had not been as committed as it should have been to a multicultural Bosnia. It had never been fundamentalist in the Iranian sense of the term, but on a cultural level at least many of its leaders had been in favor of the return of the Bosnian Muslim population to Islam. But as the fighting continued, and Bosnians suffered and died in the name of maintaining a multiethnic, multiconfessional state, the commitment of the SDA leadership to pluralism became far more serious. This did not mean that the party did not have its fundamentalists, or that the fighting had not bred a world of young fanatics who insisted on saying *"Es-salaam aleikum"* instead of *"dobar dan"* (good day), and proclaiming themselves mujahedin. But the dominant trends were in the other direction during the first two years of the fighting, no matter what those who wanted to dismiss the Bosnian conflict as one more intractable civil war might choose to imagine. It was only in late 1994, when most Bosnians had completely lost hope in any just outcome, that the Islamists began to enjoy some success in undermining the multicultural ethos of urban Bosnia, and the SDA itself began to gravitate toward Muslim nationalism.

Until then, most Bosnians capable of describing their predicament in intellectual terms did so by way of moral analogy. In this, they were not just playing to the gallery of international public opinion; they spoke that way among themselves. "If nothing is done for us," Haris Silajdzic said repeatedly on Bosnian TV, "then it will mean that there is no such thing as morality in world affairs." And he once added, "Do people in America and Britain and France really want to live in such a world? I simply cannot believe that." Had they been simply trying to curry favor with the West, or ram home the point that as civilized people they deserved special treatment, the Bosnians would not have been so quick to attribute the disaster that had befallen them to the spiritual decay of the rich world. Alia Izetbegovic was particularly prone to this kind of thinking. He once remarked to me that fifty years of comfort had made the West "morally soft." And Silajdzic liked to muse about the spiritual crisis threatening Europe; of which indifference to the Bosnian cause was, as he put it with astonishing dispassionateness, "only one, minor symptom."

Others, who were either temperamentally more pragmatic or intellectually more enamored of Western culture, just damned themselves for their naïveté and for their inability to give up hope. "Perhaps I am just a Balkan fool," the filmmaker Ademir Kenovic, who was not naive personally or politically, once remarked, "but no matter how long this goes on, I cannot accept that the world will just stand by as we are all massacred. But here we are, being massacred, and I keep hoping." And an official at the Jewish community center, a rather hard-edged businessman who had been a senior executive at one of the biggest import-export companies in the former Yugoslavia, was being only half ironic when he said to me one afternoon, "I was raised on American cowboy movies. In those films, the cavalry always comes at the end. And it may sound stupid to you, but when I look up at the sky and see the NATO planes flying overhead, I keep thinking, 'Those planes are our modern cavalry, and yet they do nothing for us.' "

What Bosnians of all stripes seemed unable to accept was the thought that nobody cared. If the West was afraid of the Serbs, or morally degenerate, as Izetbegovic and some other SDA politicians seemed to believe, that at least was comprehensible. If nonintervention was based on a lack of information, and what was required was to tell people in the West one more time about the full implications of the slaughter, that, too, was comprehensible. What was unbearable was an explanation that it was all but impossible to put forward to a Sarajevan: that far from having led to a moral softening, fifty years of prosperity had made the West immorally hard, and that if there was no intervention in Bosnia, it was because the Western powers did not care enough about Bosnia's fate to sacrifice the lives of even a few of its soldiers. Humanly, such disbelief was understandable. As Zdravko Grebo, a law professor who ran the best independent radio station in Sarajevo, Radio Zid (*zid* means "wall"), and served as the coordinator for the financier George Soros' Open Society Foundation in Bosnia, liked to say, "It's all illusion, of course, but people have to live on something." It would have been as absurd to expect many Sarajevans to follow his austere line of reasoning as it would have been to expect people to go on behaving as heroically as so many did in Sarajevo and elsewhere without being offered any hope of either victory or rescue.

Many United Nations officials, convinced that there had never been the slightest possibility of Western military intervention, believed that Bosnia's foreign supporters—the journalists, in particular—had done great harm in fostering these illusions. It was not so much what was said to the Bosnians. Rather, some UN people insisted, by making it politically unpalatable for the American government to declare once and for all that there would never be intervention, and by keeping popular indignation alive in Western Europe, particularly in France, the journalists had fostered false hopes and abetted the Bosnian authorities in a reading of the political situation that was fundamentally misguided. What would have done more to relieve the suffering of the Bosnian people, a senior UNPROFOR civilian official once remarked to me, was a stern public declaration by the Americans that they weren't coming. Instead, the Clinton administration continued until well into the spring of 1994 to hold out the hope of intervention.

If, as seems increasingly likely in retrospect, Washington was insincere about this from the start, rather than simply having been confused or incompetent, then President Clinton and his advisers have almost as much Bosnian blood on their hands as General Mladic. It *was* the prospect that military aid would eventually flow in that, time and again, stiffened the Bosnian government's resolution to fight on. The UN was right about that. Bosnia's prime minister, Haris Silajdzic, might insist that the Bosnian army would defeat the Serbs, but he knew how grim the situation of the battlefield really was. Without military intervention, the partition of Bosnia on terms unfavorable to the government—the Bosnian government having privately accepted the principle of some sort of partition since the days of the Vance-Owen plan—was sure to take place. The fact that, by the late fall of 1994, the Bosnian army began to acquit itself better on the battlefield did not alter this situation in any fundamental way.

But if one were to judge by the rhetoric coming out of Washington, and from some politicians in Paris as well—which was curious, since the French had steadfastly opposed intervention from the start—it would have been hard to conclude that Western military strikes against the Serbs had been ruled out. There were short periods between 1992 and 1994 when it looked as if the United States was gearing up either to act unilaterally or to commit itself to pressuring its allies to endorse a NATO military intervention. Then, Bosnians would be treated to the spectacle of flying visits by American NATO generals, and the arrival of the press en masse at the Holiday Inn in Sarajevo, sent by editors who apparently expected the bombs to fall at any moment. The old hands might affect cynicism, but even they would be on edge for a few days. In this atmosphere, it was difficult even for Bosnians who had finally embraced the painful conclusion that no one from abroad was going to help, to go on believing that they were to be left to their fate.

For Bosnian government officials, there was little else to do but go on trying to persuade foreign governments, the United States in particular, to intervene. Even with intervention still being held out as a possibility, Bosnian officer cadets I met in 1993 reported being routinely told by their instructors that their training was meant to prepare them for a final Bosnian offensive that would take place in 1996 at the earliest. But in the meantime, even as they longed for the intervention and waited for it, the requirements of day-to-day survival on the Bosnian government side required that Bosnians look for assistance not to NATO or to the American 82nd Airborne Division, but to the UNHCR and UNPROFOR. They were the only powers standing between the Bosnians and General Mladic's forces.

In Sarajevo, in central Bosnia, and in the eastern enclaves of Srebrenica and Gorazde, particularly after the Serbs conquered the hinterlands surrounding these pockets, this dependency grew almost complete. The more people were forced to congregate in towns, the hungrier and more uncomfortable they got, and the more they had to rely on humanitarian aid. For long periods, places like Maglaj— which had been market towns but had doubled or tripled in population after the Serb ethnic cleansing of surrounding areas—only survived thanks to supplies airdropped by American transport planes. And, by and large, except in the case of Sarajevo where the UNHCR air bridge really did save many thousands of people from starvation, only a fraction of what the UN High Commissioner for Refugees estimated people needed actually got through. As one HCR logistics officer put it succinctly at the end of 1993, one of the worst periods of shelling and shortage in the capital, "At the rate things are deteriorating everywhere else, no matter how bad things get here Sarajevo is going to be the *garden spot* of Bosnia for the rest of this winter."

Not only did the Serbs go on, as Larry Hollingworth, the white-bearded former British colonel who was one of the most effective and certainly the most outspoken UNHCR official in Bosnia, once put it, "munching up village after village," but they blocked far more convoys than they let through. For all the talk of UNPROFOR being in Bosnia to facilitate the aid program, the soldiers had no authorization to use force when passage through a roadblock was denied to a convoy they were escorting. The assumption was that while it might have been possible to shoot one's way through once, to have done so would have made the passage of future convoys impossible. Whatever the merits of this argument, the practical result was that very little aid got through to the places most in need of it. Between August 1992 and March 1993, to cite only one example, *three* UNHCR convoys made it into Srebrenica. And because the Bosnian war was not a simple morality play, much of the little that did finally make its way in was not distributed to the neediest populations but taken straight to the fighters on the front line. It was commonplace to see Bosnian government positions protected by sandbags made out of the sacking for food aid or the UNHCR plastic sheeting brought in to replace windows blown out by shellfire. And Bosnians one spoke to saw nothing wrong with this. The war came first.

And yet it was difficult on any level to keep political, diplomatic, and humanitarian efforts in their separate little boxes. If the United Nations was to go on running humanitarian relief convoys, it had to turn a blind eye to the way in which some of the supplies were used. For their part, even as they denounced it for not doing more, the Bosnian leadership in Sarajevo soon became dependent on the grace and favor of UNPROFOR, even for something as basic as getting in and out of the besieged city. Over the course of the fighting, the Bosnians had managed to dig two tunnels that ran from the city, under the Serb lines and the UN-controlled airport, and into a government-controlled village called Butmir. These tunnels, which were a closely guarded secret until 1993 when Chuck Sudetic of *The New York Times* was allowed to go through one of them (the rumor was that the UN was about to reveal their existence publicly), were the way most black market foodstuffs and arms were brought in, and the way soldiers and some private citizens got out. The passage was hardly an easy one. The tunnel was low, dark, and difficult to navigate for anyone but the young and the agile. When Alia Izetbegovic, a seventy-four-year-old man, wanted to visit his forces in central Bosnia—a trip UNPROFOR was hardly going to facilitate—it was said that he had to be wheeled through the tunnel in a barrow. In any case, for most Sarajevans the tunnel might as well have been on another planet. The ordinary experience of living in Sarajevo was of a city that was all but sealed off, by the Serbs first of all, obviously, but by UNPROFOR as well.

At first glance, it seemed quite outrageous that the United Nations could determine the rules for entry and exit to and from Sarajevo. After all, the city was the capital of a United Nations member state. Given that fact, and its corollary, that the Serbs in Pale were the illegitimate leaders of a rebellion against an internationally recognized state, one might have expected UN officials to defer to the wishes of Izetbegovic and his colleagues. Certainly it was surprising to see UN Civil Affairs officials taking it upon themselves to in effect administer the Serb siege by designating the small number of Sarajevans—mostly government people and local journalists—who could fly out on the relief flights that most foreign journalists and visiting dignitaries used to come and go. On return trips to their bases in Split, Ancona, and Frankfurt, these NATO cargo planes on loan to the

UNHCR were empty, so it was hardly a question of space. But that made no difference. According to the United Nations, it had no "mandate" to transport people, and in any case—though this was nowhere written down—preventing people from leaving had been part of the agreement between UNPROFOR and General Mladic when the Serbs had relinquished the airport to UN control in the early summer of 1992.

Not only were most Bosnians refused permission to travel on the flights, but UNPROFOR soon limited foreign journalists to carrying six letters from Sarajevans when they left. "You're a journalist, not a mailman," a Swedish UN Civil Policeman once told me as he discovered a cache of letters in my flak jacket, most of which he confiscated. "I can't let you take these. One might contain a plastic explosive." When I asked him whether he had ever found any Semtex or Formex, he replied, with perfect sincerity, "No, I haven't yet . . . thank God." He then turned to a Bosnian journalist I knew slightly and literally unpacked all the man's meager belongings, running his hands through them. Neither this policeman, who was on balance *less* arrogant than the UN "Civpol" average (only a small contingent of Colombians could be depended on to behave humanely; the Canadians and the Scandinavians behaved like prison warders), nor any of his superiors I ever spoke with seemed to see anything improper about their conduct or to question the propriety of their deciding what and who could come in and out of Sarajevo. Seeing Civpol at work, one understood why so many people from the Third World suspected the United Nations of using peacekeeping operations to establish a new form of neocolonialism. The Civil Policemen and their Civil Affairs superiors I met in Bosnia were, almost to a man, people who would have been perfectly at ease serving in some remote district of British India, imposing rules on the lesser breeds over whom they had been granted authority. Doubtless, the imperial police in 1893 were as quick to justify their conduct by an appeal to a "mandate" from the Colonial Office back in London as UN officials were to refer all inquiries to the Security Council in New York.

The UN's role as gatekeeper was not limited to humiliating and capricious displays of authority, carried out in the name of preventing a possible terrorist threat, over the few people who had permission to board one of the relief flights. UN Protection Force troops also patrolled the airport runway, turning back those people desperate enough to risk the Serb snipers in order to leave Sarajevo. And many Sarajevans died when the lights UN soldiers used to locate them on the runway served to illuminate them for nearby Serb snipers. There were also many stories of individual United Nations soldiers routinely humiliating those Sarajevans they did round up. This the UN denied. But even when something undeniable came up, like the incident in 1993 when UNPROFOR armored personnel carriers out on patrol actually ran over Bosnians cowering near the tarmac, UN officials seemed quite unrepentant, stressing that preventing people from leaving was part of their deal with the Serbs. When one said to them that, in the name of simple humanity, they might patrol less energetically, since after all there were plenty of other aspects of the mandate that they were unable or unwilling to fulfill—protecting the six Safe Havens designated by the Security Council, to name just one—they usually responded that not to patrol might bring down the ire of the Serbs and compromise the humanitarian airlift.

They may have been right, although this hardly seems likely, since when the Bosnian Serbs wanted to close the airport they never seemed to need a pretext for doing so. They just lobbed in a few shells or fired at the United Nations planes. But it was emblematic of so many United Nations decisions in Bosnia that UNPROFOR never even tried a softer approach, never waited to see if the Serbs would retaliate. The United Nations could have sent out fewer patrols; they could have turned a blind eye to the women from Dobrinja or Sarajevo who crossed the airport, their arms laden with food if they were returning to the city or with a small suitcase if they were trying to flee it, as they turned a blind eye to their own black marketeering. It was an open secret in Sarajevo that members of the Ukrainian battalion of UNPROFOR would smuggle Serbs who wanted to leave Sarajevo to Pale for a thousand Deutschemarks. The crossing was dangerous enough as it was, since Serb snipers with infrared night scopes on their rifles were shooting anyway. But UNPROFOR was for once indefatigable, sending patrols out, turning back the people they caught, and usually confiscating the foodstuffs they were bringing back to the city. What was most disquieting about all this, even more than the policy itself, was the UN's lack of shame in carrying it out. It was as if, having stipulated to themselves that they were the virtuous party—the sole virtuous party, as they construed it—in the Bosnian tragedy, anything they did was virtuous, even the petty cruelty of UNPROFOR's conduct at the Sarajevo airport. With this extraordinary self-regard rampant among United Nations officials, it was easy at times to get the sense that UNPROFOR considered itself to be the real aggrieved party in Bosnia.

And yet, of necessity, the Bosnian government was obliged to cooperate with UNPROFOR even on these questions of getting in and out of the city. If Haris Silajdzic or any other Bosnian officials needed to leave Sarajevo to attend another round of negotiations in Geneva, they could only do so aboard a United Nations aircraft. For that matter, they could only reach the airport safely by riding in a UN armored personnel carrier. When UNPROFOR officials really became annoyed, the first move they made was usually to threaten to stop letting Bosnian officials use United Nations APCs. I once witnessed a demonstration of Bosnians against the UN during which a senior French officer, Colonel Valentin, told a Bosnian official present that "if this does not stop immediately, the next time [Vice-Premier] Ganic wants to get to the airport, he can walk." Even Sadako Ogata, the United Nations High Commissioner for Refugees herself, indulged in this sort of tactic. When, after a particularly bad period of shelling, the Mayor of Sarajevo called for a hunger strike, Ogata responded, as if she had been dealing with a bunch of unruly children, by suspending the airlift until the city authorities backed down. It was a pure power play. At the time, UNHCR warehouses in Sarajevo were anything but full, and the UNHCR might have used the opportunity to restock them. But to Ogata, it seemed more important to drive home the point that while Bosnia might be a sovereign state, it was the UN Protection Force and the UN High Commissioner for Refugees who had the whip hand.

When things went wrong, even with something so simple as transporting a Bosnian official to and from the airport, the UN was quick to blame everyone but themselves. In January 1993, the Bosnian Vice-President, Dr. Hakija Turaljic, perhaps the ablest member of Izetbegovic's cabinet, was returning to Sarajevo in a French armored personnel carrier after a meeting with Turkish humanitarian officials at the airport. At the bend in the road halfway into town, a spot where the Bosnian Serbs would later establish a checkpoint—despite the fact that, according to the airport agreement, they were already allowed to inspect relief supplies at the airport and had supposedly ceded control of the road to the UN—his convoy was stopped by a hundred and fifty Serb fighters and a number of armored vehicles. A standoff ensued.

The French battalion commander, Colonel Patrice Sartre, instead of calling for help from the UNPROFOR airport garrison, actually *sent away* three British Warrior fighting vehicles that had happened on the scene. When their commander, Captain Peter Jones, offered to deploy around the armored personnel carrier in which Turaljic was sitting, Sartre dismissed him. "This is a French problem," he said. Shortly thereafter, Sartre allowed the rear hatch of the APC to be opened in order, he said later, to demonstrate to the Serbs that there were no arms or "mujahedin" riding along with Turaljic. At this point, according to a French enlisted man riding with the Vice-President, Turaljic was weeping. His terror was entirely warranted. As Sartre stood there, a Serb fighter simply pointed a machine pistol past his shoulder and into the rear of the vehicle and cut Dr. Turaljic to bits.

A UN commission of inquiry exonerated the French soldiers, and actually hinted that it was the Bosnians' fault for creating "an atmosphere of anxiety" among the Serbs that day. The Serbs, the report claimed, were "disturbed" by the arrival of the Turkish plane. The Bosnians had not given UNPROFOR proper notification of the trip. As for Colonel Sartre, far from being sent home, he was allowed to carry on in Bosnia, and, upon his return to France, was awarded the Legion of Honor. Later he would be sent to command one of the elements of the French intervention force in Rwanda. Not that the finding of the United Nations commission exonerating Sartre was surprising to anyone who knew how UNPROFOR treated its own. The UN's covering up of its own malfeasance had already been evident in its refusal to accept the possibility suggested regularly by journalists that UNPROFOR troops were engaged in widespread black marketeering. The French commander, Lieutenant General

Philippe Morillon, did send a few Ukrainian soldiers home, but he insisted their improprieties had been an isolated incident. Neither corruption nor dereliction of duty, it seemed, was cause for self-examination in the higher echelons of UNPROFOR.

So there were at least as many reasons for Bosnians to resent and mistrust UNPROFOR as there were for them to welcome it. But one of the things Bosnia taught one was that people could keep a number of opinions, not to mention several identities, in their heads at once. The most blatant and disturbing example of this, of course, was the ability of so many Bosnian Serbs to conceive of themselves as entirely modern *and* as essentially tribal at the same time. On the Bosnian government side, it was saddening to realize that no matter how often people denounced the United Nations and, in Sarajevo particularly, chafed under its only partly benign occupation, Bosnians also expected the UN to do more for them than simply send in convoys and cargo planes full of food and medicine. For the United Nations, the Bosnians were, if not the good guys, at least the most sinned-against side, who had to be compelled to surrender for their own good. For the Bosnians, UNPROFOR might behave high-handedly and ineffectively but if its troops had been deployed in Bosnia, sooner or later these troops would intervene on their side to rescue them.

General Mackenzie had been right to attribute part of this mistaken belief to the hope that UN military intervention would eventually be forthcoming, and its corollary, an acute sense of disappointment when that action did not take place, as well as to the linguistic problem of having called the UN army in Bosnia a "protection force." The more basic difficulty, however, was that if most Bosnians had believed in 1992 and many still hoped in 1994 that they would be rescued by an international force, this was because they thought that they *deserved* to be rescued. Perhaps all victim peoples the world over feel this, but what made the Bosnians different from Afghans or Rwandans was that their prewar lives had inculcated in them the assumption that what they deserved they would also get.

As Bosnia lurched toward partition, it was clear that this had been their fatal error. The Bosnian government had imagined that if it could only make the Bosnian case eloquently enough and stir public outrage in the West, then the great powers, the United States in particular, would eventually be forced to intervene. When Warren Christopher, the American Secretary of State, went to Europe in March 1993, ostensibly to try to build support for the American stand, and wound up, whether by design or incompetence (there was a school of thought in Washington that held that the Americans had never wanted to do anything in the first place but had to be seen as trying to satisfy elite domestic opinion), stiffening British and French opposition to any intervention, it should have been clear to the Bosnian authorities that the Americans had nothing in mind. For instead of telling the Foreign Office and the Quai d'Orsay what the United States planned to do, as his predecessors would have done, Christopher had invited a discussion that was bound to be fruitless.

Of course, the diplomats' round, with its seemingly endless, self-defeating discussions of options, regional implications, and domestic policy considerations, which made such little sense to the average Bosnian (the language of statecraft rarely makes sense to those who experience its effects) was by no means the only impediment to Western action. Many military planners both in UNPROFOR and in Western defense ministries, the British in particular, kept insisting on the difficulty of doing anything to thwart the Bosnian Serbs short of all-out war. Many subscribed to less elegant versions of Herbert Okun's epigrammatic formulation that "Serbs kill without compunction and die without complaint," and though they rarely came right out and said it, acted as if nothing short of a ground assault on Pale could prevent the Serbs from getting everything they coveted in Bosnia.

The martial qualities of the Bosnian Serbs were only part of the story. To frame the options available to the West as being either acquiescence to Serb war aims or total war was to determine in advance what the final choice would be, and, by setting such a maximalist goal, in effect to make the great the enemy of the good. Airpower might not have rolled back the Serbs, but it might have lifted the siege of Sarajevo. (All the cease-fire did was stop the shelling; the siege went on much as before.) It also might have prevented General Mladic from destroying the economic viability of the Gorazde pocket. But listening to UN press officers in Sarajevo

and Zagreb, and to defense analysts in London and Paris, it was hard
not to feel that the more the Bosnian Serbs humiliated UNPROFOR,
the more Western military people came to admire them. The way
briefings seemed to list toward discussions of what fine country
Bosnia made for guerrilla fighting, how easy it would be for the
Serbs to pin columns of armor down on its switchback roads, and
how the Serbs had a tradition of this kind of fighting dating back to
World War II, when they had fought twenty-seven divisions of the
German army to a standstill, only loaded a deck that was already
stacked against helping the Bosnians. And what the military people
were saying was neither entirely accurate historically nor reflective
of even the meager experience the United Nations and the Western
powers had had with the way the Bosnian Serbs had responded to
threats of force from the West since the beginning of the fighting in
1992.

That the story of the Yugoslav partisans fighting the mighty
Wehrmacht to a standstill had become almost a European folk memory did not make it true. The reality was that heroic as the partisan
resistance had been, and damaging as it was to the German war effort in the Balkans, Tito's forces had spent more of the war retreating
from the Germans than forcing them to retreat. The bulk of the fighting had involved a brutal, three-cornered war between the partisans,
the Croat and Bosnian Croat Ustasha, and the Serb monarchist
forces under General Mihailovic—not a fight with the Germans.
Bosnian Muslims had served with both the Croat fascists and the
partisans, and proportional to population had taken more casualties
than any other national group in Bosnia. As for the story of the
twenty-seven Wehrmacht divisions, it is myth. Only two frontline
German divisions were involved in the partisan war. But Churchill
had bet against his Tory principles and on the Communist Tito during the war. "All I care about is who kills the most Germans," he
said, and when a Tory politician remonstrated that Tito was a Red,
Churchill replied acidly, "Are you planning to live in Yugoslavia after the war?"

After Tito's split with Moscow in 1948, when the West became interested in propping up the Belgrade regime, echoing Titoist legends
about what had taken place between 1940 and 1945 made a useful
propaganda adjunct to all the Marshall Plan aid that was flowing into

Yugoslavia. There was no way to make Tito the Communist a palatable figure, but Tito the resistance hero was something else again. To harp on partisan victories was the positive side of a Western attitude that consistently ignored the repressive nature of the Titoist state (a similar process took place vis-à-vis Ceausescu's Romania until almost the moment "the genius of the Carpathians" was put up against the wall and shot) and chose only to emphasize its independence in foreign policy from the Soviet bloc. Once the breakup of Yugoslavia began, these same legends proved both to have been sufficiently incorporated into the thinking of some to genuinely convince them that there was no effective military recourse to stop the Serbs in Bosnia, and to be useful to others—a shifting group that at different times included most senior figures in the French and British governments—who didn't want any intervention to be undertaken or even the arms embargo against the Bosnian government to be lifted.

There were other factors. To a certain extent, the British and French officers who took such pleasure in propounding these evaluations did so because they were constantly faced with a callow, ill-informed insistence on the part of some supporters of the Bosnian government that Western intervention was bound to be relatively easy. Many of the calls for lifting the arms embargo against the Bosnians took no account of the military realities on the ground. To the question of how the weapons were going to be gotten into Sarajevo or Tuzla, supporters of this approach at best tended to respond vaguely. When pressed, they would concede that some outside force would have to bring in the arms the Bosnians needed. And yet, if one took them at their word, what they were calling for was military intervention in the strictest sense. Only NATO had the airlift capacity and the ability to suppress fire from Serb rockets and artillery batteries ranged around the Sarajevo and Tuzla airports. Only NATO had the attack aircraft capable of shooting down, or, at least, convincingly threatening to shoot down, the Serb planes that would undoubtedly be scrambled to intercept any attempt at bringing heavy weapons or even antitank missile systems in.

In reality, there was never any possibility of getting arms in sufficient quantities to Bosnian government forces without at least a limited intervention. Perhaps the Bosnian Serbs would have backed down. But no military planner in his right mind would have agreed to such a mission on the assumption that a fight could be avoided. Unless the intervening forces had the authorization to fight, there could be no question of going ahead. The soldiers who would actually have to do the dying and the killing had the right to demand that much of their governments. It was morally disingenuous of the Bosnian government to pretend that they wanted only the arms. They needed NATO soldiers to bring them to them. And it was morally reckless, however understandable it may have been, for pro-Bosnian activists abroad to pretend otherwise. Some did so because they genuinely did not understand the implications of what they were saying. This was particularly true of pro-Bosnian Westerners who came from the European and North American left, and many of whom were supporting their own governments' military for the first time in their lives. Having spent their adult lives opposing force, they had not really thought through what the use of force entailed. The choices in Bosnia were stark. Even a limited use of military power would have been governed by the laws of war—another way of saying by the cruel exigencies of war. To stop the Serbs meant killing a lot of Serbs, including, war being war, innocent noncombatants, not sending in glorified policemen to arrest them or make them cease and desist from their aggression.

Nonetheless, it was taking nothing away from the abilities of General Mladic's forces or from the Yugoslav National Army to insist that the image UN military people clung to of the Serbs being ten feet tall was as wide of the mark as the interventionists' wishful assumption that they were two feet tall. More hypocritical still was the pretense on the part of UN officials that they were drawing these conclusions strictly on the basis of objective military criteria. Legitimate opinion might differ, but there was at least as much evidence to support the view that the Serbs were extremely vulnerable to NATO air strikes, and that some knew it, as there was to assume that such attacks would have little effect on either the military disposition or the morale of the Serb forces. Senior American and Western European officers kept saying, accurately enough, that no war had ever been won from the air—the implication being that if NATO remained unwilling to commit ground troops, there was no purpose served in starting an air campaign. But the mission would not have been to defeat the Serbs but to hurt their morale, destroy a lot of their equipment, and get the kind of equipment in to the Bosnians that they needed to make General Mladic and his subordinates reconsider the wisdom of continuing their campaign.

Serbs might die without complaint, but they were not invincible. Even with the military balance so radically skewed in their favor, there were many occasions during the first two years of fighting when their morale had grown shaky. In Banja Luka, in the fall of 1993, elements of the Bosnian Serb Army had come close to mutinying. And though the Chetnik fighters, many of whom were "weekend warriors" who came into Bosnia from Serbia and Montenegro, and, in small numbers, from as far away as Germany and Austria, to serve brief stints on the front lines, might have maintained their taste for fighting, I encountered many Bosnian Serb Army soldiers as early as the winter of 1993 who were royally fed up with it. Obviously, it was better to be a Serb fighter in a bunker above Sarajevo or to sit drinking slivovitz on Mount Vis, east of Tuzla, than to be one of the outgunned, hunkered-down defenders of either of those cities. But, however much they might insist—and believe—that they were willing to go on fighting forever, life for the fighters on the Serb front lines could only be described as easy in comparative terms.

Still, if the ordinary Bosnian Serb soldier was often cold, and wet, and homesick for his family, he was also overconfident as a result of experiencing the fighting as a nearly unbroken string of victories. Except in a few places like the area around Brcko, where Bosnian army and Croat militia forces had achieved some tactical parity, even Bosnian Serb regiments that had simply been transferred as units to General Mladic's command by their former Yugoslav National Army commanders after April 1992 often took on the appearance of irregulars. Spit and polish gave way to the Rambo look. To watch these soldiers strut around in their headbands and their beards, often carrying not just an assault rifle but a submachine gun and a pistol, and an impressive assortment of knives, was frightening but not impressive. As a UN military observer once commented to me, such gear was for killing civilians, not enemy soldiers. If, he said, the Serbs had believed that they were going to face people who could effectively shoot back, they would have carried more ammunition and fewer weapons, and have fired in the short bursts necessary to hit a particular target, rather than in the wild, clip-emptying salvos of fighters who neither knew nor cared much about where their bullets would finally land.

Another foreign military man, a British member of the European Community peacekeeping monitors—the white uniformed observers, most of them ex-officers from Western armies, who were known throughout the former Yugoslavia as "the ice cream men" and suspected of being spies—once told me that what had most impressed him about the way all sides fought was that "no one seems remotely interested in digging in." His incredulity did not exactly jibe with the anxieties over Serb fighting abilities that his colleagues in UNPROFOR expressed so religiously. And yet, as he pointed out, the tactics the Bosnian Serb Army used—heavy bombardment; then shooting at random with small arms to produce the maximum amount of terror in the civilian population; rape, if one believed the stories—were perfectly chosen tactics if ethnic cleansing was the real goal. "When you fire an automatic weapon," he said, "the whole trick is to squeeze the trigger and then immediately stop squeezing. Even in that time, some of the bullets will go wide or high. But of course, these fellows are not aiming at other soldiers. They're aiming at the whole village, so you might say that from their point of view, every shot they fire hits the mark."

The soldiers of the Yugoslav National Army who made up the backbone of the Bosnian Serb Army were well trained. But during the first year of the fighting, they met almost no opposition. The Bosnian government's army only began to take shape in 1993 as something more than a citizens' militia. That would have been enough to make the Serbs overconfident. Add the fact that Bosnian Serb propaganda endlessly instilled in them the idea that the whole world was simultaneously against the Serbs and afraid of them—for all the fierce talk from Presidents Bush and Clinton, there had been no intervention—and the self-confidence veered off into complacency. The pitiful spectacle, when, in April 1994, UNPROFOR finally exercised its famous right to call in air strikes to defend United Nations personnel in Gorazde, of the attacking aircraft briefly strafing and dropping only a few bombs, and, subsequently, of not responding forcefully when the British commando who had served as a forward air controller for the strikes was targeted and killed by Serb fire, when a British Harrier jet was shot down, and a French aircraft hit repeatedly, could only appear to substantiate the boast of General Mladic's deputy, General Gvero, that the Bosnian Serb Army was "the third best army in Europe."

No wonder this army, by 1994, had become so careless in the way it positioned its heavy weapons. One conceals one's batteries when one is afraid they will be destroyed by enemy fire, not just to give privates something to do. And the Serbs obviously didn't consider the effort warranted. What must they have thought when they heard UNPROFOR briefers emphasizing the difficulty of hitting Bosnian Serb Army gun emplacements? They knew the guns were sitting ducks for air attack. Many of the correspondents based in Sarajevo who regularly moved back and forth across the line between the capital and Radovan Karadzic's headquarters in Pale had the same impression. Driving along the "war road" the Serbs had built on the ridgeline around the city, one passed seemingly endless dugouts and mortar and artillery emplacements. Far from being masked to prevent destruction from the air, the guns stood in plain view, often only a few meters from the road. Obviously, when the Serbs advanced, they set up new forward positions, but in most parts of Bosnia the lines remained static month in and month out, and the guns were not moved at all.

Even in besieged Sarajevo, which as the recipient of the largest share of attention from the world media had long been the likeliest place for NATO to strike, the Serb guns remained mostly where they had first been placed, from the moment the Yugoslav National Army pulled out of Sarajevo and the siege began in earnest until the last hour of the last day before the end of the NATO ultimatum in February 1993 that compelled the Serbs to withdraw or warehouse all their heavy weapons. The mere fact that the Serbs did withdraw, when the great powers seriously demanded that they do so, demonstrated that they were not nearly so contemptuous of NATO's power as they pretended to be.

But, for most of the period in which Sarajevo lay under siege, neither ordinary Serb soldiers nor their commanders seemed to believe that the West would ever summon the will to move against them. When one visited these emplacements, the mood was one of boredom, not embattlement. Soldiers talked about shooting down any NATO or American plane that dared to attack them, and occasionally showed off their shoulder-fired surface-to-air missiles in front of the cameras, but from their tone it was clear that they believed no such attacks would be forthcoming. What in Washington was already being called "the Mogadishu effect" had already made its way to the mountains of Bosnia. "You think the American public was upset when eighteen of your soldiers were killed in Africa," a Bosnian Serb official once boasted. "Wait until the coffins start coming back from Bosnia. You are not a strong nation anymore. You cannot stand the idea of your children dying. But we Serbs can look at death. We are not afraid. That is why we will beat you even if you come to help these Turks you love so much."

Brave words, and familiar ones to anyone who spent time on the Serb side. "We will be your next Vietnam," Karadzic liked to say. Nonetheless, every so often the mood would change and it would look for a time as if the Americans really were about to strike. And *whenever* there were such seemingly credible threats, the Serbs would back down. There would be a rhetorical climbdown in which suddenly the same officials who had boasted of Serb invincibility would start musing over the Serb vocation for martyrdom. They would move from triumphalist hectoring to plaintive demands in which they would ask why all the foreign journalists so totally misunderstood the Serbs and so viciously misrepresented what their goals were. "You must help us bring peace," Karadzic once said, at a particularly fraught moment, to CNN's Christiane Amanpour. The Serbs, he would always say, only wanted to live in peace, had long wanted to stop fighting, and only demanded the right to live among like-minded people, "like West Virginia not wanting to be part of the Confederacy during *your* Civil War."

More important, when the Serb leadership began to fear that it had gone too far, that by some particular bit of bloodthirsty behavior it really might have pushed the West into action, it responded by suddenly permitting all kinds of United Nations humanitarian aid to get through. Whether it was unblocking the relief supplies bottled up at the Sarajevo airport, or letting UNHCR convoys move freely through Bosnian Serb Army checkpoints toward besieged areas like Maglaj in north-central Bosnia, or, as in the case of Sarajevo in February 1994, and Gorazde in April 1994, withdrawing heavy guns from a NATO-proclaimed exclusion zone, the Serbs gave every evidence not only of fearing air strikes more than they said they did, but of believing in their effectiveness far more than UN military officials did themselves. From a position of complete intransigence, they would suddenly become so cooperative, often within a day, that an unschooled visitor might have wondered what the UNHCR was making such a fuss about. But then, as the attention of the world shifted away from the Bosnian slaughter, and the pressure from Western publics on their governments to bring pressure on the Serbs receded, the screws were tightened again. The convoys stopped getting through. The relief supplies at the Sarajevo airport were not permitted to pass by Serbs manning what they had started to call an international-frontier crossing point between the airport and the city—a checkpoint whose existence UNPROFOR had initially objected to but soon came to accept, as it had accepted every rewriting of every agreement it had made with the Serbs. In the villages cut off from aid, hunger began to mount again, the hospitals ran out of supplies again, and the world, once more happily relieved of the burden of its indignation over what was happening in Bosnia, turned its collective face away as the Serbs, more emboldened than ever, renewed their onslaught against those last bits of Bosnia they coveted but had not yet conquered.

VIII

The people who actually ran the United Nations peacekeeping operation from the Secretariat in New York had been opposed from the beginning to getting involved in Bosnia. The UN Protection Force operation had originally been restricted almost exclusively to Croatia and was put into effect after the signing of the cease-fire agreement that Cyrus Vance had brokered between Serbs and Croats at the end of 1991. It was, in the term of art employed at the United Nations, a classical or traditional peacekeeping operation. That is, it was a situation in which the Security Council authorized the Department of Peacekeeping Operations, the DPKO, to interpose forces between two sides that already wanted to stop fighting but needed neutral forces to oversee the cease-fire they had agreed to. Although a few United Nations military observers had been stationed in Bosnia, and, ironically, so as to be seen as favoring neither the Serbs nor the Croats, UNPROFOR had established its headquarters in Sarajevo, there was initially no intention on the part of the United Nations to propose extending the UNPROFOR mandate to Bosnia.

Not that the United Nations was not asked. Much has been made of this fact by those who believe that by declaring Bosnian independence the Izetbegovic government in effect signed its own death warrant. The thirty-two percent of the Bosnian population that were Serb, this argument runs, were never going to accept an independent Bosnia, and it was suicidal of Sarajevo to ignore this. But the reality was that Alia Izetbegovic was trapped in a Hobson's choice. Along with the President of Macedonia, Gligorov, Izetbegovic had tried desperately throughout 1991 to work out a formula for a loose Yugoslav confederation. It was Slobodan Milosevic who would have none of this, and insisted that what had to happen in Yugoslavia was increased centralization—another way of saying more power for Serbia and for himself. Staying in Yugoslavia seemed hopeless to Bosnia's SDA party leadership, but so did leaving it. In the end, under what would prove to be a tragically false impression that Europe would guarantee its sovereignty, the Bosnian government opted for a referendum on independence, which, supported by the overwhelming majority of Bosnian Muslims and Croats (except, curiously, the county of Tuzla—a left-wing stronghold whatever its ethnic makeup) and boycotted by most Serbs, passed by a wide margin.

But while Izetbegovic would prove to have been too sanguine about what the West would and would not do, he knew full well that the course he had chosen was terribly dangerous. That was why, when Vance and a number of Department of Peacekeeping Operations officials visited Sarajevo shortly before the fighting started, Izetbegovic pleaded with them to deploy United Nations peacekeepers in Bosnia. The international officials were perfectly well aware of what was to come. Back at the height of the Croatian war, while Bosnia was still at peace, Vance had written to the German Foreign Minister, Hans-Dietrich Genscher, warning him that Germany's insistence on pressing the European Community to recognize Croatia and Slovenia made war in Bosnia a virtual certainty. And yet they had not agreed to recommend the sending of the UN soldiers. As a senior UN official recalled it, "We were in effect being asked to deploy in a province of a sovereign state in order to assist in that province's secession."

It was a position that the Department of Peacekeeping Operations was to maintain even after the carnage had begun. In May 1992, a month into the siege of Sarajevo, Marrack Goulding, the UN Undersecretary General for Special Political Affairs, and former head of the Department of Peacekeeping Operations, argued in a memo to the Security Council that since there was not yet a peacekeeping mandate on which the sides agreed—a polite way of saying that both sides still wanted to fight—the situation in Bosnia was not "ripe" for peacekeeping. Most people who witnessed the deliberations agree that the permanent members of the Security Council, under pressure from domestic public opinion, chose to ignore the recommendation, even though they did not agree among themselves about what should be done in Bosnia. After issuing a series of fruitless appeals for the fighting to stop, the Council on May 30, 1992, passed a resolution imposing sanctions on the rump Yugoslavia—that is, Serbia and Montenegro. It also authorized the dispatch of humanitarian relief to Bosnia under the auspices of the UN High Commissioner for Refugees, and designated the United Nations Protection Force to assist the humanitarian agencies in this work and to secure the reopening of the Sarajevo airport, then under Serb control. On June 5, the United Nations reached an agreement with the Serbs, and on June 8, the Security Council authorized an enlarged UNPROFOR deployment in Bosnia.

Although the Security Council would pass an astonishing number of resolutions about Bosnia—more than fifty, all told, over the course of the next two and a half years—these initial moves more or less determined how the United Nations would subsequently interpret what it had and had not been authorized to do. To the Department of Peacekeeping Operations in New York and the United Nations Protection Force in the field, keeping the humanitarian effort going took precedence over everything else even though the Security Council's actions had included resolutions that made other demands on the belligerents. At least one resolution had demanded that the practice of ethnic cleansing be stopped. The UN had imposed the No Fly zone over Bosnia, declaring Sarajevo, Tuzla, Bihac, Gorazde, Zepa, and Srebrenica to be Safe Areas. These were measures that could hardly be construed in strict humanitarian terms, since when the resolution was passed, the Serbs were the ones doing all the bombing from the air, and almost all the ethnic cleansing (this was long before the HVO attempted to cleanse Muslims from around Mostar, provoking retaliatory war crimes carried out by Bosnian government forces). As for the "Safe Havens," as they soon became known, these were all Bosnian government–controlled areas under attack by the Serbs.

Because it believed that the only mandate United Nations peacekeeping forces had in Bosnia was to further humanitarian programs, and that other Security Council declarations concerning broader questions like ethnic cleansing did not specify what the United Nations was to do, the UN Secretariat steadfastly opposed every call for it to do more in Bosnia. It had bitterly opposed the Safe Areas resolution, and privately dug in its heels over the enforcement of the No Fly zone policy, believing both to represent the UN's taking sides in the fighting. That violated everything the Department of Peace-keeping Operations thought it its duty to try to maintain in its peace-keeping efforts. To have behaved otherwise, they argued, would have been to imperil the whole concept of United Nations peacekeeping. "We are not going to delegitimize our operations throughout the world," a UN official in Zagreb once told me, "in an ill-conceived effort to preserve the Bosnian state." Shashi Tharoor, a well-known Indian novelist and former UNHCR official who led the DPKO section dealing with Bosnia and Croatia, declared morosely in a speech in 1993 that enforcement of the UN's No Fly resolution was "going to put the United Nations in a position where its peacekeepers, wearing blue and not terribly heavily armed, will in effect be making war and peace at the same time."

As the international human rights organization Human Rights Watch pointed out in a report, the price of such a conception was that human rights inevitably became "the lost agenda" in UN peacekeeping work, even though "severe human rights abuses often play a critical role in fueling armed conflict and aggravating humanitarian crises." The United Nations had appointed the former Polish Prime Minister, Tadeusz Mazowiecki, to be its "special rapporteur" on human rights in the former Yugoslavia. But though he pleaded with the United Nations to enforce its own resolutions on human rights, at one point threatening to quit because, he said, he had no wish to have his office play the role of an "umbrella disguising the helplessness of the international organization," UN officials paid lip service to his efforts but made no attempt to modify what they were doing in the field to take into account his recommendations that they claimed to value so highly.

Those who ran the operation in Bosnia were not to be budged from their commitment to maintaining UNPROFOR's role as one of almost exclusively alleviating the consequences of the war. The United Nations, they argued, had not been sent there either to bring the conflict to an end or to make protecting human rights a priority. If that was what the Security Council wanted, it would have to say so explicitly. For the time being, however, if such a welcome improvement in the situation were to take place, it would have to do so through other outside pressure or through negotiation. And that task was to be left to governments, and to the heads of the joint UN-EC

negotiating team, first Vance and Owen, and later Owen and Thor-
vald Stoltenberg, the former Norwegian Foreign Minister and ex-
head of the UNHCR, who took Vance's place after the American
resigned in May 1993. And if the Council wanted a military solution
to the Bosnian crisis, then it should have intervened not under the
peacekeeping rubric of Chapter VI of the UN Charter but under the
peace enforcement rubric of Chapter VII, as it had in the case of
Kuwait. "That would have been fine with us," a Department of
Peacekeeping Operations official once said to me. "We would
hardly have complained had they taken it out of our hands, declared
that they wanted peace enforcement and not peacekeeping, and left
us to go about our business."

Such comments had the air of bureaucratic pettifogging, and to a
certain extent they were. To a very large degree, the UN Secretariat
was organized by British civil servants who gave their opaque, conformist stamp to the organization. It is emblematic of the way the
United Nations operates that no UN civil servant ever either dis-
sented publicly or resigned as a question of principle over Bosnian
policy. Indeed, to ask the officials in question why they had not resigned was more likely to invite a blank stare, as if the idea were unthinkable in a United Nations context, than a rousing defense of
UNPROFOR. In private, UN officials were capable of conceding
that, in moral terms, the Bosnians might be right, but in the terms of
the peacekeeping mission that they had to administer, it was necessary for them to remain entirely impartial. At times, such impartiality could be positively grotesque, as when Yasushi Akashi, the
Secretary General's Special Envoy, left a meeting in Pale and declared to the press that he believed Radovan Karadzic to be "a man
of peace," boasting of the "friendship" that had developed between
them. He made these extraordinary and, even from a diplomatic
point of view, quite unnecessary declarations long after most of the
civilized world, including most UN officials, had concluded that the
Serb leader was in all likelihood a war criminal.

To the journalists listening to him, many of whom had seen far too
much of how Karadzic waged war, Akashi's words were infuriating.
The nicknames disgruntled UNHCR field officers had come up with
for him, "the Mitsubishi Chetnik" and "the Senior Serb Liaison Officer," seemed particularly apposite that day. At best, he appeared as

the embodiment of that triumph of hope over experience that seemed to be the principal hallmark of UN diplomacy. More likely, like several of the UNPROFOR military officials whom the journalists had come to know and, speaking for myself, to distrust, Akashi was a two-faced apologist for the Serbs, trying with his words to forestall a firmer stand on the part of the NATO powers. And yet Akashi was said to be one of the best the United Nations had. He had been sent to the former Yugoslavia after bringing to a close one of the United Nations' most successful peacekeeping operations to date, the mission in Cambodia. If, in Bosnia, he often seemed naive, he was certainly not inexperienced. If he was willing to lie about Radovan Karadzic, to treat the murderers as being as worthy of respect and friendship (Akashi kept emphasizing his "good personal relationships" with the Bosnian Serb leaders) as their victims, it was because he remained utterly committed to a specific concept of what UN peacekeeping was all about. And, as he demonstrated when he all but single-handedly prevented NATO attacks on the Serbs after they failed to heed the ultimatum to completely withdraw from Gorazde in late April 1994, he would go to almost any lengths to preserve the integrity of that concept.

In this, as in so many other areas, Akashi proved himself to be no different from his predecessors. He might unwisely speak of his warm feelings for Karadzic, but it had been his UNPROFOR predecessors who, in the name of keeping the negotiations going, had acceded to a Serb demand that the United Nations no longer refer to Sarajevo as being under siege. The Bosnian Serbs had always claimed as much, arguing that it "just happened" that all the areas in Sarajevo that the Serbs now controlled had been Serb before the war and that, far from attacking "the Muslims," they were only defending Serbs from attack. By Pale standards, this claim was only mildly outlandish. But to hear an experienced UNPROFOR press officer, a well-liked and well-informed Canadian officer named Barry Frewer, parrot this line and inform an incredulous press corps that the Serbs were not besieging Sarajevo but were in a "tactically advantageous encirclement" was to hear the United Nations stand truth on its head.

The UN officials concerned seemed to feel no shame in having to lie on the Serbs' behalf. Theirs was an austere, self-referential creed. Stripped to its bare essentials, the dogma the UN people lived their

professional lives by required them to believe that they had no mandate to do anything more for the Bosnians than, as they put it, try to al-
leviate the humanitarian consequences of the fighting. Were they to
have supported military intervention, they kept repeating, that humanitarian mission would have been compromised. They argued that
either one delivered humanitarian aid or one used force. As for human
rights, that usually just made them shake their heads. Almost all of
them believed that all sides were committing war crimes. Indeed, it
was common to hear UNPROFOR people insisting that the only reason the government side had done less was that they had had fewer
opportunities to do so (Auden's line "Those to whom evil is done, do
evil in return" seemed more accurate a diagnosis). And in private,
while not directly repudiating the War Crimes Commission that the
UN had set up, they made it clear that they felt one either negotiated
with Milosevic, Karadzic, Mladic, and the others, or one tried to bring
them to justice. Claiming one could do both might be a pleasant thing
for Western governments to insist to their citizens, but it was puerile.

As the behavior of the United Nations demonstrated in Bosnia, its
officials believed that if they did not rigidly hew to their impartiality,
UNPROFOR's mission could not continue. In the largest sense, the
Serbs could not be expected to allow UNPROFOR and the UNHCR
to continue to operate if forces under United Nations command
were pursuing military action. Convoys would be halted, UNHCR
personnel killed or expelled, and the air bridge to Sarajevo—the humanitarian effort's most signal success—brought to a halt. After all,
the airport was surrounded by Serb guns. The United Nations could
scarcely hope to keep it open to airlift flights once the NATO bombs
started to fall. Even a more robust interpretation of the UN's own
humanitarian mandate was deemed to be impractical. Theoretically,
UNPROFOR had been given the authority to use whatever means
were required, including force, to escort relief convoys to their destination. But in practice, United Nations officials had concluded early
on that to authorize the peacekeepers to shoot (or even threaten to
shoot) their way past at a checkpoint, however satisfying that might
have been, could have destroyed everything the United Nations was
working for in Bosnia. As Sergio Vieira de Mello, who, like Akashi,
was a highly regarded veteran of the United Nations' operation in
Cambodia before he became the senior UN civilian administrator in

Sarajevo in late 1993, once put it to me, "Shooting your way through only works once. After that you're at war, and for all practical purposes the humanitarian effort is over. You've lost."

The problem with this argument was that it was a United Nations dogma, not a fact grounded in the experience UN peacekeepers had had in Bosnia. In reality, whenever individual units of UNPROFOR used force, their task was made easier, not harder. In northern Bosnia, for example, the British soldiers charged with escorting relief convoys from their own forward base in the village of Kladanj to the city of Tuzla along a road known as "Bomb Alley" decided, without fanfare, to start shooting back at the Serbs in the surrounding hills. After a few engagements, Serb attempts to harass the convoys dropped off radically. In central Bosnia, in late 1993, the combined Nordic battalion got a new commander, a Swedish fire-eater named Hendrikson. "If I'm stopped at a checkpoint," he said, "I tell them they let me through or I'll blow their fucking heads off. Sure, sometimes they don't, and I have to go back, but it doesn't hurt to try it. You have to in the Balkans. You act the tough guy or they piss all over you."

For its part, the United Nations pissed all over those who, like Hendrikson, tried to do more. When during the siege of Srebrenica, the UNPROFOR commander in Bosnia, General Philippe Morillon, decided to go to the enclave and by remaining there try to compel the Serbs to stop shelling, the Secretariat in New York was livid. Boutros-Ghali reprimanded Morillon personally, telling the French general that he was guilty of "exceeding the mandate." In other words, instead of talking about saving lives and bringing peace, for a short moment Morillon actually had saved lives and brought a measure of peace. It was not as if Morillon had ordered his soldiers to fire on the Serbs. He had simply gone where he thought he might do some good (the general, whatever his limitations, had a certain old-fashioned Gaullist sense of honor and personal grandeur). A few months later, he was dismissed from his command and sent home to France. The rumor was that the French government had acceded to a personal request from Boutros-Ghali himself.

To someone like me, who sympathized with the Bosnian cause and believed that the UN's activism in trying to prevent or, after the air strike in Gorazde in 1994, limit military intervention made them, however inadvertently and unwillingly, the handmaidens to the geno- cide of the Bosnian Muslims, it is excusing nothing to assert that the United Nations acted out of stubborn fidelity to peacekeeping as they understood it and to the mandate they believed they had been or- dered by the Security Council to carry out. But it is still important to try to understand why the UN acted in the way that it did. And while it might be comforting to attribute the policy to some inherent organi- zational malignity, the truth is that the people who run United Na- tions peacekeeping are, as a rule, among the most intelligent and sophisticated civil servants in the world, and tend to be *more* sensi- tive, not less, to the slaughterhouse that our world really is. In reality, it was the gap between the sensitivity with which many UN officials, both in the former Yugoslavia and in New York and Geneva, appre- hended what was going on and their insistence that the slaughter had to be allowed to go on that was so shocking to outsiders.

And yet the more I encountered UN officials, the more it seemed to me that not only were they trapped in an organization that is prob- ably more conformist and hierarchical than any institution except a military force, but they had grown accustomed to speaking to each other in a self-referential language that might have made sense to them but made increasingly little sense in the context of Bosnia. Surely, it was partly because of the way the UN fetishized "the man- date" that Boutros Boutros-Ghali's report to the Security Council dated March 16, 1994, evaluating whether or not to continue UNPROFOR, could brush aside all significant criticism of the oper- ation. "I am conscious," the Secretary General said, "that continuing conflict and tragedy in UNPROFOR's area of operations since its mandate was last renewed have led to considerable, but unjustified, criticism of the effectiveness of the Force."

Such criticism was unjustified, the report went on to suggest, first because certain "hopeful" developments around Sarajevo (i.e., the NATO-imposed cease-fire) meant that a settlement might finally be coming within reach. But more important, it was unfair to criticize what the United Nations had done in Bosnia because "UNPROFOR's deployment embodies the will of the international community to help arrive at such a settlement . . . It is the responsibility of the parties to seize the opportunity provided by UNPROFOR's continuation to demonstrate by their conduct that they are seriously committed to pursuing the path to peace. If they are, the United Nations stands ready, as always, to help them."

To read sentences like these after spending even a month or two in Bosnia was to enter a world in which reality seemed to have been stood on its head. Whatever Akashi and Boutros-Ghali might say publicly, the situation was *not* hopeful in mid-March 1994, and grew ever less hopeful in the ensuing months, as the NATO exclusion zone around Gorazde proved to be a porous joke, the military threat all but a hoax, and even the Sarajevo cease-fire an increasingly tenuous affair. As for the idea that UNPROFOR had been a success, that really was like the old vaudeville saw "The operation was a success. It's just that the patient died." Had UN officials simply talked, as some of the less reflective among them usually did, of the lives saved by the airlift, or else insisted, as some military officers tended to do, that the Bosnians were a bunch of savages who should be allowed to get on with the business of killing one another, that at least would have been understandable. What was odd was to hear the best people in UNPROFOR and the Department of Peacekeeping Operations sincerely maintaining in one breath that they had done a good job while in the next conceding that the whole situation in Bosnia was turning into a complete disaster.

This was where the professional deformation of the peacekeeper came in. As a UN Civil Affairs official said to me in Sarajevo, "You have to learn to compartmentalize in this job. I know what the Serbs have done in Bosnia. I've seen the corpses, heard the women weep. But it doesn't matter where my sympathies lie, or what I might say or want done if I were a journalist like you. My job is neither to fight the Serbs nor to denounce them. I'm here to help Bosnia as much as I can, and to do that I not only have to appear impartial, to treat Serbs and Muslims just the same, but, because the Serbs have all but won this war, and you need their permission to do most things here, I have to stay on good terms with them."

To many of the peacekeepers, giving vent to their moral sentiments was a luxury they could not afford. And the most reflective among them were quick to concede the ambiguous moral position this put the United Nations in. Fred Cuny had quipped that if the United Nations had been around in the 1930s, everyone in Europe would be speaking German, and to those of us who in two years had learned to despise the UN for its impartiality and its smug self-satisfaction in Bosnia, that seemed to encapsulate everything that needed to be said about UNPROFOR. (The UN High Commissioner for Refugees was another matter entirely.) But there were officials at the United Nations who could even concede *this* and still defend what they had done in Bosnia. Fred Cuny's comment was rarely far from my thoughts when I was in Sarajevo, so I was flabbergasted to hear a UN official remark almost offhandedly at a meeting, "You know, when you talk about what we have been unable to do in Bosnia, my response is, there are a great many situations for which the instrument of peacekeeping simply is not suitable. For example, I think the UN would not have been very effective in dealing with Hitler in the 1930s."

He went on. "We are accused of not having done more in Bosnia, but the truth is that since the first peacekeeping operation in 1947 we have never exceeded a Security Council mandate. And we were certainly not in a position to do so here. When you condemn us, I think it is because we are the most visible symbols of the world, and, by extension, of the world failure to prevent the terrible things that have occurred in the former Yugoslavia. But when you condemn us, you are really shooting the messenger. Blame your own governments for what has gone on; they could have given us a different mandate. Blame yourselves for not having persuaded your governments to act. But it is pointless to blame us. The UN is not the world's government. It is an organization of the world's governments. And peacekeeping is only an instrument that we in the UN can make available if called upon to do so by the Security Council. You think we are hiding behind the mandate, but the fact is that it provides us with the only legitimacy we have. It is one thing for us to do less than the Council wanted—often we have no choice—but you and your colleagues are reproaching us for not having done more. But we don't do so because we simply do not see that as our function or our right. Were we to attempt to do so, we would be usurping the authority of the member states, and I put it to you that they would not tolerate that for very long."

Implicit in such an account was the notion that the peacekeeper's brief was either to stick to being a benign, impartial bystander or not to get involved at all. It rejected any suggestion that it had a role in interpreting the mandate it had been given, and the specific resolutions it had been ordered to enforce. United Nations officials seemed quite impervious to the idea that the tactical decisions UNPROFOR had made on the ground in Bosnia had significantly influenced the decisions that the governments of the five permanent members of the Security Council had reached either at the United Nations or in the context of other supranational councils like NATO. They rightly pointed out that the Security Council kept ordering the peacekeepers to do difficult and ambitious things, but then rarely were willing to back up these new mandates with even the minimal amounts of money and manpower that they required.

A classic case in point was the so-called Safe Havens resolution passed in May 1993. UNPROFOR had estimated that thirty thousand new troops would be needed to protect the six designated areas. At a pinch, the force commander said, he could do the job with ten thousand soldiers—"Safe Havens Lite," as the joke went in UNPROFOR headquarters in Zagreb. In the end, the Security Council authorized seventy-five hundred troops and eventually appropriated the money for only thirty-five hundred. And even these forces were only committed a year later, after much backtracking by the permanent members and endless politicking by Department of Peacekeeping Operations officials. As was so often the case with United Nations resolutions on Bosnia, the stated purpose of a given decree was rarely the same as its real goal. The Safe Havens policy was adopted after the Bosnian Serbs had turned Srebrenica into an enormous killing ground. In France, in particular, there was great pressure on the Mitterrand government for military intervention, and pressure was building in Britain. In the view of many observers at the United Nations, in and out of the Secretariat, the French and the British had to be seen to be doing something, and designating some towns in Bosnia as Safe Havens demonstrated resolve without actually committing the United Nations or NATO to very much.

By contrast, the United States favored the policy because it was at least leaning toward stepped-up military engagement. Declaring Safe Havens seemed a step in that direction. As it turned out, of course, the British and French—who opposed intervention every step of the way and whose every action needed to be viewed in that light in order to be understood properly—got the better of the deal. Srebrenica became a holding pen for Bosnian refugees, as Gorazde would a year later, and nothing particular was done to protect the other areas—Bihac, Zepa, Tuzla, and Sarajevo. And the United States, for all its blustering commitment to helping the Bosnians—this was the period when President Clinton kept insisting that he "would like" to lift the arms embargo but couldn't get his European allies to go along—not only refused to commit troops but would eventually renege on its longstanding pledge to fund troop commitments by other countries. It took the Gorazde crisis, a year after the Safe Havens resolutions had been passed, to shame the Clinton administration into once more reaffirming its original commitment.

So there was blame enough to go around. Still, it was disingenuous of United Nations officials to pretend that they were the only disinterested parties in the Bosnian tragedy. In reality, UN peacekeepers had been carrying out a very specific and well-thought-out political agenda from the beginning of their deployment. Its premise was simple. The United Nations saw not just full-scale intervention in support of the Bosnians but any increased military activity, whether it was NATO air strikes or lifting the one-sided arms embargo against the Bosnian government, as putting at risk everything it had been trying to accomplish in Bosnia. Its criterion was not moral—by their own admission, UN officials felt they had no business judging the rights and wrongs of the conflict. Nor was it political, since although the Bosnian government was an internationally recognized state and the Bosnian Serb "republic" an illegitimate rebellion, the United Nations felt compelled to deal with them equally, as "the parties," or "the warring factions." Rather, the UN wanted to get the aid through and facilitate a peace. "UNPROFOR's mission is to maintain the peace," insisted General Bertrand de Lapresle, the overall commander of UN forces in the former Yugoslavia in late October 1994. "I don't have enemies, I have partners."

The terms of peace were, from the standpoint of UNPROFOR, almost irrelevant. It did not have to be a just peace, or even a peace that could be maintained. All that the United Nations required was that "the parties" agree to it. Again, the appearance the UN assumed was of an organization trying impartially to help resolve a terrible situation. And again, this facade concealed interests that the United Nations was loath to admit it stood for but that were not difficult to figure out. If the purpose of a mission is to stop a war, and one side, having won, appears ready to settle, while the other side, feeling its cause to be just but having turned out to be the loser, is determined to fight on, then those running this mission are likely to find that most of the time their interests coincide with those of the victors. They and the victors want peace. The vanquished, possessed of the notion that they have right on their side, refuse to accept their defeat. Given these convergences, it is only a small step to the victors and the international organization understanding that, when all is said and done, they share the same goal.

That was exactly what happened in Bosnia. Of course the United Nations deplored what the Bosnian Serbs had done, but since they had no mandate to do anything about that and a specific mandate to put an end to the suffering of the Bosnian people, the UN found itself trying to prod the Bosnian government to come to its senses and surrender. It might not be an ideal outcome, but at least people would stop getting killed. And if this involved essentially delegitimizing a member state of the United Nations, then so be it. It was interesting that the objection of both UNPROFOR and the Department of Peacekeeping Operations to the Safe Havens resolution had been that it was not impartial enough. That is, UN officials felt that to be truly evenhanded and "humanitarian," the resolution would have to require that Bosnian forces within the six areas be disarmed; otherwise, they argued, these areas would serve as staging and resupply areas for Bosnian government forces. In peacekeeping terms, this made sense. The problem was that if UNPROFOR had really been able to disarm Bosnian troops in the country's capital, Sarajevo, in the second largest city under its control, Tuzla, and in the enclaves that were the last areas of Bosnian resistance in a part of the country that had otherwise been all but completely ethnically cleansed, they would have effectively abolished the Bosnian state in the name of protecting Bosnian citizens from Serb attack.

Fortunately for Bosnia, the attempt to change the resolution failed. But the readiness the United Nations had exhibited to sacrifice Bosnia so as to succor Bosnians spoke volumes about what it thought it was in the country to do. And as every outsider who spent any time in Bosnia soon learned, this convergence of interest between the UN and the Chetniks was not an exceptional situation, but actually played itself out on almost a daily basis. It was most evident, however, when the Serbs would mount an offensive. Usually, when they did, the civilian casualties would be atrocious, and, egged on by press reports, pressure would mount in the West for some sort of intervention. On a number of occasions, the only thing that stopped the bombers from coming was a preemptive move by UNPROFOR.

When, for example, in July 1993, General Mladic's Romanija division seized the last two crucial high points above Sarajevo, Mount Igman and Mount Bjelisaca, it really did look as if the United States might send in attack planes to drive the Serbs back. At that point the UN Protection Force commander in Bosnia, a Belgian lieutenant general named Francis Briquemont, and his deputy, the British brigadier Guy de Vere Hayes, whose apparent good relations with Karadzic and Mladic were a source of endless amazement and indignation in Sarajevo, cobbled together an agreement under which the Serbs would allow French UN peacekeepers to be stationed on the new front line. The Serbs themselves would pull back slightly, but not far enough away to make the French and Chetnik lines separable to an attacking pilot.

To hear the United Nations tell it, this so-called disengagement agreement—which, it was widely rumored, had actually been drafted by Hayes and the UN Civil Affairs boss in Sarajevo, a Russian called Victor Andreyev—was a great victory for peace. There had, UN officials insisted to the press, been "no need" for air strikes. But in reality, by stationing peacekeepers so close to the Serbs that any air strikes would have killed as many Frenchmen as Chetniks, the United Nations had not acted as a disinterested bystander but had succeeded in making sure that its wishes—above all, the wish that there be no intervention—carried the day. There it was, that confluence of interest again. By stymieing air strikes, the United Nations got to preserve its mission and the Serbs got to keep their battlefield gains. No wonder the Serb and UNPROFOR commanders got along so well. During the battle for Igman, as during so many other battles before and after, the United Nations was almost the best friend the Serbs had. It was not as if NATO planes were going to kill French soldiers. More to the point, it was not as if either UNPROFOR or the hard men in Pale were unaware of that fact.

Nor did United Nations officials appear to be in any doubt about the correctness of such actions. The point was to avoid more fighting, full stop. This meant finding a way to defuse the situation when the Serbs went too far. This usually involved not responding at all and waiting for the crisis to blow over. When the Serbs attacked UN forces directly, as they did from time to time, either no force was used at all or, as UNPROFOR showed when it ordered two air strikes to support its people in Gorazde in April 1994, so little was used that not only was its effect of little use militarily but it showed the Serbs how little they had to fear from UNPROFOR. This encouraged them, not that they needed much goading, to feel they could do what they liked in Bosnia. No matter what the Serbs did to the UN, the UN wanted to negotiate with the Serbs. And over the course of two years, as reporters grew accustomed to cautiously optimistic communiqués from UNPROFOR declaring that this time there was really going to be a deal, Bosanski Brod fell, and Cerska, and Jajce, and Zepa. Banja Luka was cleansed, Sarajevo destroyed, and Srebrenica and Gorazde turned into glorified refugee camps for Muslims. "We are moving inexorably toward a peace settlement," David Owen said in mid-1993. He should have said that General Mladic was moving inexorably toward victory.

Examples of the UN's supine relationship with the Serbs can be culled from every period of the war. The nadir probably came in May 1994 when Akashi made a secret agreement with General Mladic to escort seven Bosnian Serb Army tanks through the exclusion zone around Sarajevo. This was a case where the United Nations was betraying not only its own peacekeeping mandate by allowing the Serbs to more conveniently reposition armor on another front, but also the NATO decision about the exclusion zone that UNPROFOR was supposed to be administering. Neither Akashi nor his bosses in New York were apologetic about the deal. They argued that the Serbs had given them something in return; specifically, the right to move a hundred and fifty more British UNPROFOR troops into Gorazde and to station UN military observers along the front line in Brcko in northeast Bosnia—the area toward which, after destroying Gorazde, General Mladic was thought at the time to be turning his attention.

What were seven extra Serb tanks, UN Protection Force and Department of Peacekeeping Operations officials reasoned, compared to these "accomplishments"? And yet these same officials insisted that they were just fulfilling the Security Council's mandates, and had no agenda of their own. Not only did the Serbs, as usual, get from the United Nations a deal they should never have been offered, but, when the deal came out, and an embarrassed Akashi tried to call it off, the Bosnian Serb Army moved its tanks through the exclusion zone anyway. Since Akashi had to authorize air power, there was nothing the United Nations or NATO could do to stop them. One tank even drove off in full view of its UN Protection Force escort. There had been a column of three vehicles: the Serb tank on its carrier truck, then a Serb escort vehicle, then the UNPROFOR escort vehicle. The UNPROFOR press office reported the next day that suddenly the Serb escort vehicle had begun to weave more and more slowly back and forth across the road, blocking the view of the people in the UNPROFOR vehicle. Meanwhile the truck transporting the tank sped off. "It has gone missing, we are looking for it everywhere within the exclusion zone," declared Lieutenant Colonel Eric Chaperon, the UNPROFOR spokesman, to the press corps.

Not only would UNPROFOR more or less feel free to let the Serbs do what they pleased to the Bosnians, but they proved themselves throughout the course of the fighting to be quite willing to let the Serbs do what they wanted to UN forces. A prize example was when, during the same period in the summer of 1993 that Generals Briquemont and Hayes were groping for a way to prevent NATO from pushing the Chetniks off Mount Igman, the Serbs chose to attack a French unit setting up camp near the ruined Zetra Olympic Stadium in Sarajevo. The Bosnian Serb Army fired more than eighty shells at the French contingent, destroying a number of their vehicles although, miraculously, not killing any of the men. General Briquemont declined to order counterfire, explaining later that he had not wanted to endanger the peace talks that were about to start up again in Geneva. As tow trucks pulled the ruined armored personnel carriers through the streets of Sarajevo, local people turned out to cheer contemptuously. "At least those are eighty shells the Chetniks won't fire at us," one of them said to me.

And yet both decisions—the deal with the Serbs and the unwillingness to reply in kind to clearly directed fire from Serb lines—were perfectly in keeping with the United Nations' operating principles and its goals in Bosnia. Without confirming that Hayes and Andreyev had actually provided Mladic with a way out of the Igman crisis, a UN official later told me that if they had done so, he saw nothing wrong with it. "In that situation we are mediators," he said. "The Serbs tell us what they can do and our role is to say, 'All right, then you should so that.' Of course, we would like them to do as much as possible. That is what our negotiations with them are about. But it is not part of our mandate to compel them to come to a certain decision, any more than it is our task to compel the Bosnian side to come to its decision. What we are doing is trying to get the parties to agree."

It was not simply a question of the United Nations finding itself objectively in accord with the Serb rather than the Bosnian government position on making peace quickly, although that was a big part of it. Indeed, many UN officials held the view that the real villains of the Yugoslav breakup were not Karadzic and Milosevic but, in descending order of culpability, Franjo Tudjman, Hans-Dietrich Genscher, and Alia Izetbegovic. They conceded that Izetbegovic had tried hard to keep Yugoslavia together. But deeming Milosevic beyond appeal, they concluded that Izetbegovic had the responsibility to accept whatever the Serb leader was willing to offer him. That they thought had been true in 1991 and was equally applicable in 1994.

It was undeniable that the Bosnian Serbs had quickly attained most of their military objectives and by the beginning of 1994 were pressing for a cease-fire in place. That effectively would have delineated the partition lines in Bosnia according to what had happened on the battlefield. But in the interests of getting a peace, any peace, the United Nations was willing to go along. Understandably, the Bosnian side, which from the UN's perspective had, as was once said of the Irish, the bad taste to be in earnest about the freedom of their country, had balked. It wanted an enforceable settlement first, and only then a cease-fire. In Croatia in 1991, the Vance plan had called for people displaced from the areas of the country under Serb occupation to be allowed to return and for the United Nations to take control of the disputed zones, the so-called UNPAs, or UN Protected Areas, until a final settlement was reached. But at the end of 1994, not a single refugee had been allowed to return and it was universally conceded that the Serbs, not the United Nations, controlled the UNPAs. Under the circumstances, the Bosnian government had every reason to reject UN pressure on them to agree to a similarly "temporary" cease-fire in their own country.

But UN Protection Force officials were far more concerned about the safety of their own people than the territorial integrity of Bosnia-Herzegovina. Not that the threat to United Nations personnel on the ground was imaginary. The thirty thousand or so UN people on the ground in Bosnia would certainly have been the Serbs' first target had there ever been a serious Western military threat, although this question of UNPROFOR people being killed or taken hostage certainly stiffened UN resolve to oppose intervention tooth and nail. As the Serbs demonstrated when they took approximately one hundred and fifty peacekeepers hostage after the NATO bombing runs over Gorazde, these threats were anything but idle ones. Akashi's subsequent refusal to authorize NATO strikes, even when it was clear that the NATO ultimatum about Gorazde had not been met, was certainly motivated in part by his anxieties over the safety of his people. Nonetheless, this was only part of the story. For at the same time that the Serbs were holding United Nations personnel, and as the NATO ultimatum was approaching, the senior UN civilian official in Sarajevo, Sergio Vieira de Mello, and the UNPROFOR sector commander, General Andre Soubirou, personally led a small force into Gorazde, in effect providing the Serbs with more targets, more prospective hostages. It is not clear that Akashi would have authorized air strikes under any circumstances, but the presence of these additional UNPROFOR troops and officials made his choice an easy one. And yet, typically, de Mello and his colleagues spoke of what they had done as a great victory for the peace process.

There were so many examples of the Serbs' having understood the UN Protection Force better than UNPROFOR understood itself that the reporters soon began assuming that, when in doubt, the outcome would be another humiliation for the United Nations. The tone had been set early on and never changed. If UNPROFOR and the Department of Peacekeeping Operations could accept, as they did on April 9, 1993, the week after the UN had passed a resolution authorizing NATO enforcement of the No Fly zone over Bosnia, the spectacle of General Mladic flying in his command helicopter for a meeting with General Morillon, then it obviously could accept anything the Serbs cared to dish out. "At the rate they're going," a friend of mine in Sarajevo quipped at that time, "they are going to give self-abasement a bad name."

But the United Nations' attempts to cozy up to the Serbs were based on more than either UNPROFOR generals' feeling more comfortable with the spit-and-polish Bosnian Serb Army than with the Bosnians, or UN civilian officials' favoring peace at almost any price and being willing to sacrifice any principle in the name of the humanitarian aid effort, although, as time went on, the contrast between UNPROFOR's attitude toward the Bosnian government and the Bosnian Serbs became all too marked. UNHCR officials who accompanied UNPROFOR officials to meetings both at the Bosnian Presidency and at Radovan Karadzic's headquarters in Pale often commented on how much more at ease the UN commanders appeared to be in the company of the Serbs. At UNHCR, one senior UN official was routinely referred to by the nickname "Mrs. Mladic."

Even members of General Rose's own staff would suggest privately that the general considered the internationally sponsored spring 1994 partition plan unfair to the Bosnian Serbs and that, in meetings with Radovan Karadzic, he had made his reservations known. The effect of such statements on the Bosnian Serbs' willingness to accept the plan was all too predictable. How could the West be serious if the senior UN official in Bosnia seemed to have his doubts? But the UN's willingness to look at what was happening in Bosnia from Radovan Karadzic's point of view was not the result simply of the private views of certain officials. Rather, it was a function of the way UN peacekeeping historically had operated since its inception.

Throughout the conflict, UN peacekeeping officials on the ground in the former Yugoslavia as well as in New York and Geneva kept trying to deal with the Bosnian Serbs (and with the Milosevic government in Belgrade as well) as if they were serious about a negotiated settlement. In doing so, they were using a series of modalities and working on assumptions that might have been appropriate for dealing with people who wanted to stop fighting, but were wholly inappropriate for treating with the bellicose commanders of the rogue state that the Srpska Republika really was.

Unsurprisingly, the Serbs were as immune to these rather wistful invitations to act like responsible citizens of the world community as they were to threats of military action they knew to be empty. From the beginning, they had been clear about their war aims, clear about their military strategy, and, most important, alive to the fact that, whatever representatives of the great powers might say, and whatever resolutions they might pass in the Security Council, there was no will at all among Western governments to back up this talk with force. The world community, as it is meretriciously called, did not know what it wanted, and, as a result, was paralyzed. It wanted the war to stop, the genocide to end, and the conflict to be contained; but only the last of these requirements, which, in the short run at least, was as consistent with a Serb victory as with a Serb defeat, could be achieved without the lives of NATO soldiers being put at risk.

It had been clear since the Serbo-Croat war in 1991 that American, British, and French troops were not going to be sent to fight in the Balkans. Helping the humanitarian aid get through was one thing; making war was something else. As for the Serbs, the West's refusal to act while Vukovar was being destroyed and Dubrovnik shelled had shown them—in Knin, in Pale, and in Belgrade—all they needed to know. And it was not just disgruntled journalists who thought this. When David Owen was accused, at a meeting in New York in early 1993, of acting as the British and French had in trying to appease Hitler in 1938, he replied icily, "Munich was last year." And whatever else can be said about Owen's diplomacy, on this he was absolutely right. Vance and Owen had been dispatched by the United Nations and the European Union to negotiate a settlement in Bosnia knowing from the start that there would be no military pressure, or even a credible threat of it, that they could bring to bear on the Serbs, and knowing that the Serbs were perfectly aware of this. The fact that, as time wore on, Owen and Vance themselves began actively to campaign against Western military intervention (arguing, time after fruitless time, that they were near a breakthrough) does not change this.

As Owen once put it to an interviewer, "There's been an effort to blame the negotiators. Blame it on your governments. I'm an agent, a negotiator. A negotiator is always going to come down on the side of peace . . . I have to maintain that impartiality. I live within that context . . . We've never been against the greater participation of governments . . . Our job was to keep the peace and wait for governments to reengage."

The problem was that there was no peace to keep, and nothing to be negotiated. What the Serbs wanted was victory. That was what the United Nations and the European Community, Vance and Owen, and the rest could never face up to. It is an old problem besetting liberals faced by totalitarians, this inability to believe that what the murderers said to their domestic audiences reflected what they planned to do better than what they said around the conference table. If one watched Radovan Karadzic or General Mladic on Belgrade or Pale television, they talked about the creation of a Greater Serbia and about victory. If they were talking to journalists, they spoke (or at least Karadzic did, anyway; Mladic mostly threatened his enemies with destruction, warned reporters and United Nations officials to watch their step, and left it at that) of the defensive nature of the war and denied the culpability of the Serbian side. With the diplomats, the Serbs bargained, while in the field their forces went on doing what they had been doing all along.

"The Serbs know how to handle the UN," Owen once said. And the trajectory of United Nations officials in Bosnia became familiar to those who could bear to go on observing it. A UN diplomat or military commander would arrive in Zagreb or Sarajevo promising renewed effort. Often, faced by a hostile audience of journalists long resident in Bosnia, he would insist that it was wrong to blame the Serbs for everything and still more wrong to be cynical about the negotiating process. Quiet confidence was projected, and the possibility that things were at last taking a turn for the better. This was either declared flatly or hinted at on background, or off the record. Then the inevitable disenchantment would take place, that ascent up the steep learning curve of disillusion that every United Nations official has gone through before leaving Bosnia, his shining reputation in tatters.

The high flyers often did worse than the time servers. When UNPROFOR's mandate was first expanded to cover Bosnia-Herzegovina as well as Croatia, the quality of regular United Nations, as opposed to UNHCR, officials was generally agreed to be rather low. The United Nations' principal civilian official in the former Yugoslavia, an Anglo-Irish diplomat named Cedric Thornberry, was viewed by many people in the Vance-Owen team and within the UNHCR as a well-spoken time server, whose basic idea was to do as little as possible and shift the blame wherever he could. When Yasushi Akashi was appointed as UN Special Representative for the former Yugoslavia, and Sergio de Mello appointed as the UN's virtual proconsul in Sarajevo, people familiar with them were quick to assume that the Secretariat in New York was finally getting serious in Bosnia. This, one was assured by United Nations people, was the first team, and it would only be a matter of time before UNPROFOR began to get very different results.

At the same time, General Briquemont, whose résumé was free of any combat experience, and who used to alternate between boasting to journalists of his unparalleled access to General Mladic (whom he claimed to have known before the breakup of Yugoslavia) and complaining to them about the UN bureaucracy in New York and his own difficulties "under fire," as he put it, in Sarajevo, was being replaced by Sir Michael Rose, a real fighting general, a former commander of the British Special Air Service commandos, a veteran of the Falklands and of the dirty war in Ireland, who had also done a course in peacekeeping at Camberley, the British military staff college. Although one United Nations official who had dealings with Rose spoke of a "faraway look" that sometimes came into the general's eyes, which he attributed to Rose's having spent too much time "breaking into rooms and icing everyone in sight," there was no doubt that Rose was an unusually competent officer. At first, as the cease-fire and the withdrawal of Serb heavy weapons was arranged around Sarajevo, it really did appear that this new civilian and military leadership was making a difference. UNHCR convoys reached places in Bosnia they had been barred from for months. In Sarajevo, Rose started clearing the garbage, repairing the tram line, and even staging a soccer match within sight of the besieging Serbs—something that would have been unthinkable before the cease-fire.

But, as should have been apparent from the outset, there was less there than met the eye. Had United Nations officials and Western governments spent more time paying attention to Pale television, those who genuinely believed they had gained a victory over the Serbs would have learned that the mood in the Srpska Republika was anything but defeatist. The Serbs had long before given up their plan to take the entire city of Sarajevo. As Owen himself commented in the wake of the withdrawal of most (though, as it would turn out, by no means all) Serb heavy weapons from around Sarajevo, "to a certain extent, the Serbs were being asked to do something they had already accepted in principle . . . You were going with the grain."

And when one visited Pale or the Serb-controlled areas of Sarajevo proper, the talk among the Bosnian Serb leaders was no longer, as it had been even six months earlier, about retaking the rest of the city, but rather all about partition. Nikola Kolievic, the literary critic turned cabinet minister, liked to greet visiting journalists in Pale with accounts of the "New Sarajevo," the neighborhoods and suburbs of the city that the Serbs planned to make their capital after a general end to hostilities in Bosnia had been brokered. Everything from the new names the streets would carry to plans for new construction was being considered. And perhaps the United Nations should have taken as a signal the fact that the opening of the Brotherhood and Unity Bridge between Bosnian government–controlled Sarajevo and Grbavica, the Serb-controlled salient within the city proper, far from representing a step toward putting Sarajevo back together, legitimized its division. Or at least it did once the UN allowed the Serbs to put up a customs post, and with the legends, "City of New Sarajevo" and "Border Crossing" written on the sign alongside it.

When the sign first went up, United Nations officials declared indignantly that its erection had not been a part of their deal with the Serbs, and that it would have to come down. Naturally, it didn't. Owen, at least, was franker. By early 1994, he was willing to acknowledge publicly that, with every passing day, "the likelihood of a permanent partition of Sarajevo becomes greater." Such an honest appraisal was refreshing, particularly when contrasted with Akashi. But Owen had come a long way from the position he had categorically and repeatedly stated throughout the second half of 1992 and almost all of 1993, that "there would be no Srpska Republika." Now the game was up, and he knew it. Only force could have compelled the Serbs to give up any part of the area around Sarajevo, and, as Owen remarked, "The Russians are in there [now]. An attack now would be an assault on their pride."

It had been to forestall NATO air strikes that the Russians had moved troops to the Serb side of the confrontation line in the days leading up to the NATO ultimatum's expiration at the end of February 1994. "NATO was willing to use air strikes," Owen said, but when the Russians deployed, such willingness evaporated. The great powers were far more interested in Russia than they ever were in

Bosnia, and an air strike in which a Russian soldier might be killed was unthinkable. The Serbs understood this. When the Russian contingent that previously had been part of the UNPROFOR deployment in eastern Croatia arrived in Pale, they had been greeted by the Bosnian Serbs as liberators. The local people flashed the three-fingered salute of the Serb nationalists and proffered slivovitz, sausage, cheese, and bread. The Russians had saluted back in the same style, helping kids up onto their armored vehicles. Later, they would jokingly trade their UN-blue berets to their Serb opposite numbers in exchange for Bosnian Serb Army forage caps. Then they moved into positions along the front line. And with their deployment, there would henceforth be no further possibility of the Bosnian government retaking an inch of Serb-controlled Sarajevo by force, as it had attempted to do as late as December 1993.

Perhaps all of this was inevitable. As Owen once put it, "We'd be hoodwinking ourselves to imagine people can return to the Serb areas." But this assessment was not the one either the United Nations or the principal Western governments concerned with Bosnia chose to emphasize. However long it had been in coming, and in the United States in particular, perhaps because elite sentiment was so pro-Bosnian and because Clinton, when he was still a presidential candidate, had promised to lift the arms embargo against the Bosnian government, where the sense of past failure was so acute, the NATO ultimatum to the Serbs and what took place subsequently in Sarajevo was presented as a great victory. It was nothing of the sort. If anything, it confirmed what the great powers had already decided: that the only solution to the Bosnian crisis was partition, with the Serbs being allowed to keep a great deal of the territory they had conquered and cleansed. Nothing might have been done for Sarajevo at all, had the great powers not been faced by a public relations crisis that televised images of the Market Massacre on February 5, 1994, had produced, however sentimentally and irrationally, with their publics. As it was, the minimum was done.

That the basic relations of force between the UN and NATO and the Serbs remained unchanged was to be demonstrated two months later, in April 1994, when General Mladic launched an attack on the Gorazde pocket in eastern Bosnia. Gorazde was one of three enclaves of Bosnian government resistance in the Drina valley, an area that before 1992 had had a Muslim majority. The other towns in the region—Foca, Cajnice, Bijeljina, and Zvornik—had been taken early in the war and ethnic cleansing had been pursued particularly ruthlessly there. But three areas, each composed of one main town—Srebrenica, Zepa, and Gorazde—and a series of surrounding villages remained in Bosnian government hands. The three enclaves stuck like a fishbone in General Mladic's throat. His plan for a Greater Serbia stretching from Serbia proper all the way across Bosnia to the Krajina did not countenance having three Bosnian outposts full of well-trained guerrilla fighters blocking his communication lines both eastward toward Croatia and south along the Drina River to Montenegro and the Adriatic.

Mladic had dealt with Srebrenica in early 1993. He deployed a large number of troops and artillery around the enclave and slowly began to push inward. As always, Mladic combined the standard Yugoslav National Army (and Warsaw Pact) military doctrine—which can be summarized as never sending a man where a bullet can go first—with the Bosnian Serb predilection for targeting hospitals, water treatment plants, and refugee centers in order to produce the maximum amount of terror in the population. Village after village fell, until Mladic's troops were on the outskirts of Srebrenica itself. On one particular day, sixty civilians in the town, including a great many children, were killed by Bosnian Serb Army shellfire. It was then that the Security Council had passed the Safe Havens resolution. Its only effect, despite a brief foray into Srebrenica by the then commander of UNPROFOR in Bosnia, General Philippe Morillon, who promised the people there, "I will never leave you," but, a week later, returned to Sarajevo, was that the town center remained, an economic cripple, in Bosnian hands.

Gorazde was a reprise of Srebrenica, this time with the distinguished diplomat Akashi and the tough soldier Rose neither able to do a thing to stop the Serbs or to accurately evaluate their intentions. "I have been lied to," General Rose declared indignantly at a certain point, as if such a tactic on the part of Karadzic and Mladic had theretofore been wholly unheard of. And Rose added, "I will never trust the Serbs again." Akashi looked equally poleaxed, as did even the Russian negotiator, Deputy Foreign Minister Vitaly Churkin, who until that moment had been defending almost everything the

Serbs did. As the bombardment of Gorazde continued, UNPROFOR called in two ineffective air strikes, and then quickly backed off. Then NATO proclaimed an exclusion zone, and, at the eleventh hour, the Serbs withdrew most of their heavy weapons. Akashi and Rose proclaimed that the crisis was over.

UNPROFOR then engaged in rewriting what had happened in Gorazde. According to them, the siege hadn't been that bad. When they were resisting pressure from the UNHCR to do something about Gorazde, members of Rose's headquarters had let it be known that they considered the UNHCR staffers to be unreliable and the reports of the Canadian head of the UN military observer team in Gorazde, Major Pat Stogran, equally worthless because, as more than one of Rose's aides told the journalists on background, it appeared the major had broken under the strain. Even after the shelling of Gorazde stopped, Rose and his staff continued to insist that the whole crisis had been exaggerated. Reporting after his first flying visit to Gorazde, General Rose gave a press conference during which he insisted that both the damage to the town and the casualty figures were vastly exaggerated. "We are evacuating wounded fighters who are hopping off our helicopters," he said angrily. In fact, his outrage was due to the fact that he believed the Bosnian government troops had set up one of the British Special Air Service soldiers serving as forward air controllers by inviting him up to one of their positions, firing on the Serbs, and letting the British officer be killed by counterfire. In any case, Rose was said to privately believe that the market massacre in Sarajevo had actually been a case of the Bosnians mortaring themselves. His aides would tell visiting journalists as much, off the record, of course. But the International Committee of the Red Cross and the UNHCR, which had had international staff in Gorazde both during and after the shelling, flatly denied Rose's account. "We are facing a humanitarian catastrophe here," said the UNHCR's Peter Kessler, who had spent a year in the former Yugoslavia for every month Rose had spent there.

In the meantime, the Bosnian Serbs demonstrated that as far as they were concerned, all the NATO ultimatum required them to do was to stop shelling Gorazde and to withdraw most of their heavy weapons. Only a few days after they had supposedly withdrawn both all their men and all their matériel, as they were required to do, the Bosnian Serbs began once more to move troops closer to the town center. Then they sent in a group of Bosnian Serb refugees, escorted by Bosnian Serb Army soldiers wearing blue policemen's uniforms. "We will never give up the Serbian part of Gorazde," Karadzic insisted, in an eerie reprise of his statements about Sarajevo itself. At first the United Nations denied reports of there being soldiers and settlers in the town. "We're not going to go to war because the Serbs have left a rusty tank lying around," General Rose said. Then UNPROFOR admitted that "a few" Serbs might still be within the exclusion zone. Finally, when reports from UNHCR personnel could not be denied any longer, General Rose admitted that there were "problems" in Gorazde. The reality, of course, was that not only was UNPROFOR impotent, but when all was said and done, Akashi and Rose preferred that to actually having to fight. The Serbs could do what they liked as far as UNPROFOR was concerned. They wouldn't try to intervene. They wouldn't even blow the whistle unless they were absolutely forced to.

One of the first things United Nations officials liked to tell visitors was that everyone in the former Yugoslavia lied. Perhaps they were right. But to those who witnessed the murder of Bosnia, it often seemed as if it was the UN officials themselves who were the greatest liars of all. By providing the humanitarian fig leaf for what was really taking place in Bosnia, and pretending that their interests were not the parochial ones of a moral and intellectually bankrupt organization that had been forced by the Security Council to take on a task it was quite incapable of coping with honorably, UNPROFOR and the Department of Peacekeeping Operations became accomplices to genocide. They were, as they said, only following their mandate. That had a nice ring to it. Could they hear the echoes of a similar sentence, uttered half a century earlier, in which the only change was that the word "orders" had been substituted for the word "mandate"? But perhaps the United Nations officials were right; perhaps all sides to the conflict did lie. What was obscene about the lies the UN told—to itself as much as to the world at large—was that they thought well of themselves as they uttered them. They thought they were the humanitarians. They thought they were the peacemakers.

IX

The honor of the world was redeemed in Bosnia by those who worked for the NGOs, the nongovernmental aid organizations, the International Committee of the Red Cross, and the Office of United Nations High Commissioner for Refugees. They worked there without any hidden agendas, and steadfastly refused to accept the idea that the interests of the great powers from which they derived so much of their funding compelled them to carry out the political agendas of those powers. If they tried to behave impartially, the NGOs did not do so in UNPROFOR's spirit of pretending that between murderers and their victims it was possible, desirable even, to maintain "balance" and, whenever possible, foster cordial relations. Rony Braumann, the cofounder of the French nongovernmental organization MSF (Médecins Sans Frontières, Doctors Without Borders), did not boast of having developed a good personal relationship with Radovan Karadzic. Nor, for that matter, did Bernard Kouchner, the former French Minister for Humanitarian Affairs under François Mitterrand, with whom, though they had originally founded MSF together, Braumann was rarely in agreement.

For them, and for most of the people in the other important NGOs working in Bosnia, at the heart of things lay the obligation to help and to be fair, not to pretend to an impartiality that had its basis only in realpolitik and the imagination of bureaucrats. At the very least, it can be said that by sticking to these principles (and even, in Kouchner's case, agitating for military intervention on humanitarian grounds and in order to stop ethnic cleansing) the NGOs did not accomplish *less* than they would have done had they chosen the UN's road in the former Yugoslavia. And, no matter how often their approach brought them into conflict with UNPROFOR and the UN Secretariat, these groups emerged from the crucible of Bosnia without having become unwitting accomplices to the genocide.

UN Protection Force officials, many of whom personally had great respect for what the nongovernmental organizations had accomplished in Croatia and Bosnia, usually attributed their differing approaches to the demands of their respective mandates. "NGO officials are free to say certain things that we cannot say," a Civil Affairs officer in Zagreb told me. "And we're happy to cooperate with them wherever we can, not because of the good work most of them do, but because someone here does need to say these things. But if UNPROFOR said them, our mission here would be over; and quite quickly, I would imagine. It's all very well to talk about being more confrontational. But imagine that was the line we took, and the result was that we got expelled for our pains. Would that really improve things in Bosnia? The truth is that you journalists would be the first to scream for us to return.

"We have not been weak in the implementation of our mandate," he continued, "although I am perfectly well aware of the difference between a mandate and a solution. You journalists keep asking us to show more spine. So do many of the NGOs. But we're at the threshold of acceptable risk already, and fighting your way through while providing humanitarian assistance is and always will be the wrong approach. They are mutually exclusive." He paused. "Look," he said, "whatever you may imagine, some of us have the strongest moral doubts about what we are doing here, or whether we should in fact remain at all. But please don't put the onus on the UN. Don't go on, as most of the journalists do, I'm afraid, blaming us exclusively. We are an organization committed to peace. That is our role, as the NGOs have theirs, and you in the press yours."

His words were representative of a certain strain of United Nations thinking, one which was deeply resentful and also somewhat taken aback by the press's harshly critical attitude toward the UN Protection Force operation. As a senior UN official put it in an anonymous letter to *Foreign Affairs* magazine, the press's determination to provoke intervention on behalf of the Bosnian government had "induced in some a personal commitment—indeed, crusade— that lay uneasily with the maintenance of true professional standards." Whether an official of the UN, an organization that had traditionally had all the transparency and openness to press inquiry of the Vatican or the old Red Army, really was qualified to pontificate about what the duties and derelictions of a free press were was debatable. More interesting was the writer's assumption that the United Nations had played no role in what he called a "forcible dismemberment of a plural society into mono-ethnic statelets"—an act, he conceded toward the end of his letter, that was indeed "inimical to accepted democratic values."

But what the press was so angry about was not the UN's failure to support democratic values, but its failure to oppose genocide. The representatives of UNPROFOR and the Secretariat understood this perfectly well, but they were rarely willing to say so openly. An exception, curiously enough, was Cedric Thornberry, who had been the head of UNPROFOR Civil Affairs in 1992 and 1993 for the former Yugoslavia. In a speech he delivered in Stockholm he said, "We have been accused, essentially, of a lack of commitment in the face of a new kind of holocaust . . . If the UN is on the spot when some horror occurs, we tend to be blamed." At least Thornberry, though he insisted that the mission had been a success in its own terms, conceded that it was culpable in at least one important sense. "The media," he said, "seeing us as symbols of the international community, blame the peoples and governments of the world for what they see as their failure to come more intimately to grips with a situation that has both traumatized and astonished Europe at the end of the twentieth century."

This was right as far as it went. The UN *was* providing the world community with a fig leaf both for the inability of some states, like the United States, to muster the will to act, and for the failure of others, like Britain and France, to come clean to their own publics about their decision to allow the murder of Bosnia to proceed. But what was puzzling about the attitude of people within UNPROFOR and the Secretariat was their ability to believe that, having offered themselves up as a fig leaf for the great powers, they could remain morally uncompromised by what they had done. In the same speech, Thornberry delivered the usual UN line that "whoever may have been the original perpetrators, today there are no innocent parties in Sarajevo or Bosnia." What needed to be kept in mind, he said, was that "atrocity debases all who are affected."

But it did not seem to trouble the senior staff of UNPROFOR or the Department of Peacekeeping Operations that this point about the outrages committed by the Bosnian side (or, as General Morillon, revealingly, had so liked to say, the "Muslim side"), which they made with such insistence, also could be applied to themselves. It was not simply, as many of them seemed to imagine, that the press was using them unfairly as a whipping boy for crimes that should be laid at the doors of the great powers, or was just too blindly interventionist to recognize UNPROFOR's accomplishments. What continued to shock and anger many in the press was the UN's lack of ability to see how morally wrong it was to choose always to mediate between killers and rapists and those who were suffering at their hands, not only at first but long after it had become clear for all to see that the murderers and rapists planned to go on murdering and raping no matter what promises they might make. Just as Cedric Thornberry thought, and, in fairness, not wrongly, that many on the Bosnian side had been debased by the fighting, so many of us who covered the slaughter soon concluded that the United Nations had become debased by what its mandate was requiring it to do and not do.

It was, I think, because many of the people in the press corps had arrived in the Balkans with more respect for the United Nations as an institution and as an ideal than the institution seemed to have for itself, that our anger and indignation over how it was conducting its operations grew so intense. This indeed may have been a case, as one senior United Nations official put it to me, of distance lending enchantment. But whether UN officials liked it or not, they represented an institution that many of us had imagined to be more than an instrument of the Security Council's will or the sum of its institutional practices and bureaucratic norms. The United Nations might not yet be the world government, but it was supposed to act, at least in so extreme a situation as a genocide, in the name of humanity as well as in the name of protecting the strategic interests of member states. If UNPROFOR and the Department of Peacekeeping Operations were choosing to interpret their mandate so narrowly, surely that had to do as much with Boutros Boutros-Ghali's abdication of his obligation to defend the moral principles that the United Nations was supposed to stand for as it did with what the five permanent members were and were not willing to authorize UNPROFOR to do.

The anger with the United Nations that this moral dereliction provoked in at least a good many of the journalists—far from coming naturally to them, as UN officials so often imagined—was actually a quite uncomfortable position to be in professionally. In my case, I know that I arrived in Bosnia having always resisted appeals to become indignant about one cause or another. Indignation, I believed, was inimical to understanding—to use a word very much favored by UN officials in New York—since in the end it was informed by a sentimental and reductive reading of events. I don't know what I think now. Of course, there is a sense in which all history, not just Balkan history, is a history of slaughter. But in Bosnia the killing need not have gone on and on. The great powers could have ended it. And the senior members of the UN Secretariat, notably the Secretary General himself, could have campaigned for them to end it instead of doing all they could to facilitate nonintervention.

The journalists with whom I traveled in Bosnia were by and large even more skeptical than I was. For most, this was not their first exposure to the horrors of intercommunal war. And yet almost to a man and woman, they soon became and remained outraged by what they witnessed in Bosnia, and by the UN's role in it. If they had "gone native," as UN officials and some of their colleagues back home liked to sneer, they were unrepentant. As John Sweeney, the correspondent for the London *Observer,* recalled, "For many journalists the defining moment of the war was when a UN spokesman told a Sarajevo press conference that a cease-fire had been agreed and he wanted to thank the Serbs for their cooperation. The next moment everyone was knocked to the floor by incoming Serb artillery rounds."

Such an episode was worse than defining, it was commonplace. There were times when it seemed as if the slogan "UNPROFOR: Working for Peace" should have read, "UNPROFOR: Working for Bosnian Surrender." After all, in Bosnia wasn't a surrender on the part of the government the surest road to peace? The United Nations thought so, however much it might dress up the belief in the pious language of humanitarianism. And the spectacle of what certainly seemed like a systematic attempt on the part of UNPROFOR and the UN Special Representative to minimize the Serbs' crimes (either by covering up the full extent of what the Serbs were doing, or by taking pains to point out that all sides were behaving criminally) was not made any more edifying by the implicit justification that it was all being done in the name of furthering the chances of peace and at the behest of the great powers. The UN kept saying that the situation was not of their making. As if that were a justification. Or as if great crimes have only ever had *witting* accomplices.

Occasionally, a United Nations official would admit, off the record of course, to feeling a certain measure of discomfort over the role UNPROFOR was being "forced" to play in Bosnia. But then, he or she would usually add, the United Nations could not do what the press did; it could not do what the nongovernmental organizations did. That sounded convincing until one remembered that in fact there was another UN organization in Bosnia which had demonstrated that there were other ways of interpreting a mandate. The UN High Commissioner for Refugees operated on a different moral plane from UNPROFOR and the Office of the UN Special Representative. With a few exceptions, its officials refused to accept the idea that there were a few things they could do while everything else was off limits. The UNHCR did not refuge behind legalistic references to its mandate. Nor did it claim, as Department of Peacekeeping Operations and UNPROFOR officials did, that because it had never faced a situation like Bosnia before, its failures there were the fault of the international community.

To the contrary, UNHCR staffers, international and local alike, fought and improvised, and, in an impossible situation for which there were no precedents, time and again pulled off what seemed like miracles. According to established UN rules, most of the places in which the UNHCR operated *routinely* in Bosnia were too dangerous to consider operating in. And yet the UNHCR stayed anyway. With or without military escorts, their convoy drivers pushed the aid through, past the feral thugs at the checkpoints, and often under fire. Unlike vehicles issued the UN Protection Force, most UNHCR vehicles were not armored. And examples of the personal courage of the international staff were so numerous that even the people at UNHCR began themselves to take them for granted. If a Marc Vachon, the young French-Canadian logistics officer at the Sarajevo airport in the fall of 1992 and the winter of 1993, drove a soft-skinned fuel truck across the siege lines at a time when UN Protection Force personnel almost never ventured out except in armored vehicles, that was normal. All he would say was, "This war sure fucks up your adrenaline." And if UNHCR protection officers, as they were called, like Pierre Ollier and Philippos Papaphilippou in Banja Luka would drive alone and unarmed into Priejdor to demand that the Mayor there do something to stop the ethnic cleansing—a journey that nearly got them killed countless times—then that, too, was just something that was part of their job. "If they wanted to sell shoes," the chief of the UNHCR for the former Yugoslavia, Jose Maria Mendiluce, once insisted, his affectionate tone belying his words, "then they should have stayed in Rio, New York, or Paris." That was what Mendiluce's staff thought too.

There was nothing in the UNHCR's past history that particularly suggested that it would conduct itself in the former Yugoslavia in the extraordinary way that it did. The UNHCR was established in 1951, and was the successor to the League of Nations' High Commission for Refugees and the UN's fledgling International Refugee Organization, the IRO. Its "mandate" was to offer international protection to refugees and people who either had been displaced within their own country or had fled across a national border. Beyond protecting the refugees wherever they were, the UNHCR concerned itself with resettling them, and, whenever possible, repatriating them after the crisis that had caused them to flee in the first place had abated. Each year, the UNHCR's task grew more difficult as the number of refugees swelled and the willingness of third countries to accept them diminished. In 1970, there were estimated to be about two and a half million refugees in the world. In 1980, the figure was eleven million. In 1993, it was almost nineteen million.

These numbers only included those who had crossed a political border in response to a clear political threat. The figure for the so-called "internally displaced"—people whom the UNHCR deemed to have the same needs for protection and assistance as refugees, but who had little hope of reaching another country where they might seek asylum—was twenty-four million. And none of this counted the estimated hundred million people who were on the move in search of some decent future for themselves and their families and who were classed as "economic migrants." As the High Commissioner for Refugees, Sadako Ogata, noted in her 1993 report, "In a world where persecution, massive human rights violations and armed conflict remain a daily reality, the need to protect refugees is greater than ever before." But, she added, "the current scale and nature of the refugee problem and limits to the absorption capacity of asylum countries mean that traditional methods of protection are no longer sufficient. They must be complemented by flexible approaches that respond to the present period of transition and upheaval in world affairs."

Although Ogata does not spell it out in her report, it was above all the UNHCR's experience in the former Yugoslavia that had brought it to recognize just how inadequate its old methods as spelled out in the UNHCR's field operations manual, its so-called Blue Book, had become. In private, Ogata was heard to remark occasionally that she was not really the High Commissioner for Refugees but the UNHCR desk officer for the former Yugoslavia. Her disquiet was understandable. By 1993, the UNHCR operation in the Balkans was taking up close to half its annual budget and using a huge number of its trained international staff. People were being brought in from refugee camps in East Asia, resettlement efforts in Malawi, and work with asylum seekers in Western Europe to work in Bosnia, Croatia, and Serbia. The joke in the UNHCR headquarters in Geneva was that people returning from Yugoslavia were almost as likely to be attacked by colleagues from other areas incensed at the way this one operation was eating up the organization's resources as they were to get shot at in Bosnia. The UNHCR had been stretched too thin before the Yugoslav crisis had started. And, as another refugee crisis along Rwanda's borders with Tanzania and Zaire in the spring and summer of 1994 was to prove—in this case, one that *in one day* involved the flight of two hundred and fifty thousand people, and in a few weeks, several million, the largest number ever to flee in so short a period—it was not as if the UNHCR could concentrate all its attention and its best people on the Balkans.

In a way, however, the UNHCR's assignment in the former Yugoslavia was a reward the organization's leaders might have been grateful to do without, for their success in the best-publicized of the UNHCR's recent operations, the relief effort in Kurdistan in the wake of the Gulf War. Just as the Security Council had turned to UN peacekeeping in both Somalia and Bosnia at least in part because of a generalized post–Cold War overestimation of what peacekeeping actually could do, the UN Secretariat chose the UNHCR to be the lead agency in the former Yugoslavia because of what it had been able to do in Kurdistan. The UNHCR's brief in the Balkans was both all-encompassing and ill-defined. And until the appointment of Yasushi Akashi as the Secretary General's Special Representative, it was Sadako Ogata's Special Representative in Zagreb who was the most senior United Nations official in the region—even though they didn't always see it that way at UNPROFOR headquarters across town.

That such a decision would have been taken at all—that is, that a humanitarian agency experienced in dealing with the needs of refugees would have been given the task of spearheading the UN's response to the first war in Europe in half a century—was an early demonstration of the UN's reluctance to face up to what was really occurring in Bosnia. This was principally a war, a genocide, not principally a humanitarian disaster. And yet, as one nongovernmental organization official put it, "for a long time the world talked and talked. But the reality was that for all practical purposes the only international institution doing anything on the ground to implement all the fine sentiments was the UNHCR. They did the best they could, but it's a tragedy that they were all the world could muster. The way to stop a genocide is not to set up a field hospital for those lucky enough to escape it."

For all their skill and dedication in dealing with the effects of war, most of the UNHCR officials who were sent to Bosnia knew little about war itself. This was not just simply because so many of them had spent their professional lives filing asylum claims for refugees in Europe or running refugee camps in Africa and East Asia. No one at the UNHCR had any experience in providing aid during a war. And yet that was precisely what they had been mustered to do—first in Croatia, and then in Bosnia. As Fred Cuny, who personally probably came to Bosnia with more experience in providing humanitarian aid in wartime than the entire senior staff of the UNHCR combined, said, "The UN agencies all lacked both the operational doctrine and the operational experience that would have allowed them to come up with an overall plan in Bosnia. There was never an overall plan in

Geneva and New York, a concept of what they wanted to accomplish. As a result, an agency like UNHCR reacted to events rather than trying to shape them."

It was not long after they began to work in the former Yugoslavia that the senior UNHCR officials concerned realized that although both Kurdistan and Bosnia could be lumped together as "second-generation" humanitarian efforts, the two operations actually had very little in common. The UNHCR had been deployed in Kurdistan at the end of the Gulf War, after almost half a million ethnic Kurds had fled Saddam Hussein's army. The United Nations had declared a military exclusion zone north of the 38th parallel, and had pledged to enforce it militarily. An initially reluctant UNHCR was given the task of coping with the Kurds within the zone. At first, despite the fact that Kurds were dying by the hundreds along the hillsides, the UNHCR officer in charge in Kurdistan, an Australian named Nicholas Morris, was said to contend that aiding displaced people in a war zone was not part of the UNHCR's mandate. But under intense American pressure, the UNHCR undertook the job of providing humanitarian relief, and to the surprise of many, not least within the organization itself, that effort was largely a success.

This experience of being able to provide aid in the midst of a war had seemed to suggest that a similar operation could be mounted in Bosnia. Making the UNHCR the lead agency was, in any case, almost the only route open to the UN Secretariat and to the five permanent members of the Security Council, once it was clear that the Security Council was not going to authorize a military intervention as it had in Iraq. It was felt, or, at least, hoped, that the experience of Kurdistan would enable the UNHCR to mount the major humanitarian effort needed in the former Yugoslavia. Above all, the great powers had to appear to be doing something. If, objectively, all that meant was trying to palliate the consequences of a slaughter they were unable to muster the political will to stop, that did not appear to trouble the leaders of the NATO countries. Within the Secretariat, the view was more sober. The choice of the UNHCR was made less because the United Nations people thought there was a great chance of its succeeding than because they felt it was the only organization that stood even a small chance of succeeding.

In reality, the UNHCR was even less well prepared for the assignment than anyone imagined. When Jose Maria Mendiluce, the Basque diplomat who had served for years in Central America and had then gone on to be the number two UNHCR official in Kurdistan before coming to the former Yugoslavia, realized what was actually going on in Bosnia when he arrived as High Commissioner Ogata's Special Representative, he understood immediately that the lessons the UNHCR had learned in the Middle East were not going to work in the Balkans. "Whatever else we do," he told his staff with that odd mix of gaiety and gloom that often seemed to animate him, "we are going to have to throw away the Blue Book." It was a phrase his aides said Mendiluce liked to repeat to most newly arriving UNHCR field officers almost as soon as he met them. Not only did people have to get Geneva out of their minds, Mendiluce insisted, they had to get Kurdistan out of them as well. In the former Yugoslavia, they would be inventing things as they went along. And it would not be easy. "Kurdistan was difficult," Mendiluce liked to say, "terribly difficult. But Kurdistan was a tea party compared to what we are facing here."

Mendiluce's first exposure to the realities of ethnic cleansing came by accident. In the early spring of 1992, he was driving back to his office in Sarajevo (like UNPROFOR, the UNHCR ran its operations during the Serbo-Croat war from the supposedly neutral Bosnian capital) after a meeting in Belgrade. By coincidence, he arrived in the town of Zvornik, on the Bosnian side of the Drina River, just at the moment when it was overrun by a Serb irregular unit known as the White Eagles. "I saw kids put under the treads of tanks, placed there by grown men, and then run over by other grown men," he recalled with a shudder. "Everywhere, people were shooting. The fighters were moving through the town, systematically killing all the Muslims they could get their hands on. It was an intoxication, sure. The Serb media had been full of reports of Muslims expelling the Serbs from Zvornik, and of the atrocities that had been committed there. And although this may have been true occasionally, usually these Serbs were pushed to do so by local leaders.

"In any case, the Serbs doing the killing in Zvornik that day did not come from Zvornik. This crisis did not begin as a war between Serbs and Muslims but as a war between fanatical nationalists. These people had a coherent strategy. The whole point was to inflict as much terror on the civilian population as possible, to destroy as much property as possible, and to target as much of the violence as possible against women and kids. After the irregulars had done their work, then the established authorities—the Yugoslav National Army, or Karadzic's forces, or the local police—would come in, ostensibly to restore order. But, of course, that would mean that the ethnic cleansing of that particular place had been successful, and the White Eagles could move on."

That day in Zvornik, Mendiluce said, he rounded up as many of the surviving Muslims as he could, declaring to the local Serb commanders that he was placing the townspeople under UNHCR protection. But what in retrospect seemed like foolhardy heroism had its price. For although Mendiluce did the miraculous and saved hundreds of lives by evacuating the Muslims from the town and arranging for their transport to Tuzla, he had, acting with the best motives, guaranteed that Zvornik would thenceforth be a Serb town—which had been the political purpose of the White Eagles' assault in the first place. Mendiluce himself all but conceded the point. "We have no mechanisms to deal with ethnic cleansing," he told me. "We can treat the symptoms of the disease, whether by improving security conditions in those areas where ethnic cleansing has not yet taken place, or by doing our best to alert the international community to the depth of the crisis, or by trying to arrange food distribution through relief convoys and aerial resupply to besieged areas. But it's not as if we can compel the parties to stop the war, or militarily intervene to prevent the ethnic cleansing from continuing.

"It's an impossible situation," he went on. "People from the beginning have liked to simplify the problem with words. They speak of the Lebanization of the Balkans today, just as a few years ago they spoke of the Balkanization of Lebanon. But the reality is that at the moment, no side is defeated, including the Bosnians, no goodwill exists, no stalemate has been achieved, and despite all the efforts of Vance and Owen, no real international pressure exists." Mendiluce said all this in the fall of 1992, when he was still comparatively optimistic. When he left, a little over a year later, heartbroken over what had happened and his health all but ruined, the situation was far worse. But the basic analysis he had brought to bear in that moment was as applicable in 1994 as it had been in 1992. One had to substitute Gorazde for Zvornik, and add NATO to the equation, but otherwise not all that much had changed.

"Sometimes," Mendiluce had said, "living in this country reminds me of Macondo, you know, in Garcia Marquez's *One Hundred Years of Solitude.* It wasn't easy in Kurdistan or Central America; it wasn't a piece of cake by any means. But there are times when all I dream of is being sent to a tropical place where things are clear-cut, a place where there are refugees, sender and receiver countries, and no other complications. Those crises are hard enough to solve. But to try to create safe zones and protected areas in the middle of a war, when the front is constantly shifting, and refugees are not the byproduct of a war, as they were in El Salvador, but rather the aim of that action in the first place—how is the UNHCR to do that? People offer us more soldiers. I never asked for a single one. At the same time, I have fifty trucks to resupply hundreds of thousands of people. Even running them around the clock, how am I supposed to do that? We have provided as many miracles as possible, but we're running out of them now, and winter is on the way, a winter when every problem we have, from keeping the trucks on the road to feeding and clothing the refugees, will be all that much harder to solve."

The UNHCR did make it through that first winter of the Bosnian slaughter, and the second winter as well. They were mild, which was lucky, and Mendiluce and his successor, who ironically turned out to be Nicholas Morris, the former UNHCR chief in Kurdistan, did have a few more miracles left up their sleeves. Refugees were housed, and a fortunate minority were even resettled abroad. More and better equipment was sent, particularly by the Nordic countries and by the British Overseas Development Administration. The air bridge to Sarajevo, which Mendiluce and his brilliant young Anglo-Chilean assistant, Fabrizio Hochchild, had run when it was a matter of unloading pallets of food by hand and often under fire, began to work more efficiently than anyone could have dreamed possible. By the end of 1993, it was clear that in most places in Bosnia the humanitarian catastrophe had been avoided. What was still killing people was not, as so many had predicted, hunger and disease, but bullets and shrapnel. Judged according to narrow humanitarian criteria, the aid effort the international community had mounted could thus be deemed a success. The problem was that it wasn't only the Bosnians who thought it had been a failure. It was many of the best people within the UNHCR as well. And it was their ability to discern this that also put the UNHCR people at such odds, morally speaking, with their UN Protection Force colleagues.

Most people who met Jose Maria Mendiluce became admirers; more often than not, on the spot. I certainly did. But there was an eloquent minority who were deeply critical of what he did in Bosnia. While Mendiluce talked a good game, they insisted, in fact he was as much a servant of UN rules as any other senior official. A correspondent I knew in Sarajevo once remarked, "Yes, he's a great guy. But I would respect him more if instead of telling gossipy tales about General Morillon or pursuing his vendetta with UN Civil Affairs, he actually stood up to the Department of Peacekeeping Operations and UNPROFOR. Mendiluce's always *about* to leave the reservation. He's always basically saying, after the latest UNPROFOR screwup, 'This is the *next* to last straw.' I know that UNHCR is in an impossible situation, and God knows they're the UN's conscience here in Bosnia. But as long as the best UN people refuse to protest what the organization is doing; as long as the idea of actually resigning over a matter of policy is unimaginable; then this fiasco is just going to go on and on."

He continued. "At the UN, maybe because they are so used to being walked all over by us, the Brits, the Russians, they've become cultists of the small victory. The UNPROFOR people say, 'Well, ethnic cleansing is still going on, but the Sarajevo airport is usually open. What should we do, leave? People are alive because of our efforts.' Mendiluce knows better than to think that answer is good enough. He knows that half the time when UNPROFOR boasted that thanks to its efforts mass expulsions have stopped in some area, it's because there are no Muslims left for the Serbs to expel. And the biggest thing he knows is what a catastrophe this operation has been, for the United Nations as much as for Bosnia. He knows it as the European intellectual that he really is under that UN-blue flak jacket of his. But he has taken refuge in his little victories, in getting a convoy in here or working out a deal there to evacuate a few people from an old folks' home on the front line. He doesn't even want to think

about how few convoys have gotten in, or how little he has been able
to do to stop ethnic cleansing. And maybe he's right. The UNHCR
people who have really understood that have burned out pretty completely. I don't blame them either. Imagine knowing what they
know!"

He might have added that even on an operational level, the
UNHCR's "little victories" had cost it. One of the criticisms most
frequently leveled against Mendiluce and his senior staff was that
unless they went personally to the checkpoints to see a particular
convoy through, it might never make it. Almost invariably, the negotiating would take several days. In the meantime, while a
Mendiluce or a Manoel de Almeida, the head of the UNHCR's External Relations Unit, was on a bridge somewhere trying to get the
Bosnian Serbs to let a convoy in, a dozen other convoys were being
blocked under the system—or nonsystem—Mendiluce had set up.
Meanwhile, while he was away from his Zagreb headquarters, the
UNHCR's program and resettlement officers, whose work was at
least as important to the UNHCR's efforts as the convoys, were basically on their own. And, as more seasoned aid workers like Fred
Cuny often pointed out, many of them were simply too inexperienced to work in so unsupervised a setting.

Even Mendiluce's most fervent admirers conceded that he was a
poor administrator. But the problem went deeper than that. In the
end, the UNHCR was being called upon to do too many jobs at once.
Mendiluce was being asked and felt obliged to play the role both of
the international diplomat and of the UNHCR official. A lesser man
would have given up, since the task was fundamentally an impossible one. But to Mendiluce's credit, he could not muster the cold-
blooded resolve of his UN Protection Force and Department of
Peacekeeping Operations colleagues not to overstep the bounds of
his mission. And he certainly had no obsessive interest in preserving
the UNHCR's "impartiality" in the face of genocide. Even if the mission was hopeless, and the mandate and resources a bad joke, even if
all that might be accomplished in any given moment was getting one
busload of refugees out of the Bosanska Krajina or getting one convoy into a town in central Bosnia where people were hungry,
Mendiluce went on trying.

I believe that he left the former Yugoslavia, though, knowing that he had failed. Some months later, he intimated as much in an article he wrote for the Madrid daily *El País* on the situation in Bosnia. Its last sentence read, "Yes to intervention." But by then, of course, it was too late for that. What was being considered were the terms of the partition of Bosnia, not how to save it. As for the UNHCR itself, though it remained nominally the lead agency in the former Yugoslavia, its agenda for some time had been effectively subordinated to the wishes of UNPROFOR. Mendiluce was probably not surprised. Much earlier, he had told me that he could feel Europe "sinking back into the mediocrity of its nationalisms." And he added, "We who believed in something better are appalled. There is the GATT fight, this fight, that fight. They much prefer to think about anything but Bosnia." And Mendiluce accepted that he too was to blame. "We were unprepared," he told me, "to think of Bosnians as people who might have something to teach us. Instead, we insisted on treating them as victims, as recipient populations."

Mendiluce had opposed the militarization of the humanitarian effort from the start. To the horror of his aides, he loved to contrast the heroism of his civilian drivers with the rule-bound pigheadedness and caution of the soldiers. Before Mendiluce left the former Yugoslavia, though, the need for a further militarization of the aid effort had become an article of faith with the United Nations. I never understood quite why, since if UN peacekeepers were not being allowed to shoot their way through checkpoints to get the aid through, it was a debatable point whether their accompanying the convoys did all that much good in the first place. Plenty of unescorted convoys, including those run by the Jewish community of Sarajevo and by Adra, the Seventh Day Adventists' humanitarian organization, got through, even during the worst periods of fighting.

The likeliest explanation was that the United Nations wanted to remain in control, and to save itself and the member states in whose name it kept asserting that it was acting the embarrassment of the kind of revelations about what was really going on in Bosnia that the UNHCR tended to go in for. The habit the UNHCR public information people had of speaking their minds could not have been welcome. UN Protection Force did not want to see statements like the one made by Louis Gentile, the head of the UNHCR's Banja Luka office in late 1993 and early 1994, in which he said that what the world had allowed to happen in Bosnia "could never be forgiven," or Larry Hollingworth's jeremiad against the Serbs shelling Srebrenica, for whom, he said, "the hottest place in hell" stood reserved. In the name of the negotiating process, UNPROFOR wanted to minimize the conflicts between the United Nations and the Serbs, not see them inflamed by UNHCR officials who didn't understand that some truths just had to be kept under wraps.

But from the beginning, Mendiluce encouraged his staffers to reveal the horrors they witnessed, whatever the political consequences. Whether they were detailing the siege of Gorazde or the continuing ethnic cleansing in Banja Luka, UNHCR officials could be relied upon to tell the truth. Perhaps that was all they could do for Bosnia. It was not as if Louis Gentile could stop the ethnic cleansing of the Bosanska Krajina, or, during the siege of Gorazde, the Irish UNHCR doctor Mary McGloughlin could do much for the wounded. But telling the truth is no negligible accomplishment, and to its eternal credit, the UNHCR staffers told the truth unswervingly. Of course, then the UN Protection Force public information people, and sometimes its senior officials, would weigh in with assertions that the UNHCR reports were exaggerated, that actually the damage (or the death toll, or the number of displaced people, or the degree of want) was much less than had been first reported. Since the victims in such cases were almost always the Bosnians, the UNPROFOR people often would hint broadly, in quite the eerie echo of the propaganda coming out of Pale and Belgrade, that the Bosnians had manufactured these reports in order to con the West into intervening militarily.

After General Michael Rose visited Gorazde in the wake of the establishment of the NATO exclusion zone in May 1994, he came back to Sarajevo and announced that all the talk about the hospital having been repeatedly shelled had turned out to be false, and that most of the wounded were young men of military age (the implication being that the Serbs had been shelling legitimate military targets, not committing war crimes against civilians). Asked why the UNHCR and doctors from the French nongovernmental organization Médecins Sans Frontières who had been in Gorazde during the Serb offensive had made many of the same accusations and offered many of the same casualty estimates as the Bosnians whom Rose was dismissing so categorically, the general said that he didn't know, but that perhaps since they had spent so much of their time in underground shelters, they had taken too much of what they thought they knew from Bosnian reports. Stonily, the UNHCR's public information officer for Bosnia, Peter Kessler, simply repeated that he stood by his estimates. Even when Dr. McGloughlin confirmed the Bosnian version of events, UN Protection Force officials once again began to confide to journalists that, like the Canadian United Nations military observer, she too must have been overwhelmed by her experience and was not a reliable witness.

Such are the responsibilities of United Nations peacekeeping. To those of us who had seen UNPROFOR make excuses for the Serbs so often in the past, there was nothing particularly surprising about General Rose's words. At least he admitted that some civilians had been killed in Gorazde. For a man who was assumed to believe that the Bosnians, not the Serbs, were responsible for the massacre in the Central Market in Sarajevo, it could even be called a step in the right direction. General Mackenzie, after all, had spent a full year denying that the breadline massacre in August 1992 could be attributed with any certainty to the Serbs. And General Briquemont had opposed making Gorazde a Safe Area, because, he claimed, "the Muslims" would only use it as a base for raiding the Serbs. Briquemont had even claimed that the Serbs were the most reliable of the groups he had had to negotiate with during his tour of duty in Bosnia, although in his farewell letter to the people of Sarajevo he had confessed that he would miss the city because it was multicultural, like his beloved Brussels.

Jose Maria Mendiluce did not say that he would miss Sarajevo. He bade emotional farewells to his colleagues in the UNHCR. He would miss *them,* he said. But by the end of his tenure as Special Representative, it was clear that Mendiluce was fed up with the cruelty and the lies. Like so many of the able people who had worked for him over the course of the previous two years and eventually had broken under the weight of the physical and psychological strain, he too was burned out. It was a common feeling shared by reporters, workers in nongovernmental organizations, and UNPROFOR officials. General Briquemont was even said to have confided to a small group that he was eager to go home because, after all, he had been under fire for three months (presumably he meant that he had been living in Sarajevo). It was just that some people had earned their burnout more than others, just as some people had earned their despair more than others.

Mendiluce and the other UNHCR people had earned their despair. The more they labored, the more it had begun to dawn on them that their future would be one of failure—no matter how great their dedication. The deepest reason for this was that they simply did not know what the world expected them to do in Bosnia. As Tony Land, a veteran UNHCR official who was in charge of its Sarajevo office in 1993 and 1994, said to me, "What kind of commitment is the West and the UN really willing to make? The Safe Havens policy could work under certain circumstances, I suppose, but not unless the people in those places can be assured some reasonable quality of life. There is no water in Srebrenica. If the Serbs won't let us restore it, does that mean we will have to truck it in? We are facing the same sorts of practical problems elsewhere. And I'm not even talking about the problem of the morale of the people in these places, which is all but nonexistent.

"We know already that the costs will be enormous, even if there is a general cease-fire tomorrow. But the question is under what set of principles we are meant to be operating here. I ask you, is water a human right for these people? You journalists talk about human rights as if it is only a question of not being beaten to a pulp by the police every week. Or you talk, rightly, about rape and ethnic cleansing. But what about education? Or electricity? And what about trying to restore these things in a situation where fighting and ethnic cleansing and rape are still going on all around? Again, the question comes down, as it has from the beginning, to what we are in fact trying to accomplish here. We have to decide, and even after two years we haven't done that yet."

Inevitably, the UNHCR itself had been compromised by what it had had to do in Bosnia. Although it was the organization that had done more than any other to publicize the facts of ethnic cleansing, there had been times when it found itself having to in effect abet it. "I prefer thirty thousand evacuees to thirty thousand bodies," Mendiluce said on one occasion. In 1993, in Srebrenica, the UNHCR had organized a massive evacuation of the civilian population through Serb-controlled areas and on to Tuzla. It was not that anyone was being pressured to leave. As one UNHCR worker put it at the time, "Everyone wants to get the hell out of Srebrenica. They know there's no future there." And yet, as a Bosnian soldier remarked bitterly as he watched the first convoy cross the no-man's-land and roll past his position toward Tuzla city, "This is just ethnic cleansing. The UNHCR is doing the Serbs' work for them."

The UNHCR official in charge of the evacuation insisted that he was fulfilling a "purely humanitarian" evacuation. And he warned that although the Srebrenica operation had been the largest the UNHCR had mounted in Bosnia to date, it was unlikely to be the last. And, as people taking the apocalyptic view tended to be in Bosnia, he was right. In the spring of 1994, when it became clear to the UNHCR that the Serbs in the Bosanska Krajina, particularly in the Priejdor area, were again beginning a systematic campaign of murder and arson against the six thousand or so Muslims who remained, there was an attempt to evacuate them en masse to Croatia. It was not as if the Muslims could have fled on their own. In the bus station in Banja Luka, a sign went up in the fall of 1993 declaring that Muslims were forbidden to ride the buses. Outside, a graffito restated that pairing peculiar to racist signs the world over: "No dogs or Muslims."

Reluctantly, the UNHCR and the International Red Cross attempted to put the evacuation together. The rumor in Zagreb was that the money that was being offered, under the table, to the local Serb authorities was insufficient, and that was why in the end the evacuation had fallen through. But the precedent set in Srebrenica, repeated in the following year on a smaller scale in places all over Bosnia, and set in motion though not completed in the Bosanska Krajina was increasingly defining what the UNHCR's mandate to "protect" refugees really amounted to. In effect, it had been put in the impossible position of either standing by and watching the murders go on, or itself facilitating the larger Serb war aim of the transfer of the non-Serb population out of Bosnian Serb Army–controlled parts of Bosnia. For UNHCR officials, who had dedicated their lives to caring for refugees, even making the choice was all but unbearable, however much they might recognize its inevitability.

In retrospect, the murder of Bosnia became a foregone conclusion after Srebrenica. As the UNHCR's Larry Hollingworth put it, "We should have been stronger from the start. In this day and age, it should be an absolute right to feed people. But instead we tried to come up with the correct arrangement that would convince the Serbs to let us through. From August 1992 to March 1993, we got only a few in. Meanwhile the Serbs were closing in on Srebrenica, taking the villages, forcing people to flee, and making the situation in the areas they had not yet taken ever more desperate." Before the UNHCR had finally opted to evacuate civilians from the enclave, Jose Maria Mendiluce had asserted angrily that what the Serbs were offering the UN in agreeing to open what they called a "humanitarian corridor" northeast through their lines was opening a corridor for ethnic cleansing. "We think people have a right to humanitarian aid in the places they live, not after they have been shelled and starved out of their homes."

The UNHCR's inability at first to fully take in what it was facing was not surprising. As Pierre Ollier, the young French UNHCR official I first met in Banja Luka in 1992, and who at one time or another volunteered for practically every dirty job there was to do in Bosnia, before being killed in a plane crash on his way to Macedonia, told me, "There has never been a war in which the principal military goal has been the wholesale creation of refugees. The result was that the UNHCR in general, and Mendiluce in particular, were thrust into a political and even a military role. It's easy to say that the UNHCR shouldn't dabble in politics—that a young man like me with no particular political experience shouldn't be negotiating with the Bosnian Serbs, the HVO, or the Bosnian government. But with refugees at the heart of the political and military crisis, there was nothing else to do. It doesn't matter whether Mendiluce wanted to, or even whether he was qualified to, play the game of high politics. The UNHCR has been stuck in that role from the beginning."

Ollier was right. Mendiluce and his colleagues had been playing politics from the beginning of the operation, but always without the resources politics requires. "Diplomacy without at least the threat of force," Herbert Okun had once quipped, "is like baseball without a bat." As Larry Hollingworth declared to a reporter from the London *Sunday Times* as he was leaving Bosnia for good in the spring of

1994, "We should have been much tougher from the beginning. The UN missed the chance to seize the initiative and be forceful, and we have seen a gradual chipping away of authority ever since . . . If we had said from the start 'Either you stop this hassle or we're off and no one will get anything,' we would have established some power."

The way UNPROFOR officials seemed to prefer to deal with their powerlessness was to pretend that the situation would soon improve, that somehow the negotiations would finally start producing results. This wish to believe in the end prevented them from telling the truth even to themselves. When reporters demanded of David Owen that he confront the Serbs about the rape camps, he smiled thinly, as if this were the most farfetched demand in the world, and told one reporter, "It is very difficult to talk about things like that with the Serbs." And yet when the Serbs demanded that the United Nations stop calling the siege of Sarajevo a siege, the UN complied instantly. At least the UNHCR held on to its outrage. Returning to Sarajevo from Srebrenica, Larry Hollingworth declared, "It's murder out there. It must be stopped. And if it takes fire to do it, so be it."

Unlike Mendiluce, Hollingworth had at first welcomed the deployment of UNPROFOR troops. "It looked as if my job would be made easier," he would say later, "and the lives of many thousands of Bosnians would be made a little more bearable. The purpose of the troops seemed clear: to escort the aid and not interfere in the war itself. On the other hand, if you send in an army but don't allow it to be aggressive, why send in firepower and tanks? I'm left, sadly, with the conclusion that the troops were sent in not to be tough but simply to look tough." In fact, this was exactly what a senior UN Protection Force commander had told a group of journalists in Zagreb in early 1994, shortly before his own posting back home. "Our mission here was not to actually do anything," he said, in a tone that blended disdain for the orders he had carried out so faithfully and contempt for those who had not understood what UNPROFOR had really been in the Balkans. "Our mission was to give the appearance of doing something." He laughed. "That is a very difficult assignment," he said.

What was gallant about the UNHCR was that however much they subscribed to the United Nations view that when all was said and done they had to remain impartial, they refused to take this to mean they were absolved from involvement in the moral sense. Mendiluce talked openly of his frustration "as a member of the international community" at not being able to do more. In other words, he did not accept the idea that his role as a UNHCR official absolved him of his moral obligations as a person. This does not mean that Mendiluce and the UNHCR could strike out on their own. And in objective terms, their humanitarian effort could be looked at as a fig leaf for the unwillingness of the great powers to get involved militarily in Bosnia. "The humanitarian trap" was what one French journalist in Sarajevo liked to call it. But in operational terms, in the daily matters of life and death that they confronted, the UNHCR officials were constantly trying to help. They knew their protection officers could do little to protect and that their convoys were unlikely to get through, but this did not make them cynical, as it did so many in UNPROFOR. Rather, it seemed to stiffen their resolve. In the head-quarters in Zagreb, senior officials chafed at being stuck in desk jobs, and used the most transparent pretexts to get back to Bosnia. Jose Maria Mendiluce was famous for preferring the company of his convoy drivers to that of the diplomats with whom he spent so much of his time. But in the end, he too lost hope.

"Frankly," Mendiluce told me, shortly before he left Bosnia, "we at UNHCR feel abandoned by the international community and by the UN in New York. We feel like orphans. When the situation deteriorated completely in eastern Bosnia, we found ourselves in the morally impossible position of furthering the goal of ethnic cleansing in order to save people's lives. And yet there have been no statements on any of this from the Security Council, the Vance-Owen negotiators, or the Secretary General. It would appear that we're on our own in this impossible situation. We're becoming a transport company, and having to ignore all the humanitarian and human rights concerns that lie at the heart of *our* mandate. We truck in food and act—no offense intended—as a travel agency for foreign visitors.

"There was a long period when, no matter how bad things were, I had hope," Mendiluce continued. "I remember thinking, 'At some point the international community will have to do something and not just talk.' When you came here in the past and I spoke to you about miracles and limits, of course it was about holding on until something was done. And I am very proud of what we in UNHCR have accomplished in the former Yugoslavia. Thanks in large measure to our efforts people have not starved in Sarajevo. But everywhere else . . ." His voice trailed off, and he shrugged. "Almost everywhere else, things are very bad." A month later, Mendiluce had gone. In Zagreb and Sarajevo, the senior staff at UNPROFOR made no secret of their relief at seeing the back of him. As they rightly surmised, his successor, Nicholas Morris, would not pursue such an independent policy, nor would he have Mendiluce's unconcealed allergy to the military in a moment when, for all practical purposes, UNPROFOR and not the UNHCR was becoming the lead UN agency in the former Yugoslavia. Under Morris, the UNHCR would again become a relief agency pure and simple.

The shift from Mendiluce to Morris was emblematic of the change in the UNHCR's role, and, perhaps, in its thinking as well. Morris was unquestionably the better administrator, the better bureaucrat, and perhaps, within the UN, the better politician as well. He was regarded as an honorable man, if also, by many, as an unimaginative and rigid one. But there was little question of his ever "going off the reservation." After all, he was the man who had opposed the expansion of the UNHCR's role in Kurdistan—a stance that had earned him the nickname "It's Not My Mandate" Morris from the reporters who had been in northern Iraq at the time. In contrast to Mendiluce, who had steadfastly resisted the idea that his job was simply to contain the catastrophe or just do what he could, Morris would take a far more conventional approach. Under him, the UNHCR in the former Yugoslavia would largely revert to being an orthodox UN agency. People who had served in the operation from the beginning complained of the loss of spirit, and, by the middle of 1994, most of them either had left or were talking of leaving. When the last member of Mendiluce's inner circle, Manoel de Almeida, left for Geneva in June 1994, it marked the symbolic end of the operation, or as he sometimes called it, "the monster," Mendiluce had created.

Mendiluce had always seen his task as not just saving lives and providing relief but keeping up people's hopes. As one of his colleagues put it after he left Bosnia, "Jose Maria may have enjoyed hollow victories, but while he was winning them people at the UNHCR could go on believing, go on hoping. Now there is a crisis, but no hope, and that has demoralized all of us." Once he had left the Balkans, Mendiluce felt free to reveal the extent of his own demoralization. "The process of peace negotiation in former Yugoslavia has attained the height of perversity," he declared. "First it was the maintaining of the State of Bosnia-Herzegovina, which had been recognized by the international community. Later, there came the proposal to divide the country into ten provinces. And finally, we have the idea of creating three ethnoreligious ministates, which forces the population to define itself according to a fascist logic." This, Mendiluce insisted, was unacceptable. "Pragmatism and dialogue have to have a limit," he said, "the one imposed by a genocide. If we were not ready to intervene, it would have been better if we had stayed at home. But we were present, we did undertake a humanitarian intervention, and we created false expectations."

The marvelous thing about watching the UNHCR people conduct themselves in the field had always been that no matter how desperate things got, they refused to be defeatist. Now Mendiluce was, in effect, accepting defeat. Later, he would leave the UNHCR and reenter Spanish politics, winning election to the European Parliament on the Socialist list. What he had called "the largest, most complex and risky operation ever undertaken by humanitarian organizations" *had* failed, at least if the measure of success was actually stopping what was going on. Even Nicholas Morris insisted in 1993 that "the failure of the international community to reverse the logic of war has meant the failure of humanitarian operations based in that logic being reversed." Larry Hollingworth put it more bluntly. Before leaving the Balkans, he remarked angrily that "the West must make up its mind about whether it wants to save the Bosnian Muslims or not." By the spring of 1994, it was clear that it had made up its mind, and the answer was that it did not.

X

In the Lion Cemetery in Sarajevo in April 1993, an old man asked me, "Why do the Americans not drop the atom bomb on the Serbs?" A moment later, a mortar bomb exploded about three hundred meters away. The mourners—they had come to bury a fourteen-year-old boy killed by a sniper two days before—ducked or, rather, went through a kind of pantomime of ducking for cover, since apart from the now shell-scarred statue of the lion and the plinth on which it stands in the center of the cemetery, there was no cover to speak of. Even the headstones in Sarajevo were being made of plywood after a year of the siege. And the gravediggers would tell you that the markers were of half the thickness they had been six months earlier. I stared edgily at two freshly dug graves ten meters down one of the burial rows. From past experience I knew they would be the safest places to crouch if the shelling began in earnest. That was always a distinct possibility since the Serb forces in the hills surrounding the city had made something of a specialty of firing on mourners as they buried their dead.

By Sarajevo standards, the Lion Cemetery was safer than the other main local graveyards. It was not nearly so exposed as the soccer pitch nearby, which had been converted into a cemetery by the local authorities in the fall of 1992 to take the overflow from the Kosevo Hospital morgue, and a year later was more than a third filled with graves. Until the cease-fire in February 1994, every part of Sarajevo was dangerous, and almost no place out of reach either of mortar or artillery fire, or of the ubiquitous snipers. At least shelling is relatively impersonal. Gunners aim at a neighborhood or, often, at a particular building. But what is especially frightening and degrading about being under sniper fire is that the sniper is picking and choosing from among the people who pass through the cross

hairs of his gunsights. He is saying to himself, "I think I will shoot
the girl in the red parka." Or he is saying, "I think I will let the tall
man cross the road, but try to bring down his friend, the short un-
shaven guy in the wool coat, when he tries to follow."

That morning, before we set out for the Lion Cemetery, a French
friend, a combat photographer of long experience, said to me,
"There are two ways of photographing funerals: on your feet with
the living, or on your knees with the dead." He might as well have
been talking about the ways of thinking about Sarajevo, or generally
about the slaughter in Bosnia. When one was in the city during the
siege, what was overwhelming (apart from the fact that one was regularly frightened half out of one's wits) was that the situation seemed
so simple. A European city was being reduced to nothing; Carthage
in slow motion, but this time with an audience and a videotaped
record. Nothing, not the complex history of the region, nor the errors
and crimes of the Bosnians themselves, nor the sometimes justified
fears of the Bosnian Serbs, can mitigate the crime that took place.
Nothing. Nothing. Nothing.

It was the conceit of journalists—made up, no doubt, partly of
corporate self-regard, partly of an unexamined belief in progress and
the pacifying effects of prosperity, and partly out of the self-congrat-
ulatory belief that Europe had become a civilized place—that if people back home could only be told and shown what was actually
happening in Sarajevo, if they had to see on their television screens
images of what a child who has just been hit by a soft-nosed bullet or
a jagged splinter of shrapnel really looks like, or the bodies of citizens massacred as they queued for bread or water, then they would
want their governments to do something. The hope of the Western
press was that an informed citizenry back home would demand that
their governments not allow the Bosnian Muslims to go on being
massacred, raped, or forced from their homes. Instead, the sound
bites and "visual bites" culled from the fighting bred casuistry and
indifference far more regularly than it succeeded in mobilizing people to act or even to be indignant.

In retrospect, those of us who believed the result could have been
otherwise were naive. There was a "CNN effect," in the broad sense
that without CNN, the BBC, and the others showing it all the time,
the Bosnian tragedy would have faded from people's minds after the

first few months of fighting, even though it was taking place a couple of hundred miles from Italy. And, in a narrower sense, it really was the television cameras and not NATO, let alone the United Nations, that saved Sarajevo after the massacre in the Central Market in early February 1994. The British and the French, as well as UNPROFOR and the Department of Peacekeeping Operations, had resisted tooth and nail any credible threat on the part of the West to use force to defend Sarajevo for the better part of two years. They had insisted that the mandate did not permit it, that the risk to the humanitarian effort was too great, that in the end military threats would be counterproductive. But in the wake of the market massacre, they realized that there was real anger back home, for once, anger that would not be dissipated as easily as it had been in the wake of past atrocities. Unsurprisingly, they came to the conclusion that a number of steps previously deemed to have been impossible actually turned out to be quite doable after all. As a diplomat from one of the so-called Permanent Five countries on the Security Council put it to me sardonically, "It is not the mandate but mass sentiments that have changed, particularly in Western Europe."

All along, it had been the task many of the journalists set themselves, consciously or unconsciously, to change the sentiments of their readers and viewers about the slaughter. That was why, throughout most of the siege, the reporters and television crews were perhaps the only dependable allies the Bosnians had. The Bosnian government, which had bet everything on foreign intervention, understood the influence of the press corps early on. It also understood that since it had been deprived by the continuation of the arms embargo of any means of defending itself effectively, eliciting foreign sympathy and raising money from the Islamic world were the only strong levers left at its disposal. But it was not true, as the United Nations people sometimes liked to suggest, that their sympathies caused the journalists to distort their stories to show the Bosnian government side in an undeservedly positive light. Indeed, the accusation testified more to the skewed morality that the commitment to impartiality in considering what they often called "the claims of the warring factions" had created among senior UN officials. For all their air of injured surprise, these officials must have known that if the Bosnian Serbs had any justice on their side, it came in about the same proportion as the Nazis' had, or the Khmer Rouge's. Again, what the Serbs were doing was *genocide.*

What was true was that, because what was happening in Bosnia was genocide, most of the journalists did come to sympathize with the Bosnian cause, in exactly the way one hopes that if representatives of the foreign press had been stationed in the Warsaw ghetto in 1943, they would have sympathized with the Jews. The logic of the United Nations' position in Bosnia seemed to suggest that had the UN existed during the Second World War, and thought it had been given a "mandate" to treat all sides impartially, it might have complained that the journalists were failing to understand that anti-Semitism was a centuries-old European problem, and that the anxieties of the Germans about Jewish influence had to be understood in their historical context. From a strictly historical standpoint, it happens that those things were true then, just as historical explanations of Serb nationalism were true in 1994. But the press, to its credit, did not accept the UN's gloss on the old French saying that to understand everything is to forgive everything. In Bosnia, reporters had seen things that they could not forgive, things UN people had seemed hell-bent to go to any lengths to cover up.

The United Nations was right in one, narrow sense to resent the interaction between the Bosnian government and the foreign press corps. Throughout the course of the fighting, the Bosnian government attempted to mobilize this sympathy as it might have mobilized its young men, treating foreign journalists almost as if they were a military asset. And as time went on, the Bosnians got quite good at doing this. But it did not stage the Bosnian tragedy for its own strategic purposes. Whatever the UN Protection Force people, from General Mackenzie in 1992 to General Rose in 1994, might have chosen to hint at in private, the case for the Bosnians having been responsible for the Sarajevo breadline massacre or the mortaring of the city's Central Market was never strong enough for the UN to make public and allow the press to investigate. The fact that they refused to produce the hard evidence they sometimes claimed to have to support the assertions they made so often in private, and yet obviously believed in them so unswervingly, suggested to many of us not that they knew more than they were letting on but that UN Protection Force and Secretariat officials so wanted to believe in

Bosnian as well as Serb guilt that they could not let go of the idea that there were no heroes but only villains in the conflict.

And that belief served them well in Bosnia. Believing in Bosnian government villainy provided the United Nations with a cheap way to absolve itself of any moral obligation to reconsider its famous impartiality. In fact, the moral question was one the people at UNPROFOR or in the Secretariat preferred to avoid. There was the mandate to consider, they tended to remind you quickly, often before you had even brought it up. UN officials did not put it this way, but their rationale for the way they had acted did not, when all was said and done, differ all that much from another once quite celebrated line of institutional self-justification: "I was only obeying orders." What they could do, though they could not demonstrate the Bosnian government's guilt, was muddy the waters by letting a few journalists who were already tempted by this view in on the so-called secret. In the wake of the market massacre, a senior member of General Rose's staff showed at least two journalists the front page of a damaging initial report by a UN bomb-crater analysis team establishing Bosnian culpability in the affair. Inside, he was reported to have insisted, there was everything you needed to draw this conclusion.

But if such proof existed, it was not enough to persuade the Secretariat people—who hardly could be called well disposed toward Izetbegovic and Silajdzic. They had ordered a second, full-scale investigation. It was inconclusive. Had there been a cover-up, it would have meant that, among other things, the Russian officials serving with the group had to have joined in. That hardly seems likely. Nor is it probable that, assuming the United Nations sat on the story for its own reasons, in an institution where almost nothing of importance remains secret for very long, some Serb sympathizer within the UN would not have leaked the story.

But General Rose's people were quite busy telling a very different tale. The same aide of Rose's who had leaked the story of who fired the shell on the Central Market in Sarajevo later confided that Rose had kept quiet so that he could maintain "some leverage" on the Sarajevo authorities. He claimed that Rose had gotten the deputy commander of the Bosnian army, General Jovan Divjak, to attend a round of UN-sponsored military negotiations at the Sarajevo airport by threatening President Izetbegovic that otherwise he would reveal "the truth" about the market massacre. The suggestion of Rose's aide was that Izetbegovic had given in immediately because he knew he had been caught out. Bosnian government officials offered quite a different version. They said that Rose hadn't really had any proof, but that it was clear he believed in what he was saying. "He wanted to think we were killers; he wanted to badly," the official said.

That was exactly the position the UN did adhere to. As one official put it to me, "The Serbs are mass murderers, the Croats are assassins, and the Muslims are killers." How convenient believing that was for UNPROFOR. It could remain in the happy position of sympathizing with the victims of the Bosnian war without having to take a position about its rights and wrongs. The alternative, in any case, was unthinkable. It had taken the International Committee of the Red Cross decades to regain its moral authority after it effectively colluded with the Nazis by sending delegations to visit show concentration camps like Theresienstadt—this as late as 1943—and returning to Geneva to pronounce that it had found the conditions in them to be hard but acceptable under the circumstances. If what the United Nations had been standing by and watching in Bosnia was genocide, then its moral authority might be similarly unseated by the actions (or nonactions) that it had taken there. The contempt people had come to feel for the League of Nations was the direct result of its uselessness as an instrument for fighting fascism in the 1930s. What the many foreign aid workers and journalists who had arrived in Bosnia as supporters of the United Nations kept trying to convey to UN officials was that its refusal to confront the ethnic fascism of the 1990s was likely to prove just as destructive to the moral authority on which, pragmatically if for no other reason, its effectiveness depended.

Individual United Nations officials, particularly within the UNHCR, did realize how debased the institution was becoming through its involvement in Bosnia, but corporately the UN simply refused to accept that this was what had happened. The fault was with the mandate, or the spinelessness of the great powers, or simply the savagery and ruthlessness of the belligerents themselves. And, inevitably, as the frustrations of the aid effort mounted and it became clear that humanitarian relief could not bring much more than what an International Committee of the Red Cross official named Thierry

Germond once called "a minimum—always inadequate—of human-ity into situations that should not exist," there was a tendency to blame the victims for their fate. Why, countless United Nations offi-cials would demand, did the Bosnians insist on fighting on when it was clear that they had lost? In the minds of many UN officials, Bosnian resistance itself became a sort of crime against humanity. If the victims would only accept their victimhood, there was so much the international community could do for them.

And since they increasingly perceived the Bosnian government side in this light, it made sense that the United Nations would seize upon every single accusation holding the Bosnian side responsible for killing its own people or of committing war crimes against the Bosnian Serbs. On October 6, 1994, Bosnian government troops launched a raid on Serb positions outside Sarajevo. The next day, the bodies of twenty Bosnian Serb soldiers were discovered with their throats cut. The Bosnian Serbs immediately issued a statement call-ing the attack "a criminal act." Yasushi Akashi seemed to agree. He flew to Sarajevo to protest personally the "mutilation" of the Serb fighters. But there had been no mutilations. As an UNPROFOR spokesman, Lieutenant Colonel Tim Spicer, admitted the next day, it had been a "commando-style operation," hardly unheard of in wartime. The UN, Spicer announced, was withdrawing its claim.

What was true was that in their desperation the Bosnian govern-ment did seem on numerous occasions to welcome not the atrocities the Serbs were committing themselves but the photo opportunities such atrocities provided. Some officials thought, understandably enough, that the sight of dead and mutilated civilians might finally galvanize the great powers to do something more to protect Bosnia than pass toothless resolutions in the Security Council demanding an end to the slaughter. In this, as in so many other hopes they di-rected westward, the Bosnians were usually wrong. The outrage pro-voked by the market massacre was entirely exceptional. That became clear when the Serbs began to shell Gorazde two months later, and the Bosnians discovered that the exclusion zone around Sarajevo had not established the precedent for cease-fires in the rest of Bosnia that Western politicians initially had claimed it would.

Had the Serbs simply been prepared to give in to this second NATO ultimatum, the United Nations would have been willing enough to enforce it. But the Serbs were not weak and they were not fools, and at Gorazde they bent slightly but they did not buckle. Within three weeks of the NATO ultimatum, UNPROFOR was admitting that Serb troops had reentered the zone, this time disguised as policemen. Some were billeted within the 1.9 mile "infantry exclusion zone" of the town center of Gorazde. That was a bit much even for the local UNPROFOR commander, a British lieutenant colonel named David Santa Olalla. But Sergio de Mello, who by entering Gorazde before the NATO ultimatum had expired had probably done more than any single United Nations official to prevent air strikes, this time overruled UNPROFOR and told the Bosnian Serbs that they could keep their policemen there, ultimatum or no ultimatum.

In this, de Mello was only acting as senior United Nations officials had acted since the fighting began. Given the UN's attitude, why shouldn't the Bosnians have turned to the press and waged the war in the media they should have been allowed to wage on the battlefield? The only weapon they had in ample supply was their own suffering. And if they sometimes waited to remove a body until the foreign journalists had arrived, or sometimes seemed almost masochistic in their refusal to negotiate agreements that might have secured a little more electricity or gas for Sarajevo, this did not mean, as UN people in Zagreb, Sarajevo, and New York sometimes liked to contend, that they were the authors of their own suffering. They were the victims. But their victimhood increasingly seemed to bore and even to disgust UN officials both in the field and in New York and Geneva. UN Protection Force officers in particular became less and less discreet in the antipathy they felt for the Bosnians.

For their part, where the Bosnians made their mistake was not in misreading UNPROFOR—they made that mistake in the beginning, but they soon understood that the UN force's missions in Bosnia did not include defending Bosnians—but in imagining that if people in the outside world could be made indignant enough by what was happening, Bosnia's future would be taken out of UNPROFOR's hands. That was why the Bosnians turned to the press. They—we—tried. They—we—failed. Sitting in a room in the Holiday Inn in Sarajevo late at night, drinking the latest bottle of malt some recent arrival had brought in from Split or Ancona, after a day spent on the front line, or in the casualty ward of the French hospital, or among the people scavenging for wood along denuded hillsides (Sarajevo used to be known for its parks), it seemed incredible to us that the world could remain indifferent to what was going on in Bosnia, or, worse, could imagine that what was going on was just some ancient ethnic conflict—just another Balkan war where no side was really all that much better than any other.

Surely one more picture, or one more story, or one more correspondent's stand-up taped in front of a shelled, smoldering building would bring people around, would force them to stop shrugging their shoulders, or, like the United Nations, blaming the victims. And so the stories were satellite-faxed to New York, Paris, London, and Washington; the photos carried out to the world's busiest agencies; and the television segments transmitted, live when the desks would go along, to CNN, and ITN, and Antenne 2. And to their credit, the editors back home gave these reports and images an enormous amount of play, at least through the first two years of the fighting. In the future, no one will be able to say, as many Germans legitimately said after the Second World War, that he or she did not know what was going on in Bosnia. The United Nations might console itself that the press was biased. In reality, no slaughter was more scrupulously and ably covered.

What the press understood and the United Nations did not was that to be fair and to be impartial are not the same thing. As someone who was never really a member of the working press—I never had to file, or argue with a desk, or report on some pointless human interest story—but who spent close to two years with them, it always seemed to me poignant that this group of professional skeptics, many of whom would have been soldiers had they not been so anarchically left-wing, turned out to believe more in "Western values" than their governments did. Such a commitment cost an astonishing number of them their lives. And even for those who never suffered any physical injury, the strain of returning again, though nothing to what the Bosnians themselves were undergoing, inevitably took its toll, both personally and professionally. But they kept coming back.

For the longest time, the landscape of Sarajevo was as pitted with dreams as it was with shellfire. By the summer of 1993, people in Bosnia had grown weary of the press and cynical about its ability to *change* anything, which finally was the only criterion that made any sense. Journalists who were once greeted as trusted friends and in whom Bosnians generally but Sarajevans in particular had placed such hopes were greeted more dispassionately. It was not that Bosnians believed that they had failed to tell the story; it was that it had done no good. And, inevitably I suppose, the presence of outsiders became an irritant where once it had been a boon. "Another safari?" a friend of mine in Sarajevo asked me when I arrived back in the city in the early winter of 1993–1994. "What do you hope to see this time? More corpses, more destruction? We should charge you admission."

All this was said with reasonable equanimity, but implacably. The media attention, my friend believed, had done no good. A few months later, as the cease-fire in Sarajevo took hold and the city limped on, as besieged as ever but no longer being shelled, the bitterness toward outsiders had became much sharper. Now that it was relatively safe to come to Sarajevo, the dignitaries were flooding the place, touring the ruins, commiserating with the natives. Their motives were usually decent, but Sarajevans could not help resenting them for their concern, and, of course, for their ability when they had seen their fill to go out to the airport in that UNPROFOR armored personnel carrier, take the plane, and fly home. The press reports were diminishing steadily as, once more, the threat of NATO intervention had faded away. When the fighting was at its height, the press's collective act of witness could do little for Sarajevo. With the fighting less acute, visitors could do little to salve its wounds, even if, eventually, they and like-minded Westerners would contribute to the physical rebuilding of Bosnia. And, of course, fatigue eventually set in among the editors back home, who became increasingly reluctant to allow their best reporters to keep returning to Bosnia. Over the course of 1994, many of the major media groups pulled their permanent staff out of Sarajevo.

And there is the question whether any outsider except a relief worker or a gunrunner can do anything very useful in Bosnia in the foreseeable future. For the fighting and the dying have not stopped, and will not stop for a long time, whatever agreements are signed, whether or not the arms embargo is lifted, and whether or not UNPROFOR remains or withdraws. The future of Bosnia, and possibly the future of much of Eastern Europe as well, holds not peace but the sword. After what the West and the UN have done, and not done, perhaps that was to have been expected. And perhaps, whatever they might have done, anything else was a dream. The fall of great empires is so often followed by cruel wars of succession. What is certain is that a lot of dreams have died in Bosnia during the past two and a half years: the dream that the world has a conscience; the dream that Europe is a civilized place; the dream that there is justice for the weak as well as for the strong. It should come as no surprise that the old millenarian dream that the truth will set us free should die there as well. And this reality, it turns out, is better apprehended in the ruined town center of Gorazde, in the cleansed villages of the Bosanska Krajina, and in the Lion Cemetery in Sarajevo than in the Palais des Nations in Geneva or in the UN Secretariat building in New York, much as we might have wished it otherwise. The defeat is total, the disgrace complete.

Index